Technology and Assessment

The Tale of Two Interpretations

by

Michael Russell
Boston College

INFORMATION AGE
P U B L I S H I N G

Greenwich, Connecticut 06830 • www.infoagepub.com

Library of Congress Cataloging-in-Publication Data

Russell, Michael, 1957-
  Technology and assessment : the tale of two interpretations / by Michael
Russell.
      p. cm. – (Research methods for educational technology)
  Includes bibliographical references and index.
  ISBN 1-59311-038-3 (pbk.) – ISBN 1-59311-039-1
  1. Educational tests and measurements–United States. 2. Educational
technology–United States. I. Title. II. Series.
  LB3060.5.R87 2006
  371.260285–dc22

                                                        2005032610

Technology and Assessment

The Tale of Two Interpretations

A volume in
Research Methods for Educational Technology
Walt Heinecke, *Series Editor*

Research Methods for Educational Technology

Walt Heinecke, *University of Virginia*
Series Editor

CONTENTS

SERIES EDITOR'S PREFACE

In *Volume I* of *Research Methods for Educational Technology* we addressed the evaluation of educational technology. *Volume II* examined what teachers should know about educational technology. In *Volume III, Technology and Assessment: The tale of two interpretations,* Michael Russell tackles the important relationship between assessment and technology.

How do the standards and assessment reform movement and the movement to reform education with technology comport? The answer to this question is, of course, related to values. There is an easy answer to this question. When the interest is in efficiency and accountability, technology may serve assessment policy by providing reinforcement for assessment-based pedagogical practices. Technology can be used, for instance, to reinforce the learning of discrete and basic skills and facts through drill and practice routines. However, if the intent is to improve quality and excellence in education by accessing content and methods in which students' meta-cognitive abilities are challenged and in which education becomes knowledge-centered and learner-centered, the answer becomes a bit less clear, for policy-makers at least. Technology can be used to foster students' access to information and data that allow them to produce history the way historians do, or to access programs allowing them to engage simulations of complex social and scientific phenomenon. However, as Russell points out in this volume, traditional standardized assessments are not particularly sensitive to these outcomes. In any event Russell reminds us that technology is not value-neutral; it can serve didactic pedagogies or constructivist pedagogies.

In recent years a special interest group in the American Educational Research Association has sprung up with the title: Technology as an Agent

Technology and Assessment: The Tale of Two Interpretations, pages vii–xiii
Copyright © 2006 by Information Age Publishing

of Change in Teaching and Learning (TACTL). The assumption among the founders was that technology is merely a catalyst for pedagogical reforms, a means for unleashing access to content and methods of teaching and learning previously inaccessible without technology. However, recent research (Wenglinsky, 2005) has traced the confluence of three reform movements occurring in American education: the standards movement, the teacher quality movement and the educational technology movement, and raised serious questions about the compatibility of these reform efforts. Michael Russell's volume, *Technology and Assessment: The tale of two interpretations,* could not come at a more propitious moment. We stand at a critical juncture in the future of educational technology and this volume provides an excellent road map.

One of the most significant changes in the context of education to occur in the past 30 years has been the national movement to increase accountability. Beginning with National At Risk (National Commission on Excellence in Education, (NCEE, 1983), and bolstered by the 1991 Governors' meeting in Charlottesville, the Goals 2000 Act, and the subsequent reauthorization of the No Child Left Behind Act, the push for improved content standards and accountability at the level of school and pupil has reached its apex. Systems of accountability, including revised state content and performance standards, high stakes testing systems, accountability reporting systems and systems of rewards and punishment have been instituted by almost every state in the Union (Heinecke, Moon & Corcoran, 2003).

However, this emphasis on accountability is not a recent phenomenon. It is actually a return to efficiency in education emphasized in the early part of the 20th century. At that time "the challenge of providing mass education was seen by many as analogous to mass production in factories" (Bransford, Brown, & Cocking, 2000). This conceptualization of education led to "the development of standardized tests for measurement of the "product" of clerical work by teachers to keep records and progress...and of management of teaching by central district authorities who had little knowledge of educational practice or philosophy (Calahan, 1962). In short, the factory model affected the design of curriculum, instruction, and assessment in schools" (p. 132).

Research in the area of standards and accountability clearly indicates that high stakes accountability systems have intended and unintended consequences for teaching and learning in classrooms. Nichols, Glass & Berliner (2005) assert that "pressure created by high stakes testing has had almost no important influence on student academic performance" (p. i). At the same time some researchers have found that high stakes testing policies have had negative impacts on retention and graduation rates. In addition, some researcher have found that high stakes testing lead to a narrowing of the curriculum (Chudowsky & Behuniak, 1997; Firestone &

Mayrowiz, 2000; Koretz et al., 1996; Jones et al. 1999; McNeil, 2000; 2004; McNeil & Valenzuuela, 2001; Shepard & Dogherty, 1991; Shepard, 2000;). Most importantly, some researchers have found that classrooms operating with the context of high stakes testing are less likely to employ constructivist pedagogical methods (Harrington-Lueker, 2000). Indeed, these negative impacts of high stakes testing on curriculum appear to be experienced to a higher degree by low income and minority populations (Barksdale-Ladd & Thomas, 2000; Darling-Hammond & Post; 2000; Hoffman et al, 2001; Firestone & Mayrowitz, 2000; Roderick & Engel; 2001; Stone & Lane, 2003).

At the same time there have been significant developments within the field of cognitive psychology leading to a reexamination of educational processes. The National Research Council (Bransford, Brown & Cocking, 2000) outlined the shift in conceptions of learning that have been occurring over the past decades due to developments in cognitive psychology. They argue that the

> meaning of knowing has shifted from being able to remember and repeat information to being able to find and use it.... (R)ather the goal of education is better conceived as helping students develop the intellectual tools and learning strategies needed to acquire the knowledge that allows people to think productively about history, science, and technology, social phenomena, mathematics, and the arts. (p. 5)

The NRC (Bransford, Cocking & Brown, 2000) report asserts that there is a new emphasis on learning with understanding. They acknowledge, however, that this approach is limited by curricula, which emphasizes memory over understanding. "Textbooks are filled with facts that students are expected to memorize, and most tests assess students' abilities to remember facts" (p.9). They argue that usable knowledge is not the same as disconnected facts. They emphasize conceptual and higher order understanding. They also assert that new learning requires "helping people take control of their own learning" (p. 12). They argue that the new science of learning requires reconceptualization of "what is taught, how it is taught, and how learning is assessed" (p. 13).

Based on their review of the research, the NRC (Bransford, Brown & Cocking, 2000) calls for school and classrooms which are learner-centered, knowledge-centered, assessment-centered and community-centered. This is challenging for schools because it calls for approaches to teaching and learning that are often times more difficult to do than simply memorizing facts. The NRC report concludes:

> Many curricula fail to support learning with understanding because they present too many disconnected facts in too short a time-the "mile wide, inch

deep" problem. Tests often reinforce memorizing rather than understanding. The knowledge-centered environment provides the necessary depth of study, assessing students understanding rather than factual memory. It incorporates the teaching of meta-cognitive strategies that further facilitate future learning. (p. 24)

Current assessment policies may interfere with the necessary educational process as redefined by the NRC (Bransford, Cocking, & Brown, 2000). The NRC points out that assessments must be learner-friendly, not the traditional type in which students regurgitate memorized facts and are then rank ordered in a classroom. "Rather, these assessments should provide students with opportunities to revise and improve their thinking..." (p. 24–25). Reframing classroom assessment to focus on learning with understanding is impeded by teachers', parents', and students' models of learning. "Many assessments developed by teachers overly emphasize memory for procedures and facts. In addition, many standardized tests that are used for accountability still overemphasize memory for isolated facts and procedures, yet teachers are often judged by how well their students do on such tests" (Bransford, Brown, & Cocking, 2000, p. 141).

Wenglinsky (2005) is pessimistic about the role of the standards movement in maximizing the potential of the educational technology movement. Wenglinsky (2005) asserts that the use of technology depends specifically on whether a teacher uses a didactic or constructivist pedagogical approach. It is not the increase in access to technology, which is important, but the quality of technology use that makes a difference for student achievement. Researchers have found that technology enhances a constructivist approach to pedagogy (Becker & Riel, 2000; Becker & Ravitz, 1999; Wenglinsky, 2005).

Wenglinsky (2005), in a national, quantitative study, using NAEP test scores as the dependent variable, found that students perform better in classrooms taught by teachers employing constructivist methods. Didactic teachers are prone to use technology for drill and practice, while constructivist teachers are more likely to use technology for real-world, problem solving. The effectiveness of educational technology depends on the type of pedagogy employed. He concludes: "When technology is used in concert with constructivist teaching practices, students tend to perform well; and when it is used in concert with didactic practices, they do not" (p. 78).

Russell's volume of Research Methods for Educational Technology informs our understanding of the crossing of two of these streams, the accountability reform movement and the technology reform movement. His volume raises important questions and attempts to answer them. How do assessment and educational technology reform movement converge or diverge? To what extent does the standards-accountability-assessment movement inhibit the use of technology for new forms of learning promoted by the National Research Council? Can we accurately assess the impact of technology on student learning under conditions of high stakes testing? He concludes:

> While it is important for all students to develop basic skills in mathematics and reading and to perform well on these standardized tests when high-stakes decisions are made based on their test scores, growing use of test preparation tutorials is likely coming at the expense of computer use aimed at enhancing learning, improving technology fluency, and developing higher order research, reasoning, and communication skills. (Russell, this volume, p. 208).

Russell is correct that beliefs about the role of assessment in the educational process matter a great deal for implementation of technology-based reforms. Most importantly, Russell reminds us that while there may be a digital divide in this country, there is also a pedagogical divide: teaching for mastery on standardized tests is not the same as teaching for understanding and higher order thinking. While not mutually exclusive, in the current environment, the former is occurring at the expense of the latter. The pedagogical divide matters a great deal when trying to understand the technological divide and when trying to understand efforts to implement technology-based educational reforms. Technology can serve as a more efficient delivery system for weapons of mass instruction: high stakes standardized assessments, or it can serve as catalyst for re-engineering education in pursuit of learner-centered, knowledge-centered, assessment-centered and community-centered educational environments.

Lee Cronbach (1988) once remarked that accountability is the first sign of pathology in a system. Michael Russell's volume in this series raises serious questions about the relationship between accountability and assessment, and the catalytic power of educational technology. He also offers concrete strategies for moving beyond any impasse. We can only hope that policy makers are reading and listening.

—Walt Heinecke, Series Editor
Charlottesville, VA
December 2005

REFERENCES

Barksdale-Ladd, M. A. & K. F. Thomas (2000). What's at stake in high stakes testing: Teachers and parents speak out. *Journal of Teacher Education, 51(5)*, 384–397.

Bransford J.D., Brown, A.L., & Cocking, R. R.(Eds.). (2000). How People Learn: brain, mind, experience and school. Washington, D.C.: National Academy Press.

Chudowsky, N. & P. Behuniak (1997). Establishing consequential validity for large-scale performance assessments. Paper presented at annual meeting of the National Council of Measurement in Education, Chicago, IL.

Cronbach, L.J. (1988). Five perspectives on the validity argument. In H Wainer & H.I. Braun (Eds.). *Test validity* (pp. 3–17). Hillsdale, NJ: Erlbaum.

Darling-Hammond, L. & L. Post (2000). Inequality in teaching and schooling: Supporting high-quality teaching and leadership in low-income schools. In R. D. Kahlenberg (Ed.), *A notion at risk: Preserving public education as an engine for social mobility.* New York: Century Foundation.

Firestone, W.A. & D. Mayrowetz (2000). Rethinking 'high stakes': Lessons from the United States and England and Wales. *Teachers College Record 102*(4), 724–729.

Harrington-Lueker, Donna (2000). The uneasy coexistence of high stakes and developmentally appropriate practice. *The School Administrator, 57*(10). Available at http://www.aasa.org/publications/sa/2000_01/harrington.htm

Heinecke, W.F., Moon, T., & Curry-Corcoran, D. (2003). U.S. schools and the new standards and accountability initiative. Chapter one in D. Duke, M. Grogan, W. F. Heinecke, & P. Tucker (Eds.), *Educational leadership in an age of accountability.* Albany: SUNY Press.

Hoffman, J. V., L. C. Assaf, & S. G. Paris (2001). High-stakes testing in reading: Today in Texas, tomorrow? *The Reading Teacher, 54*(5), 482–493.

Jones, M. G., B. D. Jones, B. Hardin, L. Chapman, T. Yarbrough, & M. Davis (1999). The impact of high-stakes testing on teachers and students in North Carolina. *Phi Delta Kappan, 81,* 199–203.

Koretz, D., S. Barron, K. Mitchell, & B. Stecher (1996). The perceived effects of the Kentucky Instructional Results Information System (KIRIS) (MR-792-PCT/FF). Santa Monica, CA: RAND.

McNeil, L. (2004). Faking equity: High-stakes testing and the education of Latino youth. In A. Valenzuela eds., *Leaving children behind: How "Texas-Style" accountability fails Latino youth.* New York: State University of New York Press.

McNeil, L. (2000). *Contradictions of reform: Educational costs of standardized testing.* New York: Routledge.

McNeil, L. & A. Valenzuela (2001). The harmful impact of the TAAS system of testing in Texas: Beneath the accountability rhetoric. In M. Kornhaber & G. Orfield, (Eds.) *Raising standards or raising barriers? Inequality and high stakes testing in public education.* New York: Century Foundation, 127–150.

National Commission on Excellence in Education (1983). A Nation At Risk: The imperative for educational reform. Washington D.C.: United States Department of Education.

Nichols, S., G. Glass, & D. Berliner (2005). High stakes testing and student achievement: Problems for the No Child Left Behind Act. Tempe: AZ: Education Policy Studies Laboratory, Education Policy research Unit.

Roderick, M. & M. Engel (2001). The grasshopper and the ant: Motivational responses of low-achieving students to high-stakes testing. *Educational Evaluation and Policy Analysis, 23*(3), 197–227.

Shepard, L. A. & K. C. Dougherty (1991). Effects of high-stakes testing on instruction. Paper presented at the Annual Meetings of the American Educational Research Association (Chicago, IL, April 307, 1991).

Shepard, L. (2000). The role of assessment in a learning culture. *Educational Researcher, 29*(7), 4–14.

Stone, C. A. & S. Lane (2003). Consequences of a state accountability program: Examining relationships between school performance gains and teacher, student, and school variables. *Applied Measurement in Education, 16*(1), 1–26.

Wenglinsky, H. (2005), *Using technology wisely: The keys to success in schools*. New York: Teachers College Press.

ACKNOWLEDGMENTS

Given the fast pace with which educational technology and testing policies are developing, the information and ideas presented in this book are more analogous to a formative assessment than a summative judgment. While the ideas expressed throughout this book are my own, they have been informed and influenced by many of my colleagues and people with whom I have worked over the past fifteen years. While the number of people who have influenced and contributed to the ideas expressed here within is too lengthy to list, I do want to formally thank several people for their direct contributions to this book.

First, I thank Walt Haney for providing multiple opportunities for me to explore the intersections of educational technology and assessment during my initial forays into educational research. I would also like to thank Walt Heineke for inviting me to author a book that explores the intersection of educational technology and assessment. While it has taken longer than I had anticipated to complete this book, Walt has provided valuable feedback throughout the process. On an almost daily, Jennifer Higgins has played an invaluable role assisting with literature reviews, tracking down reports written long ago, and reviewing multiple drafts. Damian Bebell, Laura O'Dwyer, Kathleen O'Connor, and Debra Berger also provided valuable feedback on several sections of this book. George Madaus and Al Beaton generously directed me toward documents and reports that explored early developments in testing and computer-based testing. Finally, I thank my wife, Liana Kish, for her support and feedback throughout this process.

Technology and Assessment: The Tale of Two Interpretations, page xv
Copyright © 2006 by Information Age Publishing

CHAPTER 1

THE RISE OF TECHNOLOGY AND ASSESSMENT IN K–12 EDUCATION

Computer-based technologies are pervasive throughout our society. They are ubiquitous in the workplace; have penetrated the majority of homes in the United States; are present in nearly every public school; and drive our trains, planes, and automobiles. In fact, in 2002 BMW announced that the control panel for its 7 Series will be driven by Windows CE, creating "an advanced in-car computing experience" (Microsoft, 2002). Meanwhile, it is estimated that K–12 public schools are now spending more than $5 billion a year on computer-based technologies (McCabe & Skinner, 2003), with some districts and states launching efforts to provide a laptop computer for every student and teacher.

Over the past two decades, summative assessment of student achievement also has been established as a critical and omnipresent component of the Untied States K–12 educational system. Whether occurring within individual classrooms, at the district level, or across states, the nation, or even the world, summative assessment is driving important decisions about students, schools, and specific instructional programs and practices. During the 2001 fiscal year, states spent more than $400 million developing, administering, and scoring standardized tests (Danitz, 2001). These costs will skyrocket over the next few years, some experts estimating to $2–$7 billion, as states struggle to change their assessment systems to comply with the *No Child Left Behind Act* (Danitz, 2002). Results from these tests were used to distribute $13.5 million in bonuses to principals and administrators in New York City alone (Goodnough, 2002, p. A22). But the stakes are more than just financial, in many states promotion and graduation decisions are made based on state test results. "Within the next two years, more than half the states will use student scores on these tests to determine promotion and graduation" (Futrell, & Rotberg, 2002, p.1). While reliance on summative assessment to make decisions about students and schools has led some critics to worry about increased dropout and retention rates, proponents believe that instruction will become more focused and student learning will improve (Shepard, 1990).

Separately, instructional uses of computer-based technology and assessment represent two of the most pervasive and persistent educational reform efforts introduced over the past two decades. Today, there is hardly a public K–12 school that is not equipped with computers and nearly all schools (92%) across the nation are connected to the Internet (Market Data Retrieval, 2001). Similarly, every state in the nation has a formal student assessment program. Even among other popular reform strategies like charter schools and efforts by organizations such as New American Schools to create "break-the-mold schools," technology and assessment are critical components.

GAP BETWEEN TESTING AND TECHNOLOGY

Despite the popularity of technology and assessment, these two reform tools for improving teaching and learning have been developed and implemented in an uncoordinated manner. As Walt Haney and I (Russell & Haney, 1997a, 2000) described several years ago, the result is a gap between testing and instructional technology.

At the time, our argument focused on providing more valid measures of student achievement and was based on two experiments in which students were randomly assigned to perform writing tests on paper or on computers. Both experiments found that the test scores for students who were accustomed to writing with computers severely underestimated the students' ability when they were forced to write with paper and pencil (Russell, 1999; Russell & Haney, 1997a, 2000). For this reason, we warned against reliance on paper-based tests to make inferences about the achievement of tech-savvy students.

In the years since we first identified this gap, the extent to which decision-makers depend on paper-based tests to make decisions about students and their schools has expanded rapidly. To date, all fifty states have formal testing programs that require students to take numerous standardized tests between the second and twelfth grades. Reliance on tests as a vehicle for educational accountability is also clearly evident in President Bush's *No Child Left Behind Act* (or NCLB, Public Law No: 107-110) which requires all states to demonstrate annual improvement on tests administered to students in Grades three through eight.

Recognizing the importance of computer-based technology, NCLB also calls on states to leverage the power of technology both to improve student learning and to enhance state assessment programs. To this end, $62.5 million federal dollars were made available between 2002 and 2004 to help teachers learn how to use instructional technologies in their classrooms and $17 million is available to assist states in enhancing their testing programs (U.S. Department of Education, 2002). While it is too early to know exactly how these funds will be spent, it is likely that the presence and use of technology in schools and testing programs will increase over these next few years. For this reason, it seems that the encouragement to capitalize on computer-based technologies for instruction and for testing combined with the availability of funding is a positive step toward closing the gap between testing and technology.

In reality, however, this gap represents more than the misalignment between a mode of learning and a mode of testing. Since first writing about this problem, I have come to view the gap as one between beliefs rather practices.

Many proponents of instructional technologies believe that the most valuable uses of technology in the classroom result in the development of students' higher order thinking skills, ability to conduct and assimilate research, model and solve complex problems, communicate with people within and beyond their local communities, and develop fluency with digital tools used regularly in the workplace. These proponents envision classrooms in which students are independent thinkers who develop knowledge by conducting experiments, seeking information, communicating, and collaborating with others. This vision of educational reform focuses more on *how* students learn and work than on prescribing *what* they learn.

In contrast, developers of state and national accountability systems believe that tests are an effective tool for influencing the acquisition of skills and knowledge which teachers are supposed to help students master as they progress through primary and secondary public schools. To define the skills and knowledge students are expected to develop, proponents of state-sponsored educational accountability depend on curriculum frameworks and content standards. To measure this body of skills and knowledge, states either contract test companies to develop tests or select off-the-shelf standardized tests that are aligned with their frameworks and standards. In this way, the vision of educational reform put forth by proponents of state-sponsored accountability focuses primarily on *what* students learn rather than on *how* students learn. From this perspective, emphasis is placed on developing basic skills rather than developing innovative applications of technology to develop higher-order thinking and problem solving skills.

Thus, the gap between testing and technology is more than one of modality. It is one of fundamental beliefs about how schools are expected to shape students and what role teachers and technology should play in this shaping process. To illustrate, compare a passage by Seymour Papert, one of the strongest proponents for educational technology, with text from the *Enhancing Education Through Technology Act* of 2001, Title II, Part D of the *No Child Left Behind Act.* Reflecting on his own experience working with computers, Papert writes:

> Computers should serve children as instruments to work with and to think with, as the means to carry out projects, the source of concepts to think new ideas. The last thing in the world I wanted or needed was a drill and practice program telling me to do this sum next or spell that word! Why should we impose such a thing on children? What had launched me into a new spurt of personal learning at MIT wasn't in the slightest bit like the CAI [computer assisted instruction] programs. I became obsessed with the question, 'Could access to computers allow children something like the kind of intellectual boost I felt I had gained from access to computers at MIT?' (Papert, 1993, p. 168)

In contrast, Section 2402 of the NCLB describes the purposes and goals of the *Enhancing Education Through Technology Act* as:

- [Providing] assistance to States and localities for the implementation and support of a comprehensive system that effectively uses technology in elementary schools and secondary schools to improve student academic achievement....
- [Promoting] initiatives that provide school teachers, principals, and administrators with the capacity to integrate technology effectively into curricula and instruction that are aligned with challenging State academic content and student academic achievement standards, through such means as high-quality professional development programs....
- [Supporting] the rigorous evaluation of programs funded under this part, particularly regarding the impact of such programs on student academic achievement, and ensure that timely information on the results of such evaluations is widely accessible through electronic means....
- The primary goal of this part is to improve student academic achievement through the use of technology in elementary schools and secondary schools. (Public Law No: 107-110, Section 2402)

Whereas Papert views technology as a tool that can open a child's mind to new ideas and allow children to explore ideas in such a way that their intellectual curiosity is ignited, the authors of the *No Child Left Behind Act* conceive of technology as a tool to help students master a predefined body of knowledge and skills. Whereas Papert envisions students working with computers in order to open vast expanses and to identify avenues within those expanses for exploration, NCLB conceives of computers as vehicles that carry students down a pre-paved road of content knowledge and basic skills. Whereas Papert envisions the student controlling computers, NCLB places curriculum and standards in control of teachers and teachers in control of how students use computers to achieve these curricula-based standards. Finally, whereas Papert believes that technology will reform education toward higher order, problem-based learning and thus develop skills and knowledge that are difficult to assess through large-scale testing, NCLB seeks to improve what we are currently doing to help students develop mastery of a discrete body of content which is measurable by standardized tests. It is as if what is measurable on a standardized test is defining effective technology use.

To be clear, the gap in intentions that exists between computer-based instructional technology and conventional assessment does not prevent the two from interacting. To the contrary, computer-based technology and assessment are having profound influences on each other. For example, the gap between technology and assessment is beginning to impact how and why teachers use technology in the classroom. In some cases, the fact that tests are administered on paper is driving some teachers away from using computers to develop students' writing skills (Russell & Abrams, 2004). In other cases, a desire to improve student standardized test scores is driving teachers to use instructional technology that is specifically designed to prepare students for state-mandated tests. In Massachusetts, for example, the State Department of Education has established a $300,000-per-year contract with Princeton Review to make Homeroom.com available to all students preparing for the Massachusetts Comprehensive Assessment System Exams. During the spring of 2002, Massachusetts also began pilot testing Vantage Learning's computer scoring software to provide online scoring of student writing produced during class time in preparation for the state test. Similar purchases are being made by several other states and districts.

National priorities for research on technology have also shifted to a focus on teacher-proof drill and practice software designed to develop many of the basic skills measured by state tests. In fact, the U.S. DOE recently launched a five-year, $15 million study to examine the impact of a limited number of instructional software programs on student learning as measured by standardized test scores.

As a second example, a desire to improve the efficiency of state testing programs is driving several state policy makers to transition from paper-based testing to computer-based testing. At last count, 19 states are actively exploring this transition. In most cases, these states plan to transfer paper-based tests to a web-based version with the goal of decreasing the amount of time required to distribute, collect, and score paper-based tests. In a few cases, states are exploring the use of computer adaptive tests in order to decrease the amount of testing time. A few states are also considering the use of computers to score student essays. In addition, a large percentage of states use the World Wide Web to share results of state-mandated testing programs with schools and their communities. In some cases, results are provided on the Internet as static reports. In a few cases, however, states like Michigan and Maryland capitalize on web-based database and analysis software to allow visitors to conduct dynamic analyses of the state test results.

As a third example, concern about the high costs required to place and support computers in schools and subsequent calls by educational leaders, politicians, and the general public for evidence that technology is having a positive impact on student learning is leading technology researchers to place increased emphasis on assessing student learning. Although researchers and educational leaders recognize that the type of norm- and criterion-referenced tests currently employed by state-testing programs are not sensitive to the full range of learning that occurs as students work with computers in schools (Becker & Lovitts, 2000; Means, Penuel, & Quellmalz, 2000; Russell, 2002), scores on these tests are often the measure used to examine the effect of computer use on student learning (Baker, Herman, & Gearhart 1996; Ravitz, Mergendoller, & Rush 2002; Wenglinski, 1998). This problem of misalignment between what is measured by state-mandated tests and the full range of skills and knowledge valued by many proponents of instructional technology is exacerbated by calls for scientifically- and research-based evidence of technology's impact on student achievement. Although proponents of instructional technology, like Papert, identify several ways in which technology can positively impact student learning, many of these domains are not currently measured by standardized tests. And, while NCLB does allow for the development of performance assessments and other forms of testing across all students, significant time and resources must be dedicated to developing these new assessment tools before they will be accepted as valid, reliable, and scientifically-based measurement instruments.

From my perspective, the gap between technology and assessment has emerged largely because proponents of technology and developers of student assessment instruments (i.e., tests) generally operate in separate worlds. As a result, the words "technology" and "assessment" have different meanings to members of each community.

In one world, technology proponents develop, research, and improve tools intended to alter the ways in which teaching and learning occur in the classroom. For those who work with educational technology, the words technology and assessment are most commonly interpreted to mean assessing the impact of technology on teaching and learning. While these assessments of technology's impact often utilize standardized tests designed to measures student learning in traditional content areas, it is only recently that segments of this research community have become proactive in developing assessments that are more closely aligned with the skills and knowledge students develop while learning with technology and which allow students to work on tests with the same technologies that they use while learning. As an example, Barbara Means and her colleagues have developed an assessment task for which students must find, evaluate and apply information on the World Wide Web to solve a complex problem (Means et al., 2001). These new approaches to measuring student learning have yet to be embraced by educational leaders, politicians, the general public, or major test developers, in part because their validity and reliability have not yet been well established. In addition, whereas developers of traditional standardized tests have been in operation for decades and have applied significant financial resources to develop and maintain these standardized tests, relatively little capital has been invested in developing alternative approaches to measuring student skills. As a result, technology researchers often rely on accepted, standardized measures, while admitting that these measures underestimate the full impact of technology on student learning.

In a separate world, test developers endeavor to produce tests that provide reliable measures of skills and knowledge that comprise specific domains. Increasingly, these tests are used to make high stakes decisions like college entrance, high school graduation, and retention. As a secondary goal, test developers seek ways to improve the efficiency and validity of such measures. Those who develop tests think of technology as a tool that can be used to enhance current approaches to student assessment. In fact, throughout the history of testing, test developers have relied on many forms of technology to improve the efficiency of assessment. These forms of technology include paper, the printing press, statistical and mathematical functions, and, most recently, computer-based technologies like the scanner and the Internet. Today, computers are already being used to alter how tests are delivered and scored. But current uses of computers in testing do not fully capitalize on the power and flexibility of computer-based technologies. Beyond increasing efficiency of testing, computers have the potential to alter the types of knowledge and skills that are assessed. Rather than focusing only on the end-product that students produce as they work on a test, computers make it possible to collect information about the processes and decisions students make as they solve problems. Rather than providing information about how well students can solve various problems, this process information could be used to provide more detailed information about students' current state of knowledge and their misconceptions.

When Walt Haney and I first wrote about the gap between technology and assessment, we argued that this gap needed to be bridged (Russell & Haney, 1997a, 2000). Viewing this gap from the perspective of developing more valid measures of achievement for tech-savvy students, we believed that this gap could be bridged by a thoughtful transition to computer-based testing, particularly when students are required to express their knowledge and skills through written responses. More recently, however, I have come to realize that it will take much more than simply transitioning tests from paper to computer. Bridging this gap requires a merging of two distinct communities—namely those who develop tests and those who develop and research instructional technologies. Developing sound, valid and reliable measures of the types of learning that technology researchers argue students develop as they work with technology requires the insight and knowledge of psychometricians and test developers trained in test construction. Similarly, the development of new tests that are aligned with the tools and types of skills students develop as new technologies are used in the classroom requires that test developers be informed by technology researchers and content experts about emerging instructional technologies and practices.

In this book I attempt to help bridge this gap by examining the history, recent practices, and promising developments within the field of student assessment and the field of educational technology. Given the strong emphasis placed on student assessment in the current political context, I focus first on student assessment in Chapters 2 through 7 and then on educational technology in Chapters 8 through 11. Specifically, Chapter 2 traces the development of assessment as a reform tool. Chapter 3 describes how testing is a technology itself and reviews several ways that the technology of testing has been influenced by technological advances in other fields as well as by social and political needs. In chapters four through seven, I explore several roles computer-based technologies have played in the field of testing. Chapter 4 focuses on automatic scanning machines, the many electronic devices developed during the 1940s and 1950s to augment scanners, and the current dependence on computer-based scanning services to process the incredible volume of tests administered today. In Chapter 5 I explore how instructional uses of computers in the classroom are driving testing programs to change policies regarding the use of technology and how instructional practices are being influenced by the test itself. Chapter 6 examines the application of personal computers and the Internet to deliver tests in either a linear or adaptive manner and to report test results. In Chapter 7, emerging applications of computers that have the potential to dramatically alter the content and format of tests are explored. In Chapter 8, I switch the focus from assessment to instructional technology and trace the development of technology as a reform tool. Chapter 9 documents a pattern of excitement and resistance that has accompanied the introduction of a variety of educational technologies over the past 150 years. Chapter 10 then describes many of the approaches used to examine the impact of these educational technologies and in the process traces the rise, fall, and re-emergence of large-scale experimental designs as the acid test for the effectiveness of a given educational technology. Chapter 11 focuses on some of the challenges posed by employing large-scale randomized studies to examine the effect of computer-based technology on teaching and learning and describes several alternative approaches that hold promise for understanding and supporting educational uses of computer-based technologies. The final chapter explores strategies that may help bring these two communities together in order to more fully capitalize on the power of computer-based technologies that impact teaching and learning and to more fully assess these impacts. It is my hope that by initially treating each field separately, readers who have a background in instructional technology will gain a deeper understanding of the history and current issues faced by test developers while readers with a background in test development will deepen their understanding of the challenges faced by the educational technology research community.

CHAPTER 2

THE RISE OF ASSESSMENT AS A STRATEGY FOR EDUCATIONAL REFORM

As of this writing, state-level assessment programs have been established in all 50 states and student assessment stands at the center of federal and all state-level educational accountability programs. Although many students in today's schools may not have experienced a time when state tests were not a regular school event, this level of testing is a relatively new occurrence. In this chapter, I trace the evolution of assessment as a strategy for reforming education. As I describe in greater detail below, from my perspective, this evolution was spawned in the early 1980s and grew into what has become known as the standards movement. Out of the standards movement two avenues emerged for the role of assessment in educational reform. One avenue sought to introduce new forms of assessment that would encourage teachers to alter instructional practices. The other avenue sought to use standardized tests to hold teachers responsible for teaching what is specified in state content standards. As witnessed by the dominance of student assessment in President Bush's *No Child Left Behind Act of 2001* (Public Law No: 107-110) the latter path has prevailed.

As approved by both houses of Congress in January 2002, federal education funding currently requires that states implement tests for all students in Grades 3–8 in reading and mathematics. As stated in the White House's summary of the legislation, "These systems must be based on challenging

Technology and Assessment: The Tale of Two Interpretations, pages 11–19
Copyright © 2006 by Information Age Publishing

State standards in reading and mathematics, annual testing for all students in Grades 3–8, and annual statewide progress objectives ensuring that all groups of students reach proficiency within 12 years" (The White House, 2002, p. 2). Although the President's education policy does not stipulate how states should use test scores beyond stipulating that schools must make adequate yearly progress toward increasing the percentage of students who are performing at a state-specified proficiency level, the legislation itself and rhetoric surrounding the legislation exemplify the extent to which many education and political leaders equate educational accountability with student testing.

The emphasis placed on testing, however, is not attributable solely to NCLB. In fact, this emphasis on accountability through high stakes testing existed prior to the introduction of NCLB. As an example, *Education Week*'s annual rating of the quality of each state's standards and accountability system, which was developed prior to NCLB, places strong emphasis on testing. As Orlofsky and Olson (2001) describe, six of the seven factors that influence ratings for standards and accountability focus specifically on student tests and include:

- Whether the state tests students;
- Whether the tests are norm-referenced or criterion-referenced;
- The subject areas tested (English, mathematics, science, and social studies tests are required to receive "full credit");
- The type of test items used (multiple-choice, open-ended, essay, portfolio, etc.);
- The extent to which the tests are aligned with the state standards in elementary, middle, and high school;
- Whether the state requires school report cards (ratings of schools);
- Whether the state rates, rewards, sanctions, and/or provides assistance to schools based on student test scores.

Numerous observers (Ravitch, 1995; Amrein & Berliner, 2002; Russell & Haney, 2000) have attributed the prominence of student assessment in today's educational system, particularly at the state-level, to the 1983 release of *A Nation at Risk* (National Commission on Excellence in Education, 1983). Warning that the future of the American workforce was threatened by the substandard quality of education provided by public schools, the report sparked grave concern about student learning and academic performance. As a remedy, the report recommended that states establish rigorous educational standards in order to homogenize and streamline curricula and called for the development and use of assessments that are closely tied to the standards. In addition, the report sought to hold schools responsible for meeting these new rigorous standards and viewed student assessment as the primary measure of success.

Since the report's release, the number of states that have developed their own tests linked to standards (as opposed to purchasing an off-the-shelf standardized test) increased sharply from zero in 1983 to 37 in 2001 (Meyer, Orlofsky, Skinner, & Spicer, 2002, p. 68). Similarly, the number of states that have sought to hold schools and students accountable by requiring students to pass a high school graduation test has risen steadily from four in 1983 to 18 in 2002. In addition, nine more states are slated to use tests to make decisions about graduation by the year 2008, raising the total number of states to 27 (Amrein & Berliner, 2002). On the surface, the growth in high school graduation testing and test-based accountability programs appears linear. In reality, though, the path to the current situation has taken several noteworthy turns.

At the time *A Nation at Risk* was drafted, several states employed minimum competency tests. In part, *A Nation at Risk* was a reaction to minimum competency programs and its authors argued that these programs had "diluted" the quality of education provided in many schools. Rather than teaching to a minimum level of skill and knowledge, the report sought to raise the bar. Coupled with the lingering effects of legal challenges to the validity of these testing programs (*Debra P. vs. Turlington*, 1979), the report represented the final blow to the minimum competency testing movement. To fill the void left by the elimination of minimum competency testing, and in response to the dire warnings of *A Nation at Risk*, educational reformers scrambled to develop new standards and assessments.

Professional organizations like the National Council of Teachers of Mathematics (NCTM) and the American Association for the Advancement of Science (AAAS) invested several years developing "national" standards or benchmarks. Several states and local districts followed suit, developing their own set of content and performance standards. At the same time, a revolt against multiple-choice tests erupted. Arguing that multiple-choice tests did a poor job measuring many of the higher-order cognitive skills emphasized in the emerging curriculum standards, several efforts were made to develop "alternative" forms of assessment. These alternative assessments included complex open-ended items, performance tests, portfolios, and exhibitions. Rather than presenting students with a series of discrete problems for which students select one correct answer, these alternative assessments sought to engage students in more complex problems with multiple correct responses and often required students to communicate their understanding through words, diagrams, mathematical and scientific expressions, or some combination thereof. In addition, some advocates for alternative assessments called for the use of authentic tasks that engaged students in real-world problems (Wiggins, 1993).

As one example, Lauren and Daniel Resnick formed the New Standards Project. The project invested several years developing rigorous standards in mathematics, English language arts, science and "applied learning." The new standards emphasized higher order problem-solving and communication skills. To help teachers better understand the instructional implications of the standards, several examples of student work that represented different levels of performance were assembled (Spalding, 2000). And to measure student progress toward the standards, the New Standards Reference Exams were developed for Grades 4, 8, and 10. For mathematics, these tests contained a small set of challenging open-ended problems that required students to solve complex problems that they might encounter outside of the classroom. Similarly, in language arts, the items required students to produce extended written passages and allowed students ample time over multiple days to brainstorm, outline, draft, and then finalize their responses. Unlike most standardized tests that are norm-referenced (expressing a student's performance in comparison to the performance of other students), the *New Standards Reference Exams* were criterion-referenced. On these tests, rubrics were used to score students' responses and scores represented levels of performance (e.g., developing knowledge, proficient, advanced state of understanding).

Working with individual schools, in 1985 Ted Sizer and the Coalition for Essential Schools launched a separate effort to radically reform instructional and assessment practices within schools. Rather than delivering instruction and then testing students on the content of that instruction, the Coalition of Essential Schools advocates a redefinition of what and how students learn. Rather than cover a broad and wide-ranging curriculum, the Coalition encourages schools to define a set of "Essential Skills and Areas of Knowledge." As Darling-Hammond, Ancess, and Falk (1995) explain, "While these skills and areas will, to varying degrees, reflect the traditional academic disciplines, the program's design should be shaped by the intellectual and imaginative powers and competencies that students need, rather than necessarily by 'subjects' as conventionally defined" (p. 16). Rather than administering specific tests to students to determine whether they have mastered these essential competencies, the Coalition advocates the use of formal exhibitions. Depending upon the essential skills and knowledge of which the student is attempting to demonstrate mastery, an exhibition could take the form of an extended report, an oral presentation, the creation of a product, or some combination thereof. In addition, these exhibitions are presented to several people including a group of teachers, parents, community members, and possibly fellow students, making the assessment process more public. Although the practices advocated by the Coalition are time consuming and require major restructuring of school and instructional practices, approximately 250 schools nationwide have adopted the Coalition's "Common Principles" (Coalition of Essential Schools, 2002).

Believing that there is an important distinction between knowing about a subject area and being able to solve problems in that area, several organizations also set out to create performance tests. Unlike multiple-choice tests that tend to focus on knowledge of content, performance tests required students to use tools and resources to solve extended problems. Rather than presenting students with a series of unrelated items each of which requires a small amount of time to answer, performance tests present students with a small set of tasks. Each task presents students with a unique problem. To help students solve the problem, they are given equipment and materials to work with and are usually presented with a short series of questions specific to the task. For example, one middle school performance mathematics item presents students with a balance scale, a 20-gram mass, a 50-gram mass, and a large ball of clay. Using the materials at hand, students are asked to produce a ball of clay weighing 15 grams. After doing so, students are asked to place their ball of clay into a plastic bag and then describe the process they used to produce the ball. When scoring the item, both the accuracy of the clay ball mass and the description of the process used are considered (Semple, 1992).

Although time consuming and expensive to administer and score, performance tests were employed in several states including Kentucky, California, and New York. In addition, performance tests were given to students across several nations during the 1991 International Assessment of Educational Progress and to 21 nations during the 1995 Third International Mathematics and Science Study (TIMSS). By the late 1990s, however, the use of performance tests decreased sharply for several reasons. In California, the state's testing program fell victim to politics and was sharply criticized by groups that disliked several aspects of the assessment system (see Cohen & Hill, 2001 for a detailed account of reactions to California's assessment system). Although Kentucky invested considerable resources to develop an assessment system that integrated multiple-choice items, open-ended items, and performance tasks that included group and individual activities, technical problems related to reliability and stability of scales arose while linking scores over years. In New York, the expense and effort required to administer and score performance tests were too high for the state to bear. Similarly, although performance tests were administered in 21 countries as part of the 1995 TIMSS study, the results from these tests have been largely ignored by the test developers, participating nations, and the general public. It is noteworthy that performance tests were dropped from the 1999 and 2003 TIMSS-Repeat studies, due in part to their limited focus in the first study, the high cost of developing and administering these tests, and weaker psychometric properties of the resulting scores.

Another method of assessment that became popular during the early 1990s was portfolios. Although some portfolios became little more than a repository for students' work, the push for portfolio assessment was driven by two ideas. Recognizing that students do not always produce their best work on the day of testing and that no one piece of work fully captures what a student knows and can do, portfolios were used as a tool to capture students' best work produced over a period of time. In this scenario, students, teachers, or both would purposefully select samples of work that demonstrate students' acquisition and mastery of skills and knowledge. Just as student performance on a set of test items is used to summarize their achievement, the collection of student work would be analyzed to assess student performance. A second use of portfolios was to document changes in students' skills and knowledge over time. In most cases, these changes were examined by comparing work produced during one time period (usually the fall) with work produced during a later time period (usually the spring). In general, using portfolios to document individual growth has occurred within classrooms and schools, while use of portfolios to assess the mastery of specific skills and knowledge has occurred at the classroom, school, and state level. Portfolios were a component of Kentucky's student assessment system during the 1990s and have been used in Vermont since 1992. Similarly, the Massachusetts Comprehensive Assessment System allows students with special needs to create portfolios of their work in lieu of taking the state's standardized test (Massachusetts Department of Education, 2003). While other state assessment systems have explored the possibility of using portfolios, they are commonly used within classrooms and schools. A recent search of AskERIC, which has been collecting articles and resources related to education since 1992, resulted in 3,937 articles related to portfolio assessment, indicating widespread interest in this method of assessment. Today, however, interest in portfolios is limited largely to classroom- and school-level assessment and is no longer a major component of any state-level testing programs. This disappearance of portfolios from state assessment programs results largely from the high costs associated with developing portfolios and the lower reliability of scores resulting from the evaluation of portfolios.

A fifth movement that began in the 1980s and carried into the 1990s focused on the need to develop assessments that were more diagnostic rather than summative in nature. Unlike the efforts described above which were largely led by educators and researchers working closely in schools, efforts to develop diagnostic assessments came from a small cadre of testing experts and cognitive scientists. Following the Conference of Alternative Diagnostic Assessment held in 1993, Nichols and Brennan (1995) wrote:

> The idea for the conference arose from our observations of a shift in measurement from emphasizing selection to emphasizing diagnosis. Over the

past decade or so, a number of researchers have argued that cognitive science and psychometrics could be combined in the service of instruction. They have criticized traditional testing for losing sight of the psychology of the performance being tested and for placing more emphasis on statistical technique than on the psychology of the construct being measured. (p. ix)

Efforts to develop diagnostic assessments were motivated by a desire to provide information to help teachers make specific instructional decisions. In many cases, these assessments involved complex performance-based tasks, but they also took the form of more traditional items in which students selected rather than produced responses. In a few cases, computers were used to present tasks and record each student's actions and responses. Despite a significant effort by a small community of cognitive scientists and psychometricians, the new assessments are not yet in wide use largely because their psychometric properties have not been firmly established and policy makers have yet to embrace them.

Although cognitively-based diagnostic assessments have not yet caught on, each of the other assessment efforts experienced a period of popularity. The *New Standards Reference Exams* were embraced by several individual school districts and were adopted by a handful of states during the 1990s. Following their development within the New Standards Project, the exams were also purchased and then distributed by Harcourt Brace Educational Measurement Company. As noted earlier, several schools have adopted the "Common Principles" espoused by the Coalition of Essential schools. States and international testing programs also experimented with and, in some cases, employed performance tests and portfolio-based assessments. But, in the vast majority of cases, these assessment methods are not currently used as part of state assessment and accountability programs. While several states have developed their own criterion-referenced tests that are linked to their curriculum standards and many states employ a combination of multiple-choice and short-answer items, the tests used today more closely resemble the norm-referenced, predominantly multiple-choice tests employed prior to the release of *A Nation at Risk* than the vision of assessment put forth by reformers between the mid-1980s and early 1990s.

The failure to dramatically alter the way in which students are assessed (at least at the state level) is due to at least four reasons. First, performance tests, portfolios, and exhibitions are expensive and time intensive. Second, the technical quality of these methods, especially with regard to the reliability of scores, has not been adequately established. This occurs, in part, because it is much more difficult to score open-ended responses than it is to score responses to multiple-choice items. Third, the assessment reformers have not yet been successful in persuading the educational community and political leaders of the additional value added by assessments that provide diagnostic versus summative information about student performance. Fourth, educational and political leaders, as well as the general public, are accustomed to traditional tests that contain multiple-choice and short-answer items. When confronted with the high costs and the technical challenges of alternative methods of assessment, educational leaders, politicians, and the general public question why the tests that were used throughout their formal education should not still be used today. Moreover, these tests yield scores that are familiar, and which are believed to be objective measures of student achievement. Thus, despite several efforts to generate new forms of assessment, the long-term response to *A Nation at Risk* has resulted in the wide-scale use of relatively traditional forms of assessment at the state and national level. In fact, many of the state-level tests used today are nearly identical to tests used several decades ago: They are paper-based, must be completed with pencils, focus on basic skills and knowledge in the area of mathematics and language arts (and sometimes science and social studies), and present students with a large set of fact-based multiple-choice questions, a smaller set of short-answer items, and perhaps one extended essay question.

In some cases, however, the emphasis placed on testing by national leaders is driving state testing programs to deliver tests on computers. This change is driven largely by a desire to increase the efficiency with which tests are delivered and scored, both in terms of time and money. While this move toward computer-based testing in K–12 schools has just begun, it is likely that most students currently entering kindergarten will perform several computer-based tests before they graduate from high school. In fact, over the past two years, nineteen states have taken steps to transition paper-based tests to computers (Russell, Goldberg, & O'Connor, 2003).

Not surprising, this rapidly expanding migration from paper to computer-based tests has sparked concern among many observers. Most often, these concerns relate to how computer-based testing will affect the performance of students who are not accustomed to working on computers. However, other concerns have focused on whether simply presenting today's primarily multiple-choice tests on computers fully capitalizes on the full power of computers. Some also wonder whether the speed and seeming objectiveness of computer-based tests may lead to further increases in the amount of testing.

Interestingly, neither the influence of computer-based technologies on testing that we are witnessing today nor the accompanying concerns are novel. As described in the next two chapters, since the rapid expansion of standardized testing following World War I and the subsequent invention of the electric scanning machine capable of scoring hundreds of answer sheets per hour, computer-based technologies have impacted educational testing. As I explore in detail in the next chapter, neither the political and social influences that have given rise to an unprecedented level of state testing nor the desire to apply new technology to increase the efficiency of testing are new. In fact, they have been at play since the birth of formal testing nearly two millennia ago.

CHAPTER 3

THE HISTORICAL INFLUENCE OF TECHNOLOGY, POLITICS, AND SOCIETAL NEEDS ON THE TECHNOLOGY OF TESTING

In recent years, increased attention has focused on both the use of computers to create computer-based tests and the use of tests to hold schools accountable for student learning. As I explore in greater detail below, the interactions between testing and politics, societal needs, and new technologies have occurred throughout the history of testing. In this chapter, I begin by defining what I mean by the word testing. I then trace the evolution of testing from its inception in China nearly 2,000 years ago through the early twentieth century. In doing so, several influences of politics, societal needs, and technology on the form and purpose of testing are highlighted.

THE TECHNOLOGY OF TESTING

For many readers, the word technology often evokes images of machines. Cars, televisions, robots, and computers are all recognized as technologies. Like any technology, these devices are developed to meet a specific pur-

Technology and Assessment: The Tale of Two Interpretations, pages 21–34
Copyright © 2006 by Information Age Publishing
All rights of reproduction in any form reserved.

pose and require specialized skill and knowledge to develop. But so, too, is testing a technology. As Madaus, Raczek, and Clarke (1997, p. 7) explain:

> ...testing (like any technology) is something put together for a purpose, to satisfy a pressing and immediate need, or to solve a problem. But testing, like most modern technologies, also involves specialized arcane knowledge, hidden algorithms, and technical art, and like many current technologies is a complex of standardized means for attaining a predetermined end in social, economic, administrative, and educational institutions.

Whether one focuses on a test, exhibition, examination, portfolio, or a performance assessment, the underlying technology is the same: A limited sample of behavior is taken from a specific domain in order to make inferences about the examinee's probable performance across that domain. Despite the tendency of students, parents, teachers, and the general public to focus on specific scores an examinee receives on a test, it is not the score or rating an examinee receives that is of interest. Instead, it is the inference about the examinee's performance within the sampled domain that is of value. As an example, when giving a third grade math test, what is of interest is how well that student can apply the skills and knowledge developed during third grade to solve any problem that requires these skills. Since it is not feasible to present students with all of the problems that require these skills, a sample of problems are assembled into a test. Based on how well the student performs on this sample of problems, an inference is made about how well the student can apply third grade math skills to solve any problem that requires these skills. Thus, it is the inference about how well the student can solve any problem that requires third grade math skills that is of importance rather than how well the student performed on the specific set of items that comprised the test.

Throughout the history of testing, the following four methods have been used to sample an examinee's performance within a domain:

1. A person is asked to supply an oral or written answer to a series of questions (e.g., essay, short-answer or oral exams).

2. A person is asked to create a product (e.g., conduct an experiment or build a model).

3. A person is asked to perform an act (e.g., play an instrument or perform an interpretive dance).

4. A person is presented with a series of questions or problems and is asked to select an answer from among several options (Madaus & O'Dwyer, 1999).

For the first three methods, predefined criteria are used by a person or group of people to evaluate the response, product, or act. The fourth method is evaluated by determining whether the examinee made the correct selection for each test item. It is these methods of sampling behavior, the scoring procedures, and the way in which valid inferences are made that define the technology of testing.

Today, there is growing interest in applying computer-based technology to enhance the technology of testing. In most cases, this interest is driven by a desire to make testing more efficient. Given the sharp increase in the amount of testing that has occurred since the 1960s and the continued increase that will occur over the next five years as the *No Child Left Behind Act* is implemented, any decrease in the amount of time and effort required to ship, scan and score paper-based tests will impact financial bottom lines.

Given that some states take up to six months between administration of a test and actually reporting the results of the tests, decreasing the amount of time to return results to schools could also lead to both educational benefits and more positive attitudes toward the state tests. For the sake of efficiency alone, applications of computer-based technology to testing could have an important impact on testing.

But the influence of an emerging technology on testing is not new. Since the inception of formal testing, new technologies combined with social and political issues of the time have impacted the technology of testing. To provide some perspective on the recent and potential future impact of computer-based technology on the technology of testing, it is instructive to briefly trace the history of testing.

THE BIRTH OF TESTING IN CHINA

The Han Dynasty is consistently credited with introducing the civil service examination system in 206 BC. At that time, the Dynasty was expanding its empire rapidly and was faced with three pressing political needs: (a) consolidating its government, (b) decreasing the influence of patronage, and (c) selecting civil servants based on merit (Madaus et al., 1997). In reality however, the Han Dynasty did not actually develop or administer any tests. Instead, it was during the Han Dynasty that, "[t]he first steps were taken to organize the recruitment of civil servants on the basis of merit; appointments to official posts went to 'men of talent' who had been recommended to the capital on the initiative of local officials. Later on, examinations were used to supplement recommendation as a measure of talent" (Meskill, 1963, p. vii). Thus, in response to a political need, the Han Dynasty introduced the concept that selection of civil servants should be based on merit rather than on whom a candidate knew and how well that candidate was liked (Franke, 1960).

It was not until 622 A.D. when the Tang dynasty (618–906 A.D.) actually administered exams to candidates for civil service. At the time, however, candidates were required to be recommended by a magistrate in order to take the exam. With the invention of paper by Cai Lun in 105 A.D., these first exams were written. Lasting for several days, only about 2% of examinees passed the exam and were then subjected to an oral exam by the emperor.

In comparison to the former process of local officials recommending candidates for civil service, the use of a formal written exam served to standardize the selection process and clearly defined the skills and knowledge required to enter civil service. Although it took eight centuries to implement, the use of a formal exam greatly reduced China's dependence on patronage to select civil servants. By administering the exam on paper rather than orally, the exam system allowed the emperor to narrow a large body of candidates down to a select few who were further tested through an oral exam. In this way, the first system of exams employed by the Tang Dynasty served as an efficient, standardized tool for narrowing the pool of candidates for civil service.

Over the next six centuries, both the domains tested and the way in which test results were used in China became more diverse. The civil service exam expanded its focus from a narrow set of skills and knowledge believed requisite for service to include knowledge in a number of disciplines. During the Sung Dynasty (960–1279 BC) the Letters examination emerged as the most prestigious measure of knowledge. Based on the teachings of Confucius, the Letters examination included "completing passages from memory; summarizing the meanings of the classics, composing a discussion, a poetic description, and a piece of poetry, and, finally, demonstrating reasoning ability by discussing five (seeming) conflicts within the classics" (Madaus & O'Dwyer, 1999, p. 690).

It is interesting to note, however, that in response to concerns about favoritism and the subjectivity of scoring responses to the reasoning item, examiners "revert[ed] back to questions that required more rote answers" (Madaus & O'Dwyer, 1999, p. 690). In this instance, political concerns combined with a technological shortcoming of testing influenced the process of testing.

As the importance of testing in China increased, it is interesting to note that concerns began to arise about the impact of testing on society. Specifically, Fan Zhong Yan "pointed to the negative effects of the civil-service examinations on imagination and on the pursuit of studies of practice utility because these characteristics were not assessed by the examinations" (Madaus et al., 1997, p. 11). While the Chinese civil examination was not influenced by these concerns, they are remarkably similar to concerns raised today about state testing programs.

TESTING IN EUROPE

Unlike China, testing in Europe was not introduced by the government to meet specific political needs. Instead, the use of tests arose within craft guilds and was used to determine the readiness of an apprentice to perform craftsmanship independent of his master. Although there are no written records of the exact criteria used to evaluate an apprentice's product, it is believed "that an apprentice [had] to be intimately familiar with—and emulate in the 'masterpiece'—the style of his master" (Madaus & O'Dwyer, 1999, p. 691). It was the master who determined whether or not the apprentice possessed the skills and knowledge to set out on his own. In this way, testing was a very personal and subjective process.

With the rise of industrialization in the early 1800s and the subsequent emphasis on interchangeable parts, emphasis on style was replaced by the importance of uniformity. Rather than assessing the quality and style of a craftsman's finished product, the ability to produce specific components that consistently met predefined specifications became valued. As a result, a "connoisseurship" approach to assessing the full range of skills of craftsmen was replaced by a more quantitative approach to measuring a specific subset of skills (Madaus & O'Dwyer, 1999).

Beyond assessing readiness for guild membership, tests were used throughout the Middle Ages for a variety of purposes. Churches used tests to determine readiness for priesthood, candidates had to pass tests to become knights, and school children were subjected to tests to assure that they were acquiring proper religious knowledge. Oral exams were used to assess the acquisition of knowledge, while performances were used to assess the acquisition of physical skills.

At the time, the catechism was the most common form of oral testing. As Madaus and O'Dwyer (1999) note, there are three interesting things about the catechetical method: (a) the domain of knowledge is relatively small and limited thus making it fairly easy to sample the domain, (b) it is well suited to a transmission view of teaching, and (c) it is closely linked with instruction and thus can be used easily to inform instruction.

Within academies of learning, the University of Paris and the University of Bologna first introduced formal examinations during the 12th century. These examinations were essentially "theological oral disputations" that were based on "a fixed canon consisting of Thomas Aquinas' *Summa Theologiae*, Peter the Lombard's *Sententiae*...; and Comestor's *Historia Scholastica*" (Madaus & O'Dwyer, 1999, p. 691). Similar to the reasoning exam administered in China one millennium earlier, students had to display a knowledge of these cannons and had to resolve the apparent contradictions. In the spirit of catechisms, however, the questions were known in advance, requiring examinees to memorize and reiterate predetermined answers.

While conducting research at the University of Paris in 1927, a scholar discovered documents produced between 1230 and 1240 that contained a list of answers to the questions most frequently asked during these oral exams (Madaus & O'Dwyer, 1999). Beyond emphasizing the rote nature of these oral exams, this list may represent the first form of test-preparation service—a service that today is a multimillion dollar industry.

Although qualities like eloquence required some degree of subjective judgment, the types of questions posed on most tests were easy to judge. Answers presented by an examinee either matched the fact contained in the relevant text or texts, or it did not.

Initially, these tests were used to make decisions on an individual basis about an examinee's readiness to engage in scholarly activity. During the 1740s, however, Cambridge University began using tests to make comparisons between examinees by ranking students based on their test performance. Although the practice of using test scores to compare candidates had been in use in China for centuries, this represents the first recorded use of tests to make direct comparisons between examinees in Europe.

At the time, students at Cambridge University were subjected to an oral disputation based on a book of predefined questions. As Madaus and O'Dwyer (1999) describe:

> Whether or not the question was to be disputed in the negative or affirmative was also indicated in these compendiums. The examination itself began with a 10-minute statement from the respondent on his question. The first opponent would then oppose with eight arguments of syllogistic form, each of which was rebutted in turn. Then the second opponent would produce five further arguments, and the third opponent, three. Evaluation was a qualitative judgment by the moderator on both respondent and opponents (ranging from such phrases as *satis disputasti* to a glowing *summo ingenii acumine diputasti.* (p. 692)

While these judgments were initially satisfactory for classifying student performance, they made it difficult to rank students because it was difficult to combine qualitative judgments into a single score. In addition, as the decisions made based on a student's performance on the exam increased, partiality and favoritism increasingly impacted students' scores. To overcome these problems, William Farish devised an approach to assigning quantitative rather than qualitative scores to student performances. Although quantifying performance did not necessarily eliminate bias from the scoring process, it did facilitate aggregating and averaging judgments across multiple observers. This innovation which arose from a political and social need (within Cambridge University) and was borrowed from the common practice of quantification in commerce, laid the foundation for both quantification in testing and the field of psychometrics (Madaus & O'Dwyer, 1999).

Although paper had been developed several centuries earlier, it was relatively scarce and expensive in Europe. Moreover, the domains tested, which focused largely on knowledge in a specific area, were compatible with oral exams. However, with the rise of science and machinery, the importance of mathematics increased. As a result, during the 18th century, Cambridge and Oxford began testing student achievement in mathematics. During this same time period, paper became more readily available. As it became apparent that oral exams were poorly fitted to the mathematical problems students were asked to solve, mathematical tests were administered on paper instead of in an oral format. Gradually, the use of paper-based testing spread to other domains.

TESTING IN THE UNITED STATES

Like Europe, during the early years of schooling in the United States, oral exams were used to test student knowledge. During the early 1830s, however, Horace Mann was faced with a rapid increase in student enrollment in the Boston Public Schools. In an effort to standardize test conditions by presenting all students with the same set of questions and applying the same criteria to scoring their answers to produce comparable scores, Mann supplemented oral exams with formal, written exams (Madaus et al., 1997).

Mann's movement to paper-based tests is an important event in the history of testing for three reasons. First, it marks the beginning of paper-based testing in the United States, a practice that increased rapidly and remains dominant today. Second, it represents the first attempt in the United States to standardize test conditions. Third, the use of standardized tests allowed Mann to aggregate test scores at the school level and to then make comparisons among schools. It should also be noted that Mann's use of test scores to compare schools was politically motivated: "[Mann] was engaged in a struggle with Boston's headmasters who were resisting his attempt to abolish corporal punishment. Mann and his confidant Howe recognized that school-by-school test results gave them political leverage over recalcitrant headmasters" (Madaus, 1993, p. 17).

The use of tests to evaluate schools and various educational programs increased as the 19th century progressed. For example, Joseph Rice used student test scores to formally evaluate spelling. While Rice's endeavor seems rather easy, his efforts were repeatedly frustrated by the challenges inherent in measuring cognitive processes:

Rice found that assessing spelling was far from straightforward. First, he dictated words for students to spell but found that regional accents and pronunciations made this approach problematic. He then had students pick out spelling errors embedded in texts, only to conclude that recognizing spelling errors was different from spelling correctly. Finally, he had students write texts, and he corrected their products for spelling. (Madaus & O'Dwyer, 1999, p. 693)

To this day, the desire to measure cognitive processes that cannot be observed directly challenges test developers to create tests that allow us to make valid inferences about these cognitive processes. Although this issue of validity has challenged the technology of testing since its inception, Rice's struggle provides the first formal written account of the issue.

In summary, in both Europe and the United States, the transition from the use of oral exams to written exams occurred gradually over the course of nearly a century and resulted from a confluence of technological, political, and social events. The ability to produce paper on a large-scale and at lower costs made paper more widely available. The increased importance of mathematics in industry and science led to increased instruction and assessment of mathematics in schools, which in turn proved difficult to assess with oral exams. And the desire to shape educational policy and practices through comparisons of test scores required standardization, which was facilitated by paper-based exams. By the end of the 19th century, paper-based administration was the dominant mode of testing.

THE RISE OF STATISTICS AND ITS INFLUENCE ON TESTING

During the late 19th century, two new fields of study emerged, psychology and statistics. Developments in these fields had several impacts on testing. With the importance of quantification firmly established in the industrial world, those interested in psychology undertook efforts to formally measure and quantify intelligence. As Gould (1996) recounts:

No man expressed his era's fascination with numbers so well as Darwin's celebrated cousin, Francis Galton...Galton, a pioneer of modern statistics, believed that, with sufficient labor and ingenuity, anything might be measured, and that measurement is the primary criterion of a scientific study. (p. 107)

Independently wealthy, Galton spent much of his free time quantifying just about everything imaginable. Sitting in parks, he counted the number of steps people took to travel a specific distance. He undertook studies to quantify boredom, to construct a "beauty map" of the British Isles, and to measure the efficacy of prayer.

In 1883, Galton began dabbling in "eugenics" and undertook a series of studies that explored a variety of ways to measure the worth of people. Galton's fascination with worth led him to believe that innate qualities were responsible for the social behavior of individuals. This dual fascination with quantification and innate qualities led Galton to focus specifically on intelligence. Initially, Galton attempted to explain differences in intelligence based on differences in anthropometrics. Collecting measures of skulls and body parts, Galton claimed to be able to assess the mental abilities of individuals. Capitalizing on this "ability," Gould opened a "laboratory" at the 1884 International Exposition and later at the London museum, charging people three pence for a series of tests and measures (Gould, 1996).

Through Galton's attempts to "measure" intelligence, he introduced three important statistical concepts. Building on the work of Quetelet, who had developed a method for fitting normal curves to data, Galton developed a method for displaying data such that data is ordered by increasing value and then graphed versus rank. When the data are normally distributed, the resulting graph resembles an ogive (Stigler, 1986, p. 270). Once graphed in this manner, the data can be divided into quartiles, quintiles, or percentile ranks.

This approach to data analysis led to Galton's second major concept, namely that even within homogenous populations, variation exists. As Stigler (1986) summarizes Galton's thinking:

> If data from the same species arrayed themselves according to this curve and if the unity of the species could be demonstrated by showing that measurable quantities such as stature or examination scores followed the curve, then, once such a species was identified on the basis of measurable quantities, the process could be inverted with respect to qualities that eluded direct measurement! Qualities such as talent or "genius" that were at most susceptible to a simple ordering could, by Galton's method, be assigned a value on a "statistical scale." If a hundred individuals' talents were ordered, each could be assigned the numerical value corresponding to its percentile in the curve of "deviations from an average": The middlemost (or median) talent had a value of 0 (representing mediocrity), an individual at the upper quartile was assigned the value 1 (representing one probable error above mediocrity), and so on. (p. 271)

Termed "statistics by intercomparison," this method of analysis became the dominant approach to scaling psychological tests. Ironically, the method contradicted Quetelet's original use of normal curves. Whereas Quetelet used the normal curve to demonstrate that a set of observations came from a homogenous population, and thus was indistinguishable, Galton used rank orderings within this distribution to make distinctions between individuals within a homogenous population (Stigler, 1986). This alternate application of the normal curve gave rise to several scores used by today's tests including percentile ranks and standard scores.

Galton's third major contribution to statistics grew out of his development and subsequent work with the "quincunx." Originally, Galton used the quincunx as a prop during lectures to help explain how the displacement of a given trait within an individual organism results in the trait being distributed normally within the population of organisms. Composed of a funnel at the top through which shot was dropped, several rows of pins or nails arranged in the shape of a triangle through which the shot worked its way, and a series of pockets at the bottom into which the shot accumulated, the quincunx provided a fair representation of a binomial experiment.

Outside of lecture halls, Galton used the quincunx to explore statistical patterns. Perhaps most important was his discovery that interventions made at various levels (represented by a row of pins) diverted the shot in one direction. Yet, as the shot continued through the remaining rows of pins, their dispersion again became normal. When a set of interventions were applied at various levels, each of which resulted in a normally distributed sub-population of shot, the distribution of the total population of shot also tended to be normal. This discovery laid the ground work for examining differences among groups within a single set of data. This discovery also helped Galton develop the notion of regression and ultimately resulted in his introduction of the statistical concept of correlation (Stigler, 1986).

Lacking strong mathematical skills, Galton depended upon graphs to examine correlations. Karl Pearson, however, was a mathematician by training. Influenced by Galton's concept of a correlation, Pearson applied his mathematical skills to the challenge of quantifying the extent to which two variables are correlated. Among Pearson's many contributions to statistics, perhaps the most significant was his mathematical definition of the correlation coefficient. Although several methods of calculating a correlation coefficient have since evolved, Pearson's mathematical approach laid the foundation for the development of several statistical methods commonly used today. In the field of testing, the correlation coefficient has become an important tool for examining the psychometric properties of a test.

ALFRED BINET AND THE MEASUREMENT OF INTELLIGENCE

As Galton, Pearson, and their contemporaries were focused on advancing the field of statistics, Alfred Binet was focused on developing more sophisticated measures of intelligence. Having published nine papers that explored the relationship between intelligence based on the measures of the cranium, Binet's confidence in the relationship between intelligence and anthropometrics waned due to the very small (in some cases only one millimeter) average difference in the skull size of students which deemed them as intelligent or of lesser intelligence. For some physical attributes believed to be related to intelligence, students of lesser intelligence actually had larger measures (Gould, 1996).

Abandoning physical approaches, Binet turned to psychological methods and began work on developing mental tests of intelligence. Initially, Binet attempted to estimate intelligence based on reaction time, but he soon began developing tasks that required reasoning to solve. Commissioned by the French Ministry of Public Education to develop methods for identifying those students in need of special education, Binet set out to develop a formal measure of intelligence. A year later, Binet "introduced a large series of short tasks, related to everyday problems of life (counting coins, or assessing which face is 'prettier', for example), but supposedly involving such basic processes of reasoning as 'direction (ordering), comprehension, invention and censure (correction)'" (Gould, 1996, p. 179).

These first tests of intelligence were administered individually to students by trained examiners. By combining a large set of questions that drew on a wide range of reasoning skills, Binet's tests aimed to measure a student's general intellectual aptitude. Before his death in 1911, Binet produced three versions of his intelligence scale. The version published in 1908 assigned age levels to each task and introduced the idea of comparing an examinee's performance on a series of tasks to the average performance of examinees at different age levels. Thus, the concept of "mental age" was born (Gould, 1996). But here again, the development of the intelligence test resulted from a societal need of the time—identifying students with special needs. The method of testing grew out of a technological shortcoming in the field of "psychology," namely the failure of physical measurements to provide valid estimates of intelligence.

IMMIGRATION, WAR, AND INTELLIGENCE TESTING IN THE UNITED STATES

With the large influx of immigrants into the United States at the turn of the century, two competing social and political desires emerged. Recognizing the need to help these new immigrants, especially their children, adapt to the American economy and culture, many people saw schools as an effective vehicle for "Americanizing" immigrant children. Others, however, advocated policies to limit immigration, arguing that the arrivals were intellectually inferior. For both groups, Binet's IQ tests became popular. Yet, there was one major shortcoming of Binet's approach: The large series of tasks had to be presented individually to each examinee by a specially trained administrator.

With the aim of increasing the efficiency and objectivity of testing, Kelley introduced the multiple-choice item (Madaus, 1993). This technological "advance" was adopted by Otis who set out to develop a more efficient version of Binet's IQ test. With the entry of the United States into World War I in 1917 and the subsequent need to assign massive numbers of recruits to positions, Otis convinced the U.S. Army to rely on his IQ test. Employing a series of multiple-choice items, Otis' test, which became known as the Army Alpha, was the first group-administered multiple-choice test. Although the classification of recruits based on their test score was of questionable validity, the Army Alpha was administered to more than 2 million recruits before the end of the war.

THE EXPANSION OF STANDARDIZED MULTIPLE-CHOICE TESTING IN THE UNITED STATES

As Madaus et al. (1997) describe, "This supply technology was quickly adapted to achievement tests immediately after the war and helped give commercial testing a foothold in the publishing industry" (p. 15). Perhaps most significantly, in 1926, the College Entrance Examination Board began using multiple-choice questions in addition to one written essay for a test administered to students seeking college admission. Eleven years later, the board dropped the essay test, and the admission test was composed solely of multiple-choice items.

During the 1920s, state educational agencies and educational researchers both increased their dependence on the use of tests to monitor schools and examine the impact of various educational reforms. As examples of the former, the University of Iowa launched its statewide testing program in 1929, and during the 1920s New York introduced the Regents exam which was administered to thousands of high school students each year. Similarly, researchers like Ben T. Wood and evaluators like Ralph Tyler undertook studies that included the testing of thousands of students. In one such study, William Learned and Ben Wood tested approximately 20,000 students in 1928, 1930, and 1932 (Downey, 1965). This large scale testing was possible due to the introduction and acceptance of group-administered, multiple-choice tests.

The acceptance of and dependence on multiple-choice tests led to an explosion in the development and printing of tests. By 1920, more than 100 achievement tests existed, with World Book publishing nearly half a million tests a year. By 1930, more than 2 million copies of the Stanford Achievement Test and the Stanford-Binet Intelligence Test were sold (U.S. Congress Office of Technology Assessment, 1992).

THE APPLICATION OF ITEM DISCRIMINATION AND FACTOR ANALYSIS TO TESTING

With the use of multiple-choice items, new methods emerged for selecting the set of items that comprised a test. Applying Pearson's correlation coefficient, test developers began examining the correlation between examinees' performance on a single item and their performance on the test as a whole. This focus on item level characteristics revealed that some items did a poor job discriminating between high and low performers. In some cases, poor discrimination was the result of a poorly worded item. But in other cases, the problem indicated that the item did not represent the domain of interest. This statistical approach to examining the extent to which the domain measured by an item was aligned with the domain intended to be measured by the test was advanced by the application of factor analysis. The idea of factor analysis (actually principal component analysis) was introduced by Pearson in 1901 and was first applied by Charles Spearman to educational testing in 1904. Essentially, factor analysis extends the concept of a correlation to examine the ways in which sets of variables correlate with one another. When several variables correlate highly with one another, they may be interpreted as representing a single, larger variable or factor. Spearman used factor analysis to examine the interrelationships between test scores and found that scores from several different tests tended to be highly inter-correlated. Based on this high inter-correlation, he concluded that the tests were all measuring the same dimension—a 'general intelligence.'

During the 1930s, L. L. Thurstone also applied factor analytic techniques to test scores. Rather than seeking a single factor that explained patterns across test scores, Thurstone sought clusters. To identify these clusters, Thurstone introduced the idea of rotating factor solutions in order to maximize the correlation between each factor and the variables that comprise that factor. While the mathematics behind these two approaches are too complex to present here, Thurstone's approach to factor analysis had an important impact on the development of tests in that it provided a tool for testing the dimensionality of the test.

As stated earlier, a test comprises a sample of items from a given domain. With factor analysis, it became possible to examine the extent to which the items comprising a test represented a single domain or multiple domains.

It is here that I will end this brief history of testing, since it is in the 1930s that computer-based technologies begin their influence on the technology of testing. What should be clear, however, is that technological advances—whether they are the availability of inexpensive paper in Europe or advances in psychology and statistics—have impacted the technology of testing. Similarly, testing has long been influenced by social and political needs—whether it was used to reduce patronage in China, to select candidates for the Church, rank students in universities, examine the impact of schools, identify students with special needs, or assign recruits to positions in the Army. As the next four chapters describe, the influence of computer-based technologies for testing were the result of both advances in the computer industry and an increasing reliance on computers in society.

CHAPTER 4

A BRIEF HISTORY OF COMPUTERS, TESTING, AND THE DRIVE FOR EFFICIENCY

Today's computers can perform an incredibly large number of calculations in an amazingly short period of time. Given the speed of today's computers, it is not surprising that computers are applied to increase the efficiency with which people perform a vast array of tasks. In the area of testing, applications of electronic and computer-based technologies have been developing since the mid 1930s when work on the first electronic scanning devices began. In this chapter, I describe ways in which electronic and computer-based technologies were applied to the technology of testing between the 1930s and into the 1970s. At the same time, I describe some of the ways in which the use of computer-based technologies influenced the technology of testing and trace some of the promises made and concerns raised by observers as testing evolved over this time period. In doing so, I lay the foundation for thinking critically about how computer-based technologies are being applied to testing today and how these applications may limit or create new opportunities for advancing the technology of testing.

Technology and Assessment: The Tale of Two Interpretations, pages 35–47
Copyright © 2006 by Information Age Publishing

THE INFLUENCE OF SCANNERS ON THE TECHNOLOGY OF TESTING

Ask any person to picture himself or herself taking a standardized test and the resulting image likely includes a bubble sheet. The story of how bubble sheets have become a key fixture in testing dates back to 1928 and is the product of Ben Wood, a renowned educational researcher at the time, and Reynold Johnson, a high school physics teacher. While working on the New York State Regents Examination, Wood realized that the process of hand scoring tests unnecessarily inflated the cost of the program and slowed the availability of their results. While working on a massive study that included the testing of more than 20,000 students twice over a three-year period, Wood became acutely aware of the need to mechanize the scoring of tests. In hopes of spurring the development of such a machine, he wrote to 10 high-technology companies encouraging them to take on the development of such a machine. The plea caught the attention of Thomas J. Watson, Sr., the then president of International Business Machine Corporation (IBM). After spending an afternoon discussing the potential impact on education of such a scoring machine and related machines, Watson decided to take on the project. In exchange for his consulting services, Wood was offered an annual retainer of $5,000 and was supplied with three truckloads of IBM computing equipment. Interestingly, these computers were used to establish the Columbia University Statistical Bureau on which the Bureau of Collegiate Educational Research relied for statistical analyses of their test scores.

Three years after beginning work on the development of a scoring machine, Wood and his colleagues at IBM were able to modify an IBM tabulator to score the Strong Vocational Interest Bank, an inventory used by counselors to help guide youth into a profession aligned with their interests. At the time, it cost roughly $5 to administer and score the inventory for each student largely because each student's response pattern had to be compared to the response patterns of 39 different professions. With the modified tabulator, the cost dropped to 50 cents. Despite this success, Wood believed that the machine needed further improvement so that it could further reduce the cost of scoring, could score responses even faster, and could be used for a wider range of tests. To increase the speed of scoring, Wood and the IBM engineers sought to capitalize on the speed of electricity and attempted to build a machine that could detect the number of correct answers by recording the amount of electricity that flowed through the graphite left by pencil marks. While nearly successful, they were unable to overcome one major obstacle—the amount of electricity conducted was dependent upon the darkness of the pencil mark. The darker the marks, the more correct the answers appeared to be.

Unaware of the work being conducted at IBM, in 1931 Reynold Johnson, a high school science teacher, became tired of scoring tests himself and began tinkering in his basement designing an electrical test scoring machine. Applying his knowledge of science, he developed a technique to register responses recorded with a graphite pencil by determining whether a specific location on a piece of paper could conduct electricity. Like the developers at IBM, Johnson encountered the "darkness" problem. Johnson, however, was able to overcome it by employing high resistor units which overcame problems caused by minor differences in conductivity due to variations in the graphite marks. Recognizing the incredible amount of time this scoring machine could save for routine counting and tallying procedures, Johnson attempted to market the device. Initially, there were no takers. And as the Great Depression wore on, Johnson's enthusiasm for the machine wore down. But in 1934, an IBM salesman spotted Johnson's advertisement for the machine in a newspaper. When Wood became aware of the advertisement and the method Johnson used to overcome the "darkness" problem, IBM purchased the rights to his machine for $15,000 and hired Johnson. A year later, the IBM model 805 was made commercially available. Interestingly, several years later Johnson also applied his understanding of electricity to develop the first computer disk drive.

The first large-scale use of the scoring device came with the scoring of the New York Regents exam in 1936. That same year, the machine was also the saving grace of Connecticut's testing program. Having nearly exhausted its budget after printing only 5,000 copies of its test, the state was able to print enough answer sheets to test nearly 50,000 students with only 5,000 test booklets.

It took several years for IBM to improve the machine and make it affordable. But by the early 1950s, the electronic scoring of tests was commonplace and was being used in conjunction with a variety of specialized computing and tabulating machines to improve the efficiency of testing.

Impact of Machines and Devices on Testing in the 1950s

Beginning in 1936, the Educational Testing Service (ETS) began sponsoring an annual Invitational Conference on Testing Problems. The conference held in 1953 provides a wonderful snapshot of the role machines and devices had come to play in the field of testing. At this conference, seven lectures related to automatic scoring machines were grouped under the heading: "Impact of Machines and Devices on Developments in Testing and Related Fields" (Educational Testing Service, 1954). Among the lecturers were representatives of companies that had recently developed scoring and computing devices, faculty who were heading computing and scoring centers within their universities, members of the U.S. Department of Army Personnel Research Branch, and a representative of ETS.

To provide a sense of the variety of machines being used in the 1950s, the enthusiasm for these machines, and challenges that remained unresolved, I summarize and quote liberally from several of the lectures.

The IBM Test Scoring Machine: An Evaluation

Speaking first at this conference, Arthur Traxler (1954) of the Education Records Bureau, likened the IBM scoring machine to Henry Ford's Model-T, stating, "... the test scoring machine has been to the testing business what the Model-T Ford was to the automobile industry. If the Model T put America on wheels, the test scoring machine has put the youth of America on objective-test answer sheets" (p. 138).

During his lecture, Traxler (1954) praised the IBM scoring machine for its ability to efficiently and accurately score tests. But Traxler also identified several areas in need of improvement. Among these challenges in need of solutions were:

- The need to develop a way to provide scores for several scales or sub-tests using a single answer sheet. Because the IBM scoring machine functioned by measuring the total amount of electricity transferred via all correct answers, the machine was only able to produce a single score per answer sheet.
- Although the machine was accurate within one or two points, further accuracy was required.
- The answer sheets absorbed moisture on warm, humid days which in turn affected the ability of the machine to read the tests. While a heater in the machine could be used to dry out the answer sheets, the procedure slowed down the scoring process.
- At the time, a shiny dark pencil mark absent of stray marks was required for accurate scoring. Although answer sheets were visually scanned and remarked as necessary prior to scoring, this was a labor-intensive process.

Rather than placing responsibility for overcoming this last challenge on engineers, Traxler suggested that better training of test administrators and examinees might reduce these problems. Specifically, he suggested that in addition to providing examples of well-marked answers, testing materials should also include examples of poorly marked answers. Interestingly, Traxler criticized an alternative approach that required examinees to clean up their responses after the testing time was over, but before submitting their answer sheets to the proctor. Justifying this criticism, Traxler (1954) states, "the purpose of testing, however, is measurement, not character training" (p. 143). In some ways, Traxler's concerns about character training are analogous to concerns today about handwriting and use of computers for writing tests—what should be of interest with a writing test is how well one can write, not whether they can write neatly by hand.

In addition to the IBM scoring machine, Traxler also briefly discussed the growing importance of the graphic item counter. At the time, the IBM scoring machine required a person to watch a meter that displayed the amount of current transferred through the answer sheet. The human observer would then record the reading for each answer sheet. The current reading was then converted to a single test score. The graphic item counter was a device that attached to the IBM scoring machine and could provide a graphic count of the responses to each individual item on the test. These counts were recorded directly on carbon paper that could be used later to assist in analyzing responses to individual items. Although the graphic counter slowed down the scoring process, it could provide item level responses much faster than human recorders.

The University Service Bureau and the Use of Electronic Computing Machines for Testing Problems

John Alman of Boston University and Harry Harman and Bertha Harper of the Army's Adjutant General's Office, describe several computing machines that were becoming commonplace at large universities and at ETS. As Alman (1954) describes,

> Testing makes extensive use of frequency distributions and order statistics, of bivariate distributions from coded or grouped data, of second moments [standard deviations] and product moments. All of these can be handled on the basic accounting installation—the sorter, the reproducer, the collator, and the accounting machine. These machines, together with key punches, verifiers, and the interpreter, for many years constituted the facilities of the university service bureau. In the very recent years, many have acquired punch card computers... To complete the machine potential of the present-day university service bureau there is IBM's 101 Electronic Statistical Machine which permits the high speed preparation of contingency tables from categorical or coded data, item analyses, editing and sequence checking, selective sorting, and many other tasks. (p. 148)

Similarly, Harman and Harper (1954) describe two machines being used by the Army. The first, known as the Factor Matrix Rotator, had proven time saving when conducting factor analysis of test data. According to Harman and Harper, this Factor Matrix Rotator allowed researchers and test developers to perform factor analyses 50 times faster than it would take by hand:

> The initial factor weights are set into the machine by means of a series of dials, then the positions of the points representing the tests are viewed as points of light on a scope equivalent to a 17" television screen . . . the axes are rotated by a simple manipulation of the dial . . . When the final decisions have been made about the location of the factor axes to exhibit simple structure, the elements of . . . the final factor matrix can be read out as fast as the experimenter can turn the dial and read a scale, since the computations are done electronically. (pp. 154–155)

The second machine Harman and Harper discuss is the Document-to-Card Punch. Similar to the graphic item counter, the Document-to-Card Punch was attached to the IBM scoring machine. The IBM scoring machine was extremely efficient in reading data to yield a total score and the graphic item counter provided results for each individual test item. However, to perform additional analyses, this test and item level information had to be manually recorded on punch cards that were then fed into calculating machines. The Document-to-Card Punch eliminated the need to manually record responses on punch cards, and in the process saved enormous amounts of time and increased the accuracy of data recorded on the punch cards.

Harman and Harper also introduced the Card Scoring Punch. In many ways, the Card Scoring Punch was similar to the IBM scoring machine, but instead of reading in answer sheets marked by a pencil, the Card Scoring Punch read responses punched on a card.

In addition to emphasizing the value of these machines, both lectures also highlighted the complexity and specialized skill required to operate these computing machines. Before any computations were performed, a human was required to create a series of punch cards that specified the exact operations to be performed by the calculator. These instructional punch cards then had to be properly inserted with large stacks of punch cards containing the actual data. If any card was out of order or any step in the calculation process was omitted, the computational machine produced an inaccurate solution. Some of these machines also required the operator to program the machine by literally connecting wires to form specific circuits. Clearly, improvements that simplified the set-up and use of these machines would further increase their value and wide-scale contribution to testing.

New Developments in Test Scoring Machines

Representing Testscor, a small company specializing in test scoring and analysis devices, Elmer Hankes (1954) described several new machines his company had recently developed. What is most notable about Hankes' lecture is the large number of very specialized machines that Testscor had developed, each of which was designed to meet a specific need. As an example, one complex machine that stood 4 feet wide by 8 feet long and 4 feet high and contained 1,200 double-throw switches, 300 vacuum tubes, and more than 100,000 soldered connections was designed to score a single test battery—the Strong Vocational Interest Inventory. This inventory was long and difficult to score due to the enormous number of response combinations that were used to classify a student's vocational interest. Even with this machine, it still took 30 seconds to score a test, but this was more than 70 times faster than the conventional method.

Like Trexler, Hankes (1954) also notes problems in detecting poorly marked answer sheets. To decrease this problem, he describes how Testscor began "remarking all Strong tests with a conductive ink made of a colloidial suspension graphite in water" (p. 157). As he describes, this approach "lead to the development of a very simple and reliable pick up" that was incorporated to their new machine, Testscor Universal Scorer and Computer (TUSAC). As Hankes (1954) explains:

> TUSAC is really designed to score test batteries, rather than a single test. It is too big and complex to do simple tasks. Its economic value lies in its ability to take an answer sheet, optically scan *both* sides simultaneously, gather the scores, counting both rights and wrongs, convert these scores, weight and combine the conversions and print out the resultant index scores. (p. 158, emphasis in the original)

In a trial run, it was found that working 10 hours a day with two operators, TUSAC could replace a staff of 100 people. Hankes notes, however, that TUSAC is a special machine that is only needed when large volumes of answer sheets must be scored. Recognizing that many smaller institutions, whether they are small colleges and universities or K–12 schools, do not test on a large scale, Hankes (1954) described a third machine, the Digital Universal Scorer (DUS) which cost $385 to $650 depending upon accessory items ordered:

> Like the soap of a similar name—DUS does everything. Yes, DUS does all the things outlined... Accuracy—DUS is a digital device with optical pick up. Service—DUS is made up of simple rugged components, most of which have stood the test of time. Any typewriter shop can service it. Scores are printed—Raw or Converted. Uses any kind of answer sheet and they may be

mimeographed from special stencils. No special pencils are required. It's portable—weight is under 50 pounds cased. Separate visual registers accumulate the number of tests scored and the total of scores. (p. 159)

Anticipating the development of scoring machines similar to TUSAC by other companies, Hankes (1954) suggested "the adoption of a standard format for answer sheets so that the various machines now building [sic] or under consideration will be universally useful. TUSAC is designed for flexibility in this regard and scores both Testscor and IBM answer sheets" (p. 158). Ending his sales pitch, Hankes states, "That covers our work and I hope will cover your requirements in the test scoring field" (p. 159).

The Iowa Electronic Test Processing Equipment

Not to be outdone by Testscor, Edward Lindquist (1954) of the University of Iowa followed with an extensive description of "a new 'electronic brain' for the processing of objective tests and test data" that was being installed at the State University of Iowa. Although it was not functional at the time of the conference, Lindquist indicated that the equipment was "designed to perform at one time practically *all* of the clerical and statistical operations—scoring, tabulating, computing, and reporting—involved in wide-scale testing programs using relatively long multiple-test batteries" (p.160). The combination of reading, scoring, analyzing, and reporting results with a single machine distinguished Lindquist's lecture from the single function machines described by the speakers that preceded him.

As Lindquist described, the Iowa electronic test-processing equipment consisted of a high-speed electronic scorer that sent data to a digital computer that was attached to a high-speed printer. The optical electronic scorer was designed to read up to 960 multiple-choice items organized into up to 14 sub-tests recorded on two sides of paper. Unlike the IBM scoring machine, the examinee did not need to use a special pencil and erasing answers did not interfere with the accuracy of scoring. In addition, the machine was able to detect and disallow items with multiple responses, eliminating the need for a human to pre-scan answer sheets.

Unlike other machines operational at the time, the Iowa test processor did not require a human to interact with the machine once the answer sheets were placed into it. Among the many analyses and reporting functions the machine could perform were:

- Counting correct and omitted responses as each sheet is scanned.
- Producing a score based on up to 120 items that are assigned different weights.

- Calculating correct responses for even and odd answers separately so that reliability correlation coefficients could be calculated.
- Converting raw scores to T-scores, percentile ranks, age- or grade-equivalents, or scaled scores according to pre-specified conversion tables.
- Calculating weighted total test scores based on multiple sub-test scores.
- Reading examinee names entered onto the scan sheet using alphabetic symbols and printing the examinee's actual name rather than the identification number on all reports.
- Cumulating means for groups of successive answer sheets as well as calculating squared scores and cross-products, thus enabling variances, correlations, and reliability coefficients to be easily calculated.
- Tabulating frequency distributions displayed graphically.
- Producing individual score reports and group reports.

Most impressively, all of these operations were performed with a single pass of answer sheets at a rate of up to 6000 sheets per hour. To provide a sense of the power and efficiency of the new machine, Lindquist (1954) described its intended use for Iowa's state test:

> In the Fall Testing Program for Iowa High Schools, we administer...a 56 page battery of nine tests to some 70,000 pupils in about 400 Iowa high schools. All marked answer sheets are sent to Iowa City, where we do the scoring and statistical work and prepare three types of reports for each school.... For these purposes we require a large temporary staff, provided with all of the presently available specialized equipment—such as electric typewriters, comptometers, automatic computing machines, electric accounting machines, and punched card tabulating equipment.... It takes this staff of 60 about five weeks to handle our program. The new equipment will do their work in three days, actually in 12 hours of continuous machine operation. (pp. 162–163)

Despite the amazing time and costs saved by the Iowa High School testing program, Lindquist notes that this example underestimates the actual capacity of the machine since the Iowa testing program does not require many operations such as producing frequency distributions or calculating variance and correlations.

Recognizing that the high-cost of Iowa's scoring machine would make it unaffordable for most users, Lindquist suggests that a limited number of test processing centers be established across the nation. Organizations such as school districts, colleges and universities, the military, and testing companies would then send their answer sheets to these centers for processing.

IBM's Activity in the Test Scoring Field

In contrast to the multitask, high-priced machine described by Lindquist, Philip Bradley, of IBM, dismissed the need for a small number of test processing centers. Instead, Bradley (1954) described IBM's efforts to refine its smaller and more specialized scoring machine with the aim of making it easily affordable for the many organizations that administer a limited number of tests. Bradley also described as the ideal "a machine capable of functioning as a scoring machine alone and also which could be tied in with other standard data processing units" (p. 170). In other words, whereas Lindquist saw the next generation of scoring machines as comprehensive, multifunctioning units, Bradley envisioned single-function units that could be combined to perform multiple functions.

RESERVATIONS REGARDING MACHINE SCORING

Although different visions of the how (i.e., separate peripheral units or a single mega-unit) and where (i.e., locally or centrally) scoring machines would operate, all of the lectures emphasized the importance machines had come to play in the field of testing. Yet, despite overwhelming enthusiasm for the IBM scoring device and the many machines that operated in tandem with it, Traxler (1954) noted several potential negative effects of the machine:

> The use of the kind of answer sheet required by the fixed response-position and the fixed fields of the scoring machine has tended to force objective testing into a kind of strait jacket. . . . The four- or five-choice, discrete test item has become virtually standard so that, except for differences in content, the parts of many of our standard tests are almost as interchangeable as the housing units in Levittown. The test scoring machine is not, of course, wholly responsible for this development, but I think it has accelerated a trend that might have been present regardless of mechanical means of scoring. (p. 140)

Traxler (1954) also noted that the need to develop discrete test items accompanied by four or five options occasionally led to the development of "an unnatural test situation" (p. 140). As an example, Traxler described a problem present in the then-current version of the *Cooperative English Test A: Mechanics of Expression*. As he described, "an exercise in punctuation is forced into the multiple-choice IBM answer sheet form in such a way that a considerable percent of the junior high school pupils simply do not understand what is to be done. There is introduced what seems to be a kind of closure factor, which, in all probability, influences the results of this English test considerably" (p. 140).

Reflecting criticism of standardized tests today, Traxler (1954) also describes concern by some teachers regarding "the multiple-choice mind" (p. 141). He explains that these teachers "are uncomfortable over the thought that regardless of the resourcefulness, skill, imagination, and stimulation to thinking that they bring to their teaching, in the end the achievement of their students, and indirectly their own success, is going to be judged largely by how well their students respond to a single type of test item" (p. 141).

Recognizing potential error introduced by requiring students to read questions in one booklet and to then record responses on a separate answer sheet, Traxler (1954) wondered whether this test format "introduces extraneous perceptual and spatial factors into the measurement situation" and raises questions regarding "the lowest age level at which separate answer sheet tests may successfully be used, and the question of the influence of limitations of desk space on results of tests administered with separate answer sheets" (p. 141).

Interestingly, some of Traxler's concerns were echoed seven years later by Arthur Adams of the American Council on Education. Speaking at ETS' 1961 Invitational Conference on Testing Problems, Adams (1961) warned:

> With the pace of technical advance having reached the point where from three to six thousand test papers can be scanned by a machine in an hour, one could become beguiled with the marvelous efficiency of such a process and at least momentarily forget the hopes, the aspirations and the future of the individual human being tied up in every one of those papers. (p. 80)

Foreshadowing the reliance on standardized tests which, thanks to advances in scoring and computing devices, could be administered, scored, and analyzed quickly and cost-effectively, Adams (1961) also asked:

> Is the worth of a human being to be described uniquely by an item on an IBM card? Of course not. I am fully convinced that this was never the motive nor is it the motive of those concerned with the whole process of testing. The true motive is to use all of the techniques available in order to help place the individual where he can realize his maximum potential. But, again, I say, such is the fascination of the human being with change, no matter of what sort, that this motive may not be understood by the very people who give the greatest credence to the results. (pp. 80–81)

Despite concerns captured by Traxler and Adams, over the next several decades, the use of the electronic and photo scoring machines coupled with improved calculating machines rapidly increased. By the ETS 1971 Invitational Conference on Testing Problems, the multiple uses of machines in the field of testing were accepted and well known. As outlined by Albert Hieronymus (1972) of the University of Iowa, these uses and impacts included:

- Increasing the efficiency with which tests were developed by making "[v]ery complete, complex, and inexpensive analyses of tryout data...almost routinely available to the test constructor."
- Developing "item types previously regarded as impracticable because of scoring problems."
- Weighting items and sub-tests to produce total test scores in a timely manner.
- Assembling and printing entire tests composed of subsets of items contained in large item banks.
- Producing multiple norms.
- Efficiently selecting accurate samples based on school characteristic data stored in computer databases.
- Producing a large variety of reports for different users (Hieronymus notes that "the test user is deluged with information, much of which he may not be in a position to interpret wisely").
- Aiding in psychometric analyses such as factor analysis, understanding sample distributions, and large-scale research projects like the National Assessment of Educational Progress and the International Project for the Evaluation of Educational Achievement (pp. 59–60).

In addition to the impact outlined by Heironymus (1972), scoring and computing devices had an additional impact in four areas. First, because the device required examinees to record their responses on a specially formatted answer sheet, testing programs could re-use the question booklets. This presented an additional cost savings to testing programs, if they did not make any changes to their tests over time. Thus, a second impact of the device was that it encouraged testing programs to develop a given test and then use that same test over several years. The combined impact of increased efficiency of scoring and the ability to reuse test booklets over time spurred the growth of large-scale testing programs.

In some respects, reliance on scoring machines and the use of objective answer sheets also harmed instruction. As one test publisher relates (H. Miller, personal communication, December 14, 1990, cited in U.S. Congress, 1992), the scoring machine decreased the role of teachers in the testing process:

...[before machine scoring] most standardized tests were hand-scored by the teachers...Under that system, tests corrected and scored by the teacher provided opportunity for careful pupil analysis by the teachers. In turn that analysis, pupil by pupil and class by class, provided meaningful measures for individualizing pupil instruction, improving instruction, reassessing the curriculum, and making appropriate textbook selections...As the machine-scoring movement grew, the activities related to testing changed. Certainly, the scoring activity left the classroom and often as not the school system itself. Test results moved increasingly into the hands of administrative staff...the hands-on dimension for teachers receded and in due course disappeared almost entirely. (p. 255)

Thus, while the speed of scoring was a boom for the testing industry, it decreased the instructional value of testing for teachers.

Finally, and perhaps most significantly, the scoring device increased reliance on multiple-choice test items and decreased use of open-ended and essay items. The widespread use of multiple-choice exams limited the content of what could be assessed:

> From the earliest days of application of these technologies, critics lamented the loss of richness in detail that had been a feature of open-ended questions scored by human judges, and contended that machine-scored tests encouraged memorization of unrelated facts, guessing, and other distortions in teaching and learning. (U.S. Congress Office of Technology Assessment, 1992, p. 253)

In addition, primitive scoring machines allowed only four or five response options per item and provided only basic summaries of the data. These factors further limited test construction and analysis.

As described in greater detail in Chapter 6, some of these shortcomings are being overcome through more modern applications of computers to testing. As an example, the development of automated computer scoring of written responses increases the speed with which essays and short answer responses can be scored and holds potential to increase the presence of these types of items on tests. Looking back on the evolution of applications of electronic and computer-based devices to testing, the enthusiasm expressed by many leaders in the testing industry during the 1950s and 1960s parallels the strong interest many of today's test developers have for computer-based testing. Yet, as explored in the next chapter, many of the concerns regarding the influence of testing and test formats on teaching and learning raised by Traxler (1954) and Adams (1961) are just as applicable today.

CHAPTER 5

COMPUTERS, TESTING, AND CLASSROOM PRACTICES

The Modern Day Push-me Pull-you

As the use of computer-based technologies continues to become a regular component of classroom teaching and learning, the tools with which students solve problems and produce work are transitioning from pencil-and-paper-based to computer-based. Yet, as students become increasingly accustomed to learning and working with these computer-based tools, there is misalignment between the tools some students use to learn and the tools students are allowed to use while their achievement is tested. In response, some students, teachers, and educational administrators argue that testing programs should allow the use of these instructional tools during testing. In other cases, particularly in the area of writing, teachers alter their instructional practices in response to the types of technology students are allowed to use during testing. In this way, instructional uses of technology and testing practices are pushing and pulling each other in an uncoordinated manner.

In this chapter, I explore how the use of some technologies in the classroom have led testing programs to alter the types of tools students are able to use during testing. I also explore how the tools students are allowed to use on state tests are pushing teachers to alter their instructional practices.

Technology and Assessment: The Tale of Two Interpretations, pages 49–75
Copyright © 2006 by Information Age Publishing
All rights of reproduction in any form reserved.

Specifically, I focus on the use of calculators for mathematics instruction and testing, the use of computer-based tools to provide some students with learning and testing accommodations, and the use of word processors for writing and writing tests. Through these three topics, I explore the tension that arises as new technologies shape the way students learn and display their knowledge in the classroom and how the slow adoption of these technologies for testing can influence the instructional use of such tools.

CALCULATORS AND MATHEMATICS TESTS

During the mid 1990s there was much debate about whether students should be provided access to calculators during testing (Dunham & Dick, 1994; Kenelly, 1990). When the debate about calculators first arose, several concerns were raised. These concerns related to:

- Equity issues: Do all students have access to calculators both in the classroom and during testing?
- Standardization: Should all students use the same type of calculator during testing?
- Construct validity: Is the construct measured the same when students do and do not use calculators?

While test developers and those who use test results are still concerned about these issues, the widespread and regular use of calculators in the classroom has led many testing programs to allow students to use calculators during mathematics tests.

To overcome equity issues, some states like Florida provide calculators to schools in which most students lack access to calculators. Although no states require all students to use the exact same calculator, several testing programs specify the arithmetic functions the calculator can and cannot perform. To limit effects on construct validity, testing programs limit use of calculators to those items that do not specifically measure students' arithmetic skills.

Since the controversy over the use of traditional calculators during testing first arose, graphing calculators have emerged as common tools used in high school mathematics courses. As the price of graphing calculators continues to drop and their interfaces become easier to use, graphing calculators are also being used in middle schools.

Similarly, with computers present in the vast majority of schools, many teachers are also having students use spreadsheets to develop mathematical skills. With the recent introduction of the *Dana*, a new computing device that combines a small, portable word processor with a Palm interface and includes a simple spreadsheet application and an easy to use graphing calculator, the use of graphing calculators and spreadsheets is likely to increase. Already, the widespread use of graphing calculators is leading some testing programs to allow their use during testing. The use of spreadsheets and other computer-based tools, however, has yet to be allowed as a tool during mathematics testing.

North Carolina's philosophy regarding the use of calculators provides a good example of the current thinking about the use of computer-based tools during mathematics tests.

> All North Carolina tests assess the goals and objectives in the North Carolina Standard Course of Study. For multiple-choice tests, items are written to test specific objectives; on open-ended tests, items are written to span across the objectives and/or goals. If a student is asked to solve a problem, the focus of all items written for the objective and/or goal should be problem solving, regardless of the process used to solve the problem. If a student is asked to solve a problem using a specific procedure, the focus of all items written for the objective and/or goal should be the procedure. This difference in focus can be enhanced or hindered by the use of specific tools or technology, i.e., calculators, since more sophisticated technology may interfere with the assessment of specific procedures necessary to solve problems. (North Carolina Department of Public Instruction, 2000)

Beyond specifying the general class of problem solving items for which calculators may be used, North Carolina's policy also acknowledges that while more sophisticated technologies like spreadsheets may be used during instruction, their complexity may interfere with the performance of students who are not accustomed to their use. As Table 5.1 displays, North Carolina's policy continues by specifying the minimum calculator requirements for each mathematics test administered by the state. Note that graphing calculators are required for two high school mathematics tests.

North Carolina's policy also notes that calculators with additional functions are allowed, but that "keyboarding or symbol manipulation calculators are prohibited" (NCPublicSchools.org, 2000, Minimum Calculator Requirements, para. 1). In effect, this policy prohibits the use of a multi-function machine, like a computer or Dana, which has a calculator built into it. Moreover, since a spreadsheet requires the use of a keyboard to input formulas, this policy effectively prohibits their use during testing.

As tools like spreadsheets, laptops, and Danas become commonplace in the classroom one might think that testing policies will gradually allow their use during testing. But, if word processors are any indication of how testing policies regarding the use of computers will evolve, the transition from calculators to full-fledge computers may be long in coming.

Table 5.1.   Calculator Requirements for North Carolina Mathematics Tests

Test	*Minimum Calculator Requirement*
Grade 3 Pretest Mathematics	Calculator Active: four function calculator with memory key
Open-Ended Assessment, Grades 4 & 8 Mathematics	Grade 4: four function calculator with memory
	Grade 8: Any four function calculator with square root function, y^x, π(pi), and algebraic logic
End-of-Grade Mathematics Tests Grades 3–8	Calculator Active at Grades 3–5: four function calculator with memory
	Calculator Active at Grades 6–8: Any four function calculator with square root function, y^x, π(pi), and algebraic logic
Competency Test Mathematics (Form F, G, H)	Mathematics Computation: Calculator use is not allowed.
	Mathematics Applications: Any four function calculator with square root function, y^x, π(pi), and algebraic logic
High School Comprehensive Test Mathematics	Graphing Calculator
End-of-Course Tests	Algebra I and Algebra II: Graphing Calculator
	Chemistry, Geometry, Physical Science, and Physics: Scientific Calculator
High School Exit Exam Beginning Spring 2002 at 11th grade	Graphing Calculator

COMPUTERS AND ACCOMMODATIONS FOR STUDENTS WITH SPECIAL NEEDS

Increasingly, computers are being used in classrooms to help students with various special needs access the curriculum. For students who are challenged by fine motor skills, word processors and speech-to-text software are used. Text-to-speech, text magnifiers, Braille displays, and text highlighters are used to help blind and visually impaired students access written material. To provide better access to pictures, maps and diagrams, devices like Touch Graphics' *Talking Tactile Tablet* are being used by blind and visually impaired students and students who have difficulty interpreting visual images. For students who have difficulty with word retrieval or are dyslexic, word prediction software, pop-up dictionaries, and spell-checkers are used to assist with the writing process. And devices like *Eagle Eyes* and oversized keyboards allow students who have difficulty using a mouse or keyboard to interact with computers.

These, and other computer-based tools, have proven useful as learning tools in the classroom. But increasingly, educators are requesting that students be allowed to use these tools during testing. This push to allow students with special needs to access the same tools they use in the classroom when they are tested is supported by the *No Child Left Behind Act.* Among the many programs funded through the NCLB Act is the Enhanced Assessment Instruments Competitive Grant Program (Title VI, section 6112) that provides up to $17 million to state testing programs to "evaluate student academic achievement through the development of comprehensive academic assessment instruments, such as performance and technology-based academic assessments." The Enhanced Assessment Program gives preference to "alternatives for assessing students with disabilities and limited English proficient students" (United States Department of Education, http://www.ed.gov/policy/elsec/leg/esea02/pg87.html) Already, 28 states allow students with special needs to use computers in some form as an accommodation during testing. The Enhanced Assessment Program creates an opportunity for all states to explore new ways of assessing students with special needs, in part through the use of technology-based assessments.

A Brief History of Test Accommodations

Concern about how to test students with disabilities has been debated for several decades. As noted by Bennett (1999a), the foundation for providing accommodations for students with disabilities was established by Section 504 of the 1973 Rehabilitation Act which required nondiscrimination on the basis of disability for all programs receiving federal funding. Four years later, federal regulations stipulated that tests must measure the capabilities of disabled students and not their impairments, with the exception of tests that measured skills that overlapped with the impairment.

While this policy opened the door for providing students with appropriate test accommodations, it also raised questions about the comparability of scores achieved under different conditions, and whether scores for students with disabilities should be aggregated with scores for students without disabilities (Thurlow, Scott, & Ysseldyke, 1995a,b). In response, several testing programs began to flag scores for students who received accommodations. In many cases, students with disabilities were systematically excluded from state testing programs, thus corrupting the aggregate performance of schools and states (McDonnell, McLaughlin, & Morison, 1997; McGrew, Thurlow, Shriner, & Spiegel, 1992; Shriner & Thurlow, 1992). In addition, several states recorded rapid increases in the number of students identified for special education or retained in a grade, possibly to avoid participation in state testing programs (Allington & McGill-Franzen, 1992; Haney, 2000; Ysseldyke, Thurlow, McGrew, & Shriner, 1994; Zlatos, 1994).

Concerned that flagging the results of students with disabilities or excluding them outright from state testing programs may decrease attention, funding and ultimately services provided to students with disabilities, the 1997 Individuals with Disabilities Education Act (IDEA) required that states and districts include students with disabilities in their assessment and accountability programs. As Tindal and Fuchs (1999) summarize:

> The assumption is that if schools are to consider the needs of students with disabilities deliberately and proactively in reform and improvement activities, the outcomes of students with disabilities must be represented in public accountability systems. (p. 6)

Computer-based Test Accommodations

As a result of federal legislation and desires to provide valid measures of students with special needs, a wide variety of test accommodations are in use. In many cases, however, these accommodations are inadequate. As an example of the types of problems encountered, a focus group asked to describe problems they or their blind or visually impaired students encounter while taking math tests using standard accommodations identified the following issues:

- Wide variation in the quality of the person who read the test aloud.
- Use of readers who did not speak English as a first language and who occasionally mispronounced words.
- Use of readers who were not familiar with the test content or terms and would also mispronounce or misread words.
- Readers intentionally providing hints by making comments such as "Are you sure" or "You might want to check that again."
- Readers unintentionally giving hints by pronouncing an option or key word with more emphasis or with a different tone to their voice.
- Examinees being reluctant to ask proctors to reread parts of an item when they were not sure what was being asked or what a response was, particularly for language arts items that required examinees to read extended passages.
- Examinees experiencing difficulty reading diagrams and other graphical elements (Landau, Russell, Gourgey, Erin, & Cowan, 2003).

To overcome these and other problems associated with current methods of providing test accommodations, many observers are embracing computer delivery of tests. As Thompson, Thurlow, Quenemoen, and Lehr (2002) write, "computer-based testing has been viewed as a vehicle to increase the participation of students with disabilities in assessment programs" (p. 4). Among the many advantages to using computers to provide accommodations, Thompson and her colleagues include:

- The large number of adaptive devices that already exist and work in tandem with current computer operating systems.
- Standardizing the administration of tests that are currently proctored or read by a human.
- Allowing a student to work at his or her own pace (Brown-Chidsey & Boscardin, 1999).
- Allowing students to have the computer reread items multiple times without exhausting a sometimes impatient human reader.
- Making obsolete specialized equipment such as audio recorders and video tape players due to the built-in video and audio capabilities of the computer.
- Encoding directions and help functions as text, audio, video, and Braille and allowing the examinee to select the options most useful to him/her (Bennett, 1995).
- Providing immediate feedback to students and teachers, thus increasing the educational value of tests.

Despite the many advantages of using computer-based tests to provide accommodations to students with special needs, several additional challenges arise. Among these challenges are:

- Issues of equity in terms of access to and ability to use computers.
- Lack of expertise and standards for designing web pages and other computer-based material that are equally accessible for all students.
- Unfamiliarity with and variable quality of navigation and help tools.
- The placement of more demands on skills like typing, mouse navigation, and accessing and recalling information presented on multiple screens or in multiple text boxes.
- Fatigue due to reading on the screen, particularly long passages (Haas & Hayes, 1986; Mouran, Lakshmanan, & Chantadisai, 1981).
- Difficulty accessing an entire problem on a single page, particularly ones involving graphics (Hollenbeck, Tindal, Harniss, & Almond, 1999).
- Lack of standardized equipment across schools which in turn affects the presentation of information on screens and the speed with which

students can progress through a test (National Governors Association, 2002).

Challenges such as the lack of standardized equipment may be difficult to overcome as long as individual districts remain responsible for making decisions and providing resources for purchasing computer equipment for their schools. But many of the other challenges can be addressed if test developers adopt a common standard for presenting and delivering tests on computers.

Universal Design

Since 1997, the Center for Universal Design (1997) has been working with a variety of organizations to develop standards for the design and delivery of information on computers. Rather than specifying the wide variety of ways in which computers can be used to provide accommodations that allow people with different needs to access information after it has been produced in a traditional format, the concept of universal design encourages the development of products and environments "usable by all people, to the greatest extent possible, without the need for adaptation or specialized design" (p. 1).

Two important components of sound universal design relate to the content presented and the design features used to present that content. As Thompson et al. (2002) explain:

> Test developers need to carefully examine *what* is to be tested and design items that offer the greatest opportunity for success within those constructs. Just as universally designed architecture removes physical, sensory, and cognitive barriers to all types of people in public and private structures, universally designed assessments need to remove all non-construct-oriented cognitive, sensory, emotional, and physical barriers. (p. 8)

This implies that instructions, navigation tools, menu options, and methods of recording responses must be clearly apparent, easy to understand, and user-friendly regardless of how an examinee interacts with the test interface. It is here that design features play an important role. Visual, oral and tactile information must be presented cleanly and clearly. Information must be laid out in a manner that does not distract examinees from the task at hand and does not obscure information that is needed in order to perform the problem presented. And tools required to solve a problem or to navigate between problems must require minimal physical and mental effort to use.

Clearly, tests developed with these principles in mind will increase accessibility and improve the validity of the inferences made for many students with disabilities. However, some students will still require additional accommodations in order to access and perform the test material. For this reason, when designing tests that meet standards of universal design, test developers should also consider and plan for the integration of additional assistive devices. As Almond, Steinberg, and Mislevy (2002) describe more fully, conceptualizing an assessment as a modular system that selects, delivers, analyzes, and reports results allow test developers to build in a variety of delivery options which will allow the use of different assistive devices depending upon the examinee's needs.

As all state testing programs are currently experiencing, the variety of computer-based tools being used by teachers to help students with special needs access the curriculum is expanding rapidly. In turn, advocates for students with special needs are proactively requesting approval to allow students to use these same tools during testing. In response, state testing programs are allowing an increasing variety of accommodations. In some cases, these accommodations are very costly because they require the development of an entirely new form of the test. As an example, in response to a request to allow students to use a text reader on the state test, Massachusetts had to scan its paper-based tests into computerized text and then develop a secure mechanism for uploading this text onto the computer so that students could perform the test using the text-reader. While successful in allowing students to use the text-reader on one set of items that were to be released following the test administration, the state did not allow students to use the text-reader for a secure set of items that were to be reused the next year. In addition, while students were able to use computers to "read" items and extended written passages, they had to record their responses on paper. It is still unclear whether this need to work simultaneously in two modes—computer and paper—interfered with students' performances. Rather than reacting to requests and then developing specialized versions of tests, it would be more efficient for states to develop tests that can flexibly integrate a variety of accommodations.

By being proactive in designing tests that can flexibly meet the needs of examinees, many of the advantages identified by Thompson and her colleagues (2002) will be realized. In addition, given the many ways in which tests influence teachers' instructional practices, planning for and encouraging the use of accommodations during testing may make more teachers aware of these accommodations, and in turn encourage them to use the accommodations with students in their classrooms.

Just as the use of accommodations on paper/pencil tests has increased awareness and use of accommodations in the classroom, so can opportunities to use the built-in accommodation features of computer-based tests encourage and increase the use of those features in classroom and other environments. (Thompson et al., 2002, p. 4)

COMPUTERS, WRITING AND TESTING

By far, the most common educational use of computers by students is for writing. In 1998, a national survey of teachers found that 50% of K–12 teachers reported that they have students use word processors (Becker, 1999). Similarly, during the spring of 2002, a survey of more than 4,000 K–12 teachers and 13,000 students in 144 Massachusetts schools found that 86% of teachers reported that they have students use computers or portable word processors for writing in class at least one time during the year, 79% have students do projects or papers using computers outside of class, and 81% of fifth-graders and 94% of middle and high school students report having produced first drafts on computers during the past year (Goldberg, O'Connor, & Russell, 2002).

Despite considerable debate as to the impact computer use has on student learning, there is a growing body of research that suggests that the impact is generally positive, particularly in the area of writing (Goldberg, Russell, & Cook, 2003). The research on computers and writing suggests many ways in which writing on computers may help students produce better work. Although much of this research was performed before large numbers of computers were present in schools, formal studies report that when students write on computers they tend to produce more text and make more revisions. Studies that compare student work produced on computers with work produced on paper find that for some groups of students writing on computers also has a positive effect on the quality of student writing. This positive effect is strongest for students with learning disabilities, early elementary students, and college students. Additionally, when applied to meet curricular goals, education technology provides alternative approaches to sustaining student interest, developing student knowledge and skill, and provides supplementary materials that teachers can use to extend student learning. As one example, several studies have shown that writing with computers can increase the amount of writing students perform, the extent to which students edit their writing (Dauite, 1986; Etchinson, 1989; Vacc, 1987), and, in turn, leads to higher quality writing (Hannafin & Dalton, 1987; Kerchner & Kistinger, 1984; Williamson & Pence, 1989). More recently, a meta-analysis of studies conducted between 1990 and 2001 also shows that the quality of student writing improves when students use computers for writing over an extended period of time (Goldberg et al., 2003).

Mode of Administration Effect and Computer-Savvy Students

Despite the increasing presence and use of computers in schools, particularly for writing, state testing programs require that students produce responses to open-ended and essay questions using paper and pencil. Several studies have shown that the mode of administration, which is paper versus computer, has little impact on students' performance on multiple-choice tests (Bunderson, Inouye, & Olsen, 1989; Mead & Drasgow, 1993). More recent research, however, shows that young people who are accustomed to writing with computers perform significantly worse on open-ended (that is, not multiple choice) questions administered on paper as compared with the same questions administered via computer (Russell, 1999; Russell & Haney, 1997a; Russell & Plati, 2000).

Research on this topic began with a puzzle. While evaluating the progress of student learning in the Accelerated Learning Laboratory (ALL), a high-tech school in Worcester, Massachusetts, teachers were surprised by the results from the second year of assessments. Since infusing the school with computers, the amount of writing students performed in school had increased sharply. Yet, student scores on writing tests declined significantly during the second year of the new program.

To help solve the puzzle, a randomized experiment was conducted, with one group of 68 students taking math, science and language arts tests, including both multiple-choice and open-ended items, on paper, and another group of 46 students taking the same tests on computers (but without access to word processing tools, such as spell-checking or grammar-checking). Before scoring, answers written by hand were transcribed to computer text so that raters could not distinguish them from those done on computers. There were two major findings. First, the multiple-choice test results did not differ much by mode of administration. Second, the results for the open-ended tests differed significantly by mode of administration. For the ALL School students who were accustomed to writing on the computer, responses written on computers were much better than those written by hand. This finding occurred across all three subjects tested and on both short answer and extended answer items. The effects were so large that when students wrote on paper, only 30% performed at a "passing" level—when they wrote on computers, 67% "passed" (Russell & Haney, 1997a).

Two years later, a more sophisticated study was conducted, this time using open-ended items from the new Massachusetts state test (the Massachusetts Comprehensive Assessment System or MCAS) and the National Assessment of Educational Progress (NAEP) in the areas of language arts, science, and math. Again, eighth-grade students from two middle schools in Worcester were randomly assigned to groups. Within each subject area, each group was given the same test items, with one group answering on paper and the other on a computer. In addition, data were collected on students' keyboarding speed and prior computer use. As in the first study, all answers written by hand were transcribed to computer text before scoring.

In the second study, which included about 200 students, large differences between computer and paper-and-pencil administration were again evident on the language arts tests. For students who could keyboard moderately well (20 words per minute or more), performance on a computer was much better than on paper. For these students, the difference between performance on a computer and on paper was roughly a half standard deviation. According to test norms, this difference is larger than the amount students' scores typically change between Grade 7 and Grade 8 on standardized tests (Haney, Madaus, & Lyons, 1993). For the MCAS, this difference in performance could easily raise students' scores from the "failing" to the "passing" level (Russell, 1999).

In the second study, however, findings were not consistent across all levels of keyboarding proficiency. As keyboarding speed decreased, the benefit of computer administration became smaller. And at very low levels of keyboarding speed, taking the test on a computer diminished students' performance. Similarly, taking the math test on a computer had a negative effect on students' scores. This effect, however, became less pronounced as keyboarding speed increased.

A third study, conducted during the spring of 2000 (Russell & Plati, 2000), found similar effects for students in Grades 4, 8 and 10. In addition, this most recent study also found that students accustomed to writing with eMates (portable writing devices capable of displaying about 20 lines of text) also performed significantly worse when forced to perform a state writing test on paper. Furthermore, this study found that the mode of administration effect was about 1.5 times larger for eighth-grade students with special education plans for language arts than for all other eighth-grade students.

The effect was so large that eliminating the mode of administration effect by allowing students to write with computers for all five written items on the state language arts test would have a dramatic impact on district-level results. As Figure 5.1 indicates, based on 1999 MCAS results, 19% of the fourth-graders classified as "Needs Improvement" would move up to the "Proficient" performance level. An additional 5% of students who were classified as "Proficient" would be deemed "Advanced." Similarly, Figure 5.2 shows that in Grade 8, 4% of students would move from the "Needs Improvement" category to the "Proficient" category and that 13% more students would be deemed "Advanced." And within one elementary school (Figure 5.3), the percentage of students performing at or above the "Proficient" level would nearly double from 39% to 67%.

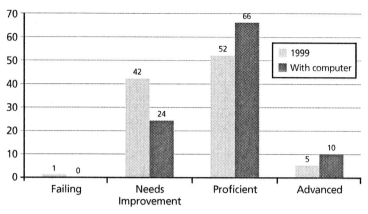

Figure 5.1. Mode of administration effect on grade 4 1999 MCAS results.

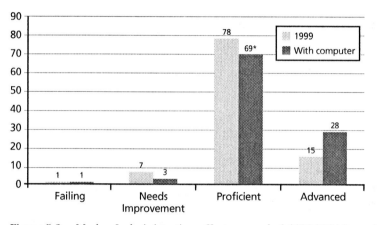

Figure 5.2. Mode of administration effect on grade 8 1999 MCAS results.

Despite this body of evidence that consistently indicates that paper-based writing tests underestimate the writing performance of students who are accustomed to writing with computers, Massachusetts and most other states have resisted requests to allow students to use computers on essay items. The rationale for refusing to allow students to use computers for during testing falls into three categories. First, testing officials cite concerns about item security and suggest that because most schools do not have enough computers for all students to use simultaneously, essay questions may become exposed during testing. Second, state educational leaders express concern that the inequitable distribution of computers in homes and in schools may place some students at a disadvantage if comput-

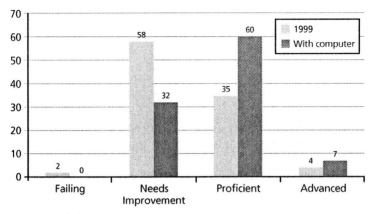

Figure 5.3.   Mode of administration effect on Bates Elementary School 1999 MCAS results.

ers are allowed. And third, some state officials fear that use of computers during testing will lead to the degradation of students' handwriting skills.

While the first two concerns are legitimate, it is important to note that not all students would be more validly measured if they used computers. As found in the second study summarized above, only students who are accustomed to drafting on computers and who have adequate keyboarding skills are systematically mismeasured by paper-based written tests. It is unlikely that students who do not have easy access to computers at home or at school will have developed comfort writing with computers. For these students, producing written responses on computers would result in underestimating their performance. Thus, these students are currently better off taking the written tests on paper and would not need access to computers.

Without question, for schools in which large numbers of students do have access to computers at home or in school and have become accustomed to drafting on computers, the need to provide large numbers of students access to computers during testing applies. Yet, these schools are also likely to have the largest numbers of computers available to students. With a little forethought and careful planning, it would be possible to rotate students onto the computers in such a way that essay questions are not exposed. In fact, Alberta, Canada adopted this strategy a decade ago for its high school exit exam system.

Without question, the systematic and severe underestimates of the performance of students accustomed to writing with computers are cause for concern. But, as described more fully below, the way in which some teachers and schools are adjusting their instructional practices in response to this mode of administration effect is even more problematic.

IMPACT OF STATE TESTING PROGRAMS ON COMPUTER USE IN SCHOOLS

Russell and Haney (2000) discuss at length several problems that result from the mode of administration effect. Among these problems are:

1. Mismeasuring the performance of students and, in turn, misclassifying the achievement level of students accustomed to writing with computers;
2. Underestimating the impact that the use of computers for writing has on students' writing skills;
3. Decreasing the use of computers for writing to minimize the mode of administration effect.

With respect to the third issue, Russell and Haney (2000) provided two lines of evidence that teachers in two schools have already begun to reduce instructional uses of computers so that students do not become accustomed to writing on computers. In one case, following the introduction of the new paper-and-pencil test in Massachusetts, the Accelerated Learning Laboratory required students to write more on paper and less on computers. Fearing that students who write regularly with computers might lose penmanship skills, a principal in another school increased the amount of time teachers spent teaching penmanship and decreased the amount of time students wrote using computers.

To examine the extent to which teachers are altering instructional uses of computers for writing in response to state-level testing programs, data collected as part of a larger national survey of teachers was recently examined (Russell & Abrams, 2004). Among the several questions administered to a representative sample of more than 4,000 teachers nationwide during the winter of 2001 by the National Board on Educational Testing and Public Policy, two focused specifically on instructional uses of technology. These items asked teachers to indicate the extent to which they agreed with the following statements:

- Teachers in my school do not use computers when teaching writing because the state-mandated writing test is handwritten.
- My school's (district) policy forbids using computers when teaching writing because it does not match the format of the state-mandated writing test.

Three other items also focused on the use of computers. These items included:

- What percent of your students have a computer at home?

- What percent of your students prefer to write first drafts using computers?
- What percent of your students can keyboard moderately well (20 words per minute or more)? (Russell & Abrams, 2004, p. 7)

Given that the research on the mode of administration effect was conducted in Massachusetts, analyses of these items focused both on Massachusetts, which was over-sampled in the national study, and on the nationwide sample. To develop an understanding of how the decisions made about students and schools based on state test scores impact teachers' instructional uses of computers for writing, Russell and Abrams also examined the relationship between the stakes associated with the accountability program and teachers' instructional uses of technology for writing.

Results for Massachusetts

As Table 5.2 indicates, 22.4% of the Massachusetts teachers agreed or strongly agreed that they do not use computers when teaching writing because the state-mandated writing test is handwritten. Eight point three percent of the Massachusetts teachers also agree or strongly agree that their school or district forbids using computers when teaching writing because it does not match the format of the state writing test.

Table 5.2.   Computer Use and Testing in Massachusetts

	N	Do Not Use Computers		Policy Forbids Computer Use	
		Agree	Disagree	Agree	Disagree
All MA Teachers	381	22.4%	77.6%	8.3%	91.7%
School Location					
Urban Teachers	115	20.4	79.6	14.8	85.2
Suburban Teachers	202	25.2	74.8	5.2	94.8
Rural Teachers	64	17.7	82.3	6.8	93.2
School Performance					
Above Average	98	19.9	80.1	2.8	97.2
Average	156	23.3	76.7	6.6	93.4
Below Average	112	24.2	73.8	14.6	85.4
School Type					
Elementary School	230	27.0	73.0	11.4	88.6
Middle School	59	16.5	83.5	3.9	96.1
High School	93	15.1	84.9	3.5	96.5

A Chi-square was performed to test for statistical differences within each set of comparisons. Shaded cells indicate statistically significant differences at the .05 level.

When disaggregated by the location of the school, the percentage of teachers agreeing that they do not use computers because the state test is handwritten ranged from 17.7% of teachers in rural schools, to 20.4% in urban schools and 25.2% in suburban schools. The percentage of teachers reporting that their school or district forbids use of computers for writing shows a different pattern. The percentage of teachers agreeing or strongly agreeing ranged from 6.8% in rural schools, to 5.2% in suburban schools, and 14.8% in urban schools. Based on this data, it appears that:

- A small but meaningful percentage of teachers are not using computers to teach writing because the state test is handwritten.
- Decisions by teachers or administrators not to use computers for writing because of the state test occur less frequently in rural schools.

Based on these findings, it also appears that:

- Urban schools are nearly three times more likely than suburban schools to have policies in place that forbid use of computers to teach writing.
- Suburban teachers are more likely to decide on their own not to use computers to teach writing because the test requires students to handwrite their responses.

Nationwide Analyses

As Table 5.3 indicates, 30.2% of the teachers nationwide[1] agree or strongly agree that they do not use computers when teaching writing because the state-mandated writing test is handwritten. Four point four percent of teachers also agree or strongly agree that their school or district forbids using computers when teaching writing because it does not match the format of the state writing test.

When disaggregated by the location of the school, the percentage of teachers agreeing that they do not use computers because the state test is handwritten is similar across urban and rural schools and is lower in suburban schools. However, as seen in Massachusetts, teachers in urban schools are more likely to report that their school or district has a policy that forbids use of computers for writing because of the state test. When disaggregated by performance level, teachers in high performing schools are the least likely not to use computers for writing because of the test while teachers in average performing schools are the most likely. However, a lower percentage of teachers in average schools report policies that forbid use of computers for writing. Conversely, a higher percentage of teachers in low performing schools report policies that forbid computer use for writing.

Table 5.3.   Computer Use and Testing Nationwide

	N^a	Do Not Use Computers		Policy Forbids Computer Use	
		Agree	*Disagree*	*Agree*	*Disagree*
All Teachers Nationwide	4100	30.2%	69.8%	4.4%	95.6%
School Location					
Urban Teachers	1080	32.0	68.0	7.1	92.9
Suburban Teachers	1732	27.4	72.6	2.8	97.2
Rural Teachers	1288	32.3	67.7	4.3	95.7
School Performance					
Above Average	1417	27.0	73.0	4.2	95.8
Average	1437	33.8	66.2	3.8	96.2
Below Average	912	31.1	68.9	6.0	94.0
School Type					
Elementary School	2395	33.1	68.9	4.4	95.6
Middle School	723	30.5	69.5	4.8	95.2
High School	827	21.7	78.3	4.2	95.8

[a] Note that the N's for the national sample are weighted. Although the 381 MA teachers are excluded from the national analyses, their weighted contribution to the national sample represented 95 teachers.
A Chi-square was performed to test for statistical differences within each set of comparisons. Shaded cells indicate statistical differences at the .05 level.

The differences among high-, average-, and low-performing schools are smaller within the national sample as compared to Massachusetts.

Differences Among Test Stakes

It is important to note that the type of testing program and the stakes associated with testing programs vary widely across states. To develop a sense of how practices and policies might vary across types of testing programs, teachers were grouped by the stakes associated with their state's testing program. To this end, state testing programs were placed into one of three categories based on the ways test scores were used to make decisions at the student-level. The three groups included (a) High stakes, including decisions about diplomas or retention in grade level; (b) Moderate stakes, including college tuition credit and eligibility for driver's license; and (c) Low stakes, indicating that no known decisions about individual students are made based on state test scores.

State testing programs were placed into one of three categories based on the ways test scores were used to make decisions at the school-level, teacher-level or both. The three groups included (a) High stakes, including sanctions, receivership, and financial awards; (b) Moderate stakes, including public display of school averages, ranking, or both absent decisions or actions directed at individual schools or teachers; and (c) Low stakes, indicating that results are not publicized or used to make decisions about schools or teachers.

Table 5.4 shows that as the stakes for students associated with a state testing program increase, the percentage of teachers who opt not to allow their students to use computers for writing also increases. Similarly, teachers who work in states that place high stakes on schools and teachers based on the state-testing program are much more likely not to have students use computers for writing than are teachers in moderate-stake states. Contrasting states with the high stakes for schools and students (High/High) with those that have moderate stakes for schools and no stakes for students (Mod/Low), Table 5.4 shows that teachers in High/High states are more than 1.5 times more likely not to use computers for writing because the state test requires students to write by hand.

Table 5.4. Computer Use and Testing Nationwide by Stakes

	N	*Do Not Use Computers*		*Policy Forbids Computer Use*	
		Agree	*Disagree*	*Agree*	*Disagree*
Student Stakes					
High	3018	31.3%	68.7%	4.4%	95.6%
Mod	642	28.9	71.1	5.3	94.7
Low	535	24.1	75.9	4.2	95.8
School/Teacher Stakes					
High	3449	31.6	69.4	4.8	95.2
Mod	651	22.7	77.3	2.6	97.4
Student/School Stakes					
High/High	655	33.1	68.9	4.7	95.3
High/Mod	753	28.9	71.1	5.3	94.7
High/Low	766	26.1	73.9	4.5	95.5
Mod/High	800	23.5	76.5	2.2	97.8
Mod/Low	837	20.1	79.9	3.7	96.3

A Chi-square was performed to test for statistical differences within each set of comparisons. Shaded cells indicate statistical differences at the .05 level.

Although the pattern is less clear regarding school policies that forbid computer use for writing, a higher percentage of teachers who work in states that place high stakes at the school level indicate that their schools have policies forbidding computer use.

STUDENTS AND COMPUTERS

The results presented above indicate a clear relationship between the stakes associated with a state-level testing program and instructional uses of computers. The higher the stakes, whether for students or for schools, the more likely teachers are *not* to use computers for writing. Similarly, the higher the stakes, the more likely schools or districts are to create policies that forbid instructional uses of computers for writing. Across all states that have high stakes for both students and schools, the decision not to use computers for writing because of the format of the test occurs more often in urban schools than in suburban schools. In Massachusetts, the school policies forbidding instructional uses of computers occurs more often in urban and low performing schools.

To explore how these decisions might be impacting the development of basic computing skills and practices of students, student access to computers at home, preferences regarding computer use for writing, and keyboarding skills (as reported by teachers) were compared across school location, school performance, and school type.

Students and Computers in High/High States

Table 5.5 displays the percentage of students in High/High states with home computers, who prefer to write first drafts with computers and who can keyboard moderately well. Note that these percentages were reported by teachers.

Table 5.5 indicates that approximately two-thirds of the teachers (68.3%) in High/High states teach in classrooms in which fewer than 60% of students are reported to have computers at home. The majority of teachers (72.2%) also report that fewer than 30% of their students prefer to write first drafts with computers. Similarly, the majority of teachers (69.6%) report that fewer than 30% of their students keyboard moderately well.

Most notably, approximately 20% fewer teachers in High/High states indicated that more than 60% of their students had computers at home. Similarly, about half as many teachers in High/High states report that more than 60% of their students prefer to write first drafts with computers. Keyboarding skills are also reported to be slightly better in Massachusetts as compared to all High/High states, although this difference is relatively small.

Table 5.5. Students and Computers in High/High States

	N	Home Computer			Write with Computer			Moderate Keyboarders		
		0–30	31–60	61–100	0–30	31–60	61–100	0–30	31–60	61–100
All High/High	1034	39.8%	28.5%	31.7%	72.2%	13.9%	13.9%	69.6%	16.2%	13.9%
School Location										
Urban Teachers	269	59.9	23.7	16.3	76.2	12.7	11.2	78.1	14.8	7.1
Suburban Teachers	454	23.5	28.5	48.0	64.4	15.2	20.3	62.6	17.3	20
Rural Teachers	256	47.7	33.	18.7	81.9	12.7	5.3	72.4	17.1	10.6
School Performance										
Above Average	364	21.7	31	47.3	63.8	16.4	19.8	61.8	16.4	21.9
Average	355	44.0	30.2	25.9	75.4	12.7	11.9	70.5	18.3	11.0
Below Average	216	65.7	22.2	12.1	80.8	11.1	8.2	82.1	12.1	5.8
School Type										
Elementary School	611	45.1	29.1	25.9	83.9	9.9	6.3	85.3	10.8	3.9
Middle School	172	34.3	25.5	40.1	57.8	19.3	23.0	53.9	22.7	23.2
High School	197	27.9	29.0	43.2	49.4	20.7	29.8	35.0	28.8	36.0

Note. Percentages represent the percentage of teachers. As an example, 24.6% of teachers indicate that fewer than 30% of their students have computers in their homes.

The responses for teachers in High/High states differ noticeably across school location, performance level, and school type. A much higher percentage of teachers in urban schools and in low performing schools report that fewer than 30% of their students have computers at home as compared to teachers in suburban and rural schools or in high and average performing schools. Conversely, a higher percentage of teachers in suburban and rural schools report that their students prefer to draft with computers and can keyboard moderately well. Similarly, a higher percentage of teachers in high performing schools report that their students prefer to draft with computers and can keyboard moderately well as compared to teachers in either average or low performing schools. Teachers across all High/High states report that fewer elementary students have computers at home than middle and high school students. However, more students in upper grade levels are reported to prefer to draft with computers and are moderate keyboarders.

In summary, practices, policies, preferences, and skills regarding use of computers for writing seem to differ among schools. In general, urban and low performing schools are more likely to have policies that prohibit use of computers for writing due to the state test. These same schools are also most likely to have students who do not have access to computers at home, who prefer not to draft with computers, and who cannot keyboard moderately well. While students in elementary schools are reported to be slightly less likely to have computers at home, they are less likely to prefer to write first drafts with computers and keyboard more slowly than do students in middle and high schools.

THE BIG PICTURE

Test-based accountability programs are intended to improve teaching and learning in schools and to increase the preparedness of students to compete in the workplace. Both the workplace and schools, however, are becoming increasingly technological. While the aim of state test-based accountability programs is to improve learning in all schools, attention often focuses on the achievement of students in urban and low performing schools. While many states have reported increases in students' scores on state tests (e.g., Texas, Massachusetts, and California among others have all celebrated gains over the past few years), the analyses above suggest that these gains come at the expense of students' opportunity in school to develop skills in using computers, particularly for writing. This pattern is cause for concern for a confluence of reasons.

In the workplace, computers are the primary tool used to compose text and communicate written ideas. In many schools, use of computers for writing is also rapidly increasing. Beyond providing students with the technological skills commonly used in the workplace, an extensive body of research documents that the use of computers can have several positive impacts on students' writing skills. Students write more, are more willing to write more often, edit more frequently, share their work with fellow students and critique each others' work more often, and, when used regularly for an extended period of time, become better writers when they use computers throughout the writing process. Although computers are expensive and most school districts do not have enough computers for all students in a given grade to write on computers at the same time, schools are beginning to acquire relatively inexpensive writing devices like AlphaSmarts (a portable word processor that can up- and down-load text to a computer or printer) in large enough quantities for large numbers of students to write using computer-based technologies. In Massachusetts, these investments are consistent with the Department of Education's benchmark for technology, which sets a student to computer ratio of 5:1 for 2003. Whether it is full-featured computers or devices like AlphaSmarts, it is clear that schools are investing in computer-based technologies with the hope of impacting student learning.

Unfortunately, the fact that state tests administered on paper mismeasure the achievement of students who regularly use computers for writing makes it difficult for schools and districts to assess the impact this use of technology is having on student achievement. Even more troubling, the analyses presented above indicate that the mismatch between how some students regularly produce writing in the classroom and how they are required to produce writing on tests is leading many teachers and some schools to prohibit or dissuade students from writing with computers in schools.

As part of a separate study, researchers in the Technology and Assessment Study Collaborative have interviewed more than 200 district and school leaders (including superintendents, curriculum directors, principals, department heads, and head librarians) in 20 Massachusetts districts about issues related to district technology programs. Although none of the questions focused on or mentioned the state testing programs, at least one leader in eight of the districts mentioned that teachers were not using or had decreased use of computers because of the MCAS. In one district, the superintendent spoke at length about how teachers stop using the writing lab several weeks before the test and instead require students to write using paper in order to prepare for the test. In another district, the English Department Head recounted the story of a teacher whose classroom was equipped with 21 computers several years ago so that all students could write with computers at the same time. Over the past few years, the teacher "severely backtracked on having kids write constantly with technology due to the MCAS exam and AP English essays. Kids came back initially from exams and expressed frustration that they did not know how to write with paper and pencil. So now they are being provided with many of their writing experiences without technology" (Personal Communication, March 21, 2002).

To reduce the mode of administration effect and to promote instructional uses of computers for writing, Russell and his colleagues (Russell & Haney, 2000; Russell & Plati, 2000) have suggested that students be given the option of composing written responses for state-level tests on paper or with a word processor. As noted above, state educational officials, however, have raised concerns that this policy might place students in urban or underfunded districts at a disadvantage because they might not have computers available to them in school if they were given the option of using them during testing. The data presented above, however, suggests that these students are already being placed at a disadvantage because their teachers discourage them from using computers for writing in school and their schools are nearly three times as likely to have policies that prohibit use of computers for writing. Moreover, these same students are significantly less likely to have computers in their homes and therefore are less able to develop proficiency in writing with computers (or working with computers more generally) outside of school. Despite rising test scores, teachers and school policies that decrease the use of computers coupled with limited access to computers at home is under preparing many students in urban and poorly performing schools for the workplace.

In addition, since the mode of administration effect reported by Russell and his colleagues (Russell, 1999; Russell & Haney, 1997a; Russell & Plati, 2000) only occurs for students who are accustomed to writing with computers, and because students in suburban and high-performing schools are much more likely to be accustomed to writing with computers, state tests are likely under-representing the difference in academic achievement between urban and suburban schools. Despite concerns about the need to close the gap between urban and suburban schools, the current policy that prohibits use of computers during state tests calls into question the use of these tests to examine the achievement gap.

OTHER IMPACTS OF STATE TESTS ON TECHNOLOGY USE IN SCHOOLS

In addition to influencing use of computers for writing in some classrooms and schools, state tests are influencing other uses of computers in schools. Perhaps the most dramatic influence is seen in how the Co-NECT Model of School Reform has changed its emphasis over the past decade.

Developed by BBN, Inc., a Boston-based communications technology firm, Co-NECT was one of nine models for innovative schooling funded by the New American Schools Development Corporation. Working with BBN, the original Co-NECT schools restructured many aspects of their educational environment. Among other reforms, the traditional middle school grade structure (that is, separately organized Grade 6, 7, and 8 classes) was replaced with blocks that combined into a single cluster of students who otherwise would be divided into Grades 6, 7, and 8. In place of traditional subject-based classes (such as English class, math class, social studies, etc.), all subjects were integrated and taught through project-based activities. To support this cooperative learning structure, several networked computers were placed in each classroom, allowing students to perform research via the Internet and CD-ROM titles; write reports, papers and journals; and create computer-based presentations using several software applications.

To help evaluate the effects the restructuring at the ALL School had on its students as a whole, the Center for the Study of Testing, Evaluation and Educational Policy (CSTEEP) at Boston College helped teachers gather baseline data in the fall of 1993 with plans to perform follow-up assessments in the spring of 1994 and each spring thereafter. To acquire a broad picture of students' strengths and weaknesses, the types of tests included in the baseline assessment ranged from multiple choice tests to short and long answer open-ended assessments to hands-on performance assessments covering a wide range of reading, writing, science, and math skills. To acquire insight into how cooperative projects affected the development of group skills, some of the performance assessments required students to work together to solve a problem and/or answer specific questions. Finally, to evaluate how the Co-NECT model, as implemented in the ALL School, affected students' feelings about their school, a student survey was administered. Assessments and surveys were administered to representative samples of the whole school's student population.

During the first six years, the Co-NECT model was occasionally modified to meet the needs of individual school districts. In some cases, these modifications included a reduced focus on multiple-grade clusters. In other cases, state assessments were used instead of some of the instruments developed by the CSTEEP researchers. Yet, regular use of computers was emphasized and remained an important design element for several years.

Today, the Co-NECT model is very different. In response to frequent inquiries by school leaders about its impact on state test scores, the Co-NECT design has decreased its focus on project-based learning and regular use of computers to assist with these projects. Instead, Co-NECT has formed a partnership with Princeton Review to support the use of Homeroom.com in their partner schools. In effect, Homeroom.com provides K–12 students test preparation tailored to each state test. To measure Co-

NECT's impact, state tests have become the sole student learning outcome measure. And, to increase the likelihood of improved state test scores, Co-NECT has shifted its emphasis from using computers to engage students in open-ended, project-based inquiries to using computers for test preparation. In essence, this transformation results from two factors. First, in order to remain financially solvent, Co-NECT had to provide a service that met the needs of the educational community. Second, in response to the use of tests to hold schools accountable for student learning, school leaders began seeking programs and services that would boost student achievement as measured by state tests. Since multiple modes of student assessment were not valued by accountability systems, Co-NECT replaced its multiple measure assessment system with services that were more closely aligned with the types of tests employed by state and federal accountability systems.

Co-NECT, however, is not alone in this move toward using computers for test preparation. Over the past few years, the market has become flooded with computer-based test preparation materials. At the 2002 National Educational Computing Conference, 20 of the 80 vendors were marketing at least one product as computer-based tool that would help improve student test scores. Meanwhile, local districts and state department of educations have invested in programs like TestU to help improve students' test scores. While it is unclear just how often these test-preparation programs are being used by students in classrooms, it is certain that whenever computers are used for test-preparation, they are not available to be used to develop skills like problem-solving, research, and writing.

SEEKING A SOLUTION

Clearly, there is not an easy solution to the multiple problems caused by administering tests, especially essay items, only on paper. While I have advocated that state-level testing programs give students the option of using paper-and-pencil or computers (without access to spell- and grammar-checkers) for written tests, this solution presents additional challenges. Students need access to computers. In many cases, it is likely that those students who use computers regularly for writing in school will attend schools that have large numbers of computers available for testing. But this will not always be the case.

As first noted by Powers, Fowles, Farnum, and Ramsey (1994), allowing examinees to produce responses in handwritten form or as computer-text also complicates the scoring process. Although conventional wisdom is that readers give preference to neatly formatted computer-printed responses, several studies have documented that readers tend to award higher scores to handwritten responses. However, research has shown that this presentation effect can be reduced or eliminated with careful training prior to scoring (Powers et al., 1994; Russell & Tao, 2004a,b).

A third problem arises due to the way in which most testing companies score open-ended responses. While the practices vary to some extent, careful procedures are employed to maintain the link between a student's identification, his or her response, and the scores awarded to the response. In Massachusetts, student identifications are placed onto a test booklet. So as to preserve the link between the student and his or her response, students are required to write their entire response in the test booklet. In fact, if students run out of room in their test booklet, they are instructed to erase and rewrite their work so that it will fit into the test booklet. Additional sheets attached to the test booklet are not accepted. Allowing students to compose responses using computers would require testing programs to alter their current administration procedures in order to preserve the link between students and their responses.

Similarly, just as state-testing programs were pushed to respond to instructional uses of calculators by allowing students to use calculators for some types of mathematics test items, these testing programs must continue to be pushed to expand the types of computer-based accommodation tools that students are able to use. As described earlier, allowing a larger variety of accommodation tools to be used during testing will complicate the test development and delivery process. However, whether one focuses on the issue of allowing students to use computers to compose responses to open-ended items or to provide accommodations, state-testing programs should begin to address the challenges immediately. To do anything less will likely lead to a continued inability to adequately examine the impact instructional uses of computers for writing has on student writing performance, lead to continued mismeasurment of achievement for some students, lead more teachers and schools to decrease use of computers for writing, further exacerbate the technology-use gap between urban and suburban students, and under-prepare a portion of the student population for an increasingly technological workplace. As I explore in detail in the next chapter, the potential to employ computer-based technologies to increase the validity of inferences made based on state tests is currently overshadowed by desires to increase the efficiency of state testing systems.

NOTE

1.   Note that the nationwide sample excluded teachers from Massachusetts in order to allow trends in Massachusetts to be compared with trends across the nation.

CHAPTER 6

PERSONAL COMPUTERS, THE INTERNET REVOLUTION, AND TESTING

During the 1984 Super Bowl XVIII, a one-minute commercial introduced the Macintosh computer. Although an extremely powerless computer by today's standards, the Macintosh sparked an explosion in the desktop computer industry. Sixteen years later 51% of households had at least one computer (Newburger, 2001), nearly every public school has several computers, and the vast majority of classrooms have at least one computer (National Center for Education Statistics, 2002). During the mid-1990s, access to the Internet experienced a similar explosion.

The widespread availability of desktop computers, their increasing power, and rapidly expanding access to high-speed Internet connections is enabling testing programs to capitalize on the efficiencies afforded by today's computer-based technologies. As the tests are increasingly being used to make decisions about students and their schools, computers and the Internet are also increasingly being used to provide teachers and parents with access to test results and to prepare students for these tests.

In this chapter, I describe in greater detail the several ways in which computers are being applied to increase the efficiency of testing. I also examine how the testing industry is responding to the rise of testing and computers to provide a variety of services and products to students and schools. Additionally, I describe efforts by several states to transition their

Technology and Assessment: The Tale of Two Interpretations, pages 77–97
Copyright © 2006 by Information Age Publishing
77

testing programs to computers. These efforts include the delivery of tests, the scoring of essays, preparation for tests, and making results available to the general public in a variety of formats. As this chapter progresses, it should become clear that it is no longer a question of whether testing programs will transition to computers, but how rapidly.

RISE OF COMPUTER-BASED TESTING

Computer-based testing (CBT) is a deceptively broad term that simply refers to the delivery mechanism for a test. The test and its component parts can vary widely. In the simplest case, multiple-choice items are transferred directly from their paper-based version to a computer. Rather than turning pages to access items and recording responses with a pencil, examinees refresh the screen to move between items and use a mouse to select responses. In this form of computer-based testing, the only feature of the test that is altered is the delivery mechanism.

In more sophisticated examples, the computer might adapt the items presented to an examinee to match that examinee's ability, closely monitor the amount of time spent on each item, present video and audio clips as part of an item's prompt or responses, allow examinees to perform simple or complex simulations, or record every action an examinee performs while working on an item (Bennett, 1998b; Drasgow & Olson-Buchanan, 1999; Mills, Potenza, Fremer, & Ward, 2002). Each of these applications of computers to testing has the potential to add value to the information collected about examinees through a test.

In the simplest example, presentation of paper-based, multiple-choice items on a computer allows for automatic and immediate scoring of examinee responses. This information can be returned immediately to the examinee, test administrator, and teachers. This information also can be aggregated efficiently with test results from other examinees and returned to schools in a timely manner.

In the more complex examples, computers are used to improve the information provided about an examinee. As described more fully below, computer-adaptive tests provide more refined estimates of an examinee's ability. In most cases, these improved measures of examinee ability are also produced with greater efficiency.

The presentation of video and audio can increase the authenticity of the problems posed in test items. As an example, a test of foreign language skills might use audio and video to provide more meaningful measures of an examinee's oral language skills. Similarly, an Advanced Placement American History test might include audio and video clips of famous speeches or other historical documents, thus increasing the range of historical artifacts students are required to work with during the testing process (Bennett, 1998b).

Requiring students to work in a simulated environment can also increase the authenticity of the test items and provide more useful information about how an examinee might perform when confronted with similar problems outside the testing venue. As an example, obtaining a valid measure of the skills required by an air traffic controller is difficult to accomplish with traditional paper-based test items. By simulating various situations that tap the skills required for successful air traffic control, more meaningful measures can be acquired (Hanson, Borman, Mogilka, Manning, & Hedge, 1999).

Finally, monitoring, and in some cases limiting, the time and actions examinees take while solving a problem can provide insight into the examinee's depth of understanding and problem-solving strategies. As an example, Vendlinski and Stevens (2002) have demonstrated how the steps students take as they solve a complex problem, such as performing a series of physical and chemical tests to identify a chemical, can be used to classify their problem-solving strategies. Once classified, problem-solving strategies can provide insight into the depth of an examinee's understanding and can reveal misconceptions.[1]

When considering the various ways in which computers can be applied to testing, Bennett (1998b) describes three stages or generations of computer-based testing. During the first generation, computers are used to increase the efficiency of testing. Both linear and adaptive computer-based testing are examples of first-generation applications, in that they are intended to increase the efficiency of item delivery, scoring, and production of results. During the second generation, item types are expanded. This expansion includes the integration of multimedia elements to increase the authenticity of the items presented to students. In addition, this expansion allows examinees to provide responses in a wider variety of formats including extended essays, verbal recordings, and manipulation of elements presented on the screen. During the third generation, Bennett argues that computers will be used to deliver tests anywhere and at any time. This will open up online learning and will enable testing to become more integrated with instruction.

As this integration occurs, computers will also be used to develop tests that provide more diagnostic information about a student's skill and knowledge. As Mislevy (1993) argues, this move toward diagnostic testing will require the development of new psychometric models. In this way, the third-generation tests will not only impact how test information is used in the classroom—it will also impact the theories and models upon which tests are developed. Whereas the fundamental advantage of first-generation computer-based testing is efficiency, second-generation tests will enhance authenticity, and the third generation will alter the technology of testing and the ways in which this testing technology is used. In the remainder of this chapter, I focus on first-generation applications of computers to testing. The next chapter explores second and third-generation applications.

COMPUTER-ADAPTIVE TESTING

Computer-adaptive testing is perhaps the most misunderstood application of computers to testing. Whereas the linear presentation of items on a computer increases the efficiency of the test delivery and scoring process, computer-adaptive testing increases the efficiency of estimating examinee ability. In essence, computer-adaptive testing decreases the number of items to which an examinee must respond before a reliable estimate of their ability is reached. To do so, the computer adapts or tailors the items presented to each examinee. As a result, examinees are presented with a larger percentage of items that are close to their ability and fewer items that are either too easy or too hard, given their ability. By most estimates, computer-adaptive testing can cut the amount of testing time in about half without affecting the reliability of an examinee's test score.

Today, computer-adaptive testing has been used primarily for tests administered to adults such as the Graduate Record Exam (GRE) and a variety of tests administered by the military. Over the past few years, however, some state-sponsored K–12 testing programs have begun to explore the use of computer-adaptive testing (Bennett, 2002). Given growing interest in the use of computer adaptive tests in K–12 schools (Trotter, 2003) coupled with the seemingly magical way in which items are tailored for each examinee, the process for adapting items is described in detail below. The process begins with item response theory.

Item Response Theory[2]

Item response theory, as it is known today, grew out of work by George Rasch. A mathematician by training, Rasch became intrigued by statistics. Unlike most statisticians of his time, however, Rasch's interest in statistics was not driven by a desire to understand differences within and among groups of people, but on the study of individuals. Reflecting on his career, Rasch explains:

> Fairly early I got around to the problem of dealing with individuals. I had tried to do that for the growth of children already before I came to London.

But meeting Julian Huxley showed me that this was really an important line of research. I continued to stick, as far as I could, to the study of individuals ever since. It meant quite a lot to me to realize the meaning and importance of dealing with individuals and not with demography. Later on I realized that test psychologists were not dealing with the testing of individuals but what they were studying was how traits, such as intelligence, were distributed in a population. (Andrich, in press)

Rasch's conceptualization of a test as a measure of an individual's trait rather than that individual's standing within the population laid the foundation for Rasch's contribution to test theory (Rasch, 1980). While working for the Danish Department of Defense to develop a group intelligence test, Rasch became aware of a major limitation of the then- current approach to test development, namely the influence of item difficulty on perceived group performance and of group performance on perceived item difficulty. This shortcoming of classical test theory is summed up best by Wright and Stone (1979) who write: "Even that noble achievement, 100 percent, [is] ambiguous. One hundred might signify the welcome news that we were smart. Or it might mean the test was easy" (p. xi).

At the heart of the problem was an interdependence of the testing group and the test items. Depending upon the mean performance or ability of the group being tested, the difficulty of the test and each of its component items could vary widely. Conversely, depending upon the difficulty of the test, the ability of a given group of test takers could appear to vary widely.

As an example, imagine a test of addition containing ten items and imagine two groups of students. The first group of students consists of second-graders that have just begun to study addition. The second group is composed of fourth-graders who are well grounded in addition. When the group of second-grade students takes the test, the mean score might be 4 or 40% correct. For the fourth-graders group, the mean might be 9 or 90% correct. Without knowing anything about the two groups, the difficulty of the test appears very different. In the first case, it seems like a fairly difficult test. In the second case, the test seems fairly easy.

Now, also imagine a new student who has studied addition, but is not particularly strong in addition and scores a seven on the test. If this student takes the test with the first group, the student would score three points above the mean. If the student were part of the second group, he or she would score two points below the mean. Again, without knowing anything about the two groups, the ability of the student appears very different. In the first case, the student seems to excel in addition relative to his or her peers. In the second case, it seems that the student is not very strong in addition.

Finally, imagine a new item that is added to the test. When the first group encounters the item, only 30% of the students get it correct. When the second group takes the item, 95% succeed. Again, without knowing anything about the two groups, the item appears rather difficult or very easy.

Rasch resolved the problem of interdependence by developing a model that yielded estimates of item difficulty that did not vary across groups and yielded estimates of an examinee's ability that did not vary across items. In other words, regardless of the ability of the examinees that took an exam, the estimated item difficulty would be the same. Similarly, regardless of the group of items an examinee responded to, the examinee's estimated ability would be the same.

Rasch's model was probabilistic in nature and expressed an examinee's ability with respect to the probability that a given individual would succeed on an item or set of items with known difficulties. Conversely, item difficulty was expressed with respect to the probability that an examinee or set of examinees with known abilities would succeed on the item. From a mathematical perspective, the challenge to creating such a model was in simultaneously obtaining estimates of item difficulties given examinee abilities and of examinee abilities given item difficulties. Although an extraordinarily large number of calculations are required to obtain simultaneous estimates of item difficulty and examine ability, once accomplished a measurement model is produced which (a) places the ability estimates for different examinees on the same scale without all examinees having to complete the same set of items, and (b) places difficulty estimates for all items on the same scale without all items having to be completed by the same set of examinees.

When Rasch first introduced his probabilistic model in 1960, he applied the model to dichotomous data derived from multiple-choice test items. At its core, Rasch's probabilistic model estimates an examinee's ability based upon the difficulty of the items on which the examinee succeeds. Both examinee ability and item difficulty are expressed on the same scale. On this scale, items are ordered by their difficulty. When the model works perfectly, an examinee will succeed on items whose difficulty is below the examinee's ability and the examinee will fail on items whose difficulty is above the examinee's ability. As the difference between an examinee's ability and an item's difficulty increases, the probability that the examinee fails or succeeds also increases. And, when an item's difficulty is exactly the same as the examinee's ability, the examinee will have a 50:50 chance of succeeding or failing on that item.

For example, imagine a test that measures a student's ability to perform addition. As depicted in Figure 6.1, the test might contain 10 items that range in difficulty. The easiest item asks students to add 1 + 1. An item of medium difficulty asks examinees to add 22 + 32. And a very difficult item

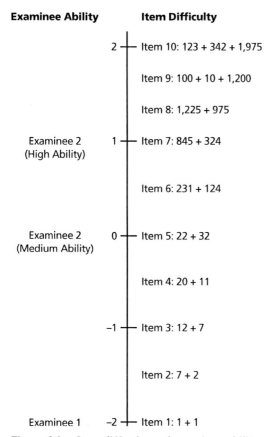

Examinee Ability   **Item Difficulty**

Figure 6.1.   Item difficulty and examinee ability scale.

requires examinees to add 123 + 342 + 1,975. For this test, the item difficulty scale ranges from –2 to +2, with 0 representing medium or average difficulty.

Now, imagine three examinees, one with a low ability of –1.0, one with medium ability of 0.0, and one with high ability of 1.0. When the examinee with low ability encounters the first two items, he or she will most likely succeed. However, since item one is the easiest item, his or her probability of success is higher on item one than on item two. Conversely, since the difficulty of items four through ten are all above the examinee's ability, his or her probability of success on these items is low. However, since item ten is much more difficult than item four, the examinee's probability of failure is much higher on item ten than on item four. Finally, the difficulty of item three is exactly the same as the examinee's ability. Thus, for item three, the examinee has a 50:50 chance of succeeding.

The examinee with medium ability will likely succeed on items one through four. However, his/her chances of succeeding are much higher on item one than on item four. Conversely, the examinee will likely fail on items six through ten, but will be more likely to fail on item ten than on item six. And, for item five, whose difficulty matches the examinee's ability, the examinee has a 50:50 chance of success.

Finally, the high-ability examinee will likely succeed on items one through six, will likely fail on items eight through ten, and has a 50:50 chance of succeeding on item seven. Moreover, when the chances of the three examinees succeeding on item one are compared, the high ability examinee has the highest probability of success, followed by the medium ability examinee. While the low ability examinee is likely to succeed, his or her chances of success are much lower than the other two examinees. Conversely, when the chances of each examinee failing on item ten are compared, examinee one has the highest probability of failure, followed by the medium examinee, and then the high-ability examinee.

From a measurement perspective, the Rasch model is attractive for at least three reasons. First, an examinee's ability estimate does not depend on the set of items that comprise a test. Second, once difficulty estimates for a set of items are obtained, different subsets of items can be used to obtain reliable estimates of different examinees' abilities. Third, an estimate of an examinee's ability can be made based on only one piece of information about the items, namely their difficulty.

Over time, several variants of Rasch's original model have been developed. In addition to considering success on an item, some of these models also consider the extent to which an item distinguishes or discriminates between examinees with different ability. Other models refine ability estimates based on the probability of success on an item due to guessing. Several models have also been developed for partial-credit items (e.g., an essay that can receive between 0 and 4 points). Still other models adjust ability and item difficulty to account for differences between the severity and leniency with which raters score examinees' open-ended responses. This general class of probabilistic models, each of which provides estimates of examinee ability that are invariant across items and estimates of item difficulty that are invariant across examinees, are based on what has become known as Item Response Theory (IRT).

Not surprisingly, as the complexity of an IRT model increases, the dependence on computers to perform complex calculations increases. In this way, computers have been vital to the development of new IRT models. But, rather than simply employing computers to perform the calculations necessary to produce an IRT model, the most powerful application of item response theory comes from the marrying of computers and an IRT model. It is this marriage of computers and IRT that has given birth to computer adaptive testing.

Item Response Theory and Adaptive Testing

Computer adaptive testing (CAT) capitalizes on item response theory to tailor the presentation of test items to more closely match the ability level of each examinee. Although several variants of CAT have been developed over the past decade, the same four-step process is used across all variants.

First, a large set or bank of items is developed. Like items on most paper-based tests, a computer adaptive item bank contains items that range widely in difficulty, from very easy to very difficult. But, unlike a paper-based test that typically contains one or two items that have the same (or very similar) difficulty, several items with the same (or very similar) difficulty are developed for a computer adaptive item bank. Typically, an item bank for a computer adaptive test contains many times more items than would be presented in a paper-based test.

Second, a small set of items that range in difficulty is presented to an examinee. These items are used to calculate an initial estimate of the examinee's ability. Based on this initial ability estimate, the adaptive aspect of the test begins.

Third, an item that has the same difficulty as the examinee's initial ability estimate is selected from the item pool and presented to the examinee. Recall that item response theory assumes that an examinee will have a 50:50 chance of succeeding on an item that has the same difficulty as the examinee's ability. Thus, if the examinee succeeds on the presented item, the adaptive test assumes that the examinee's ability is higher than the item's difficulty and the examinee's initial ability estimate is replaced by a higher ability estimate. Based on this higher ability estimate, the adaptive test then selects an item that has the same difficulty as the examinee's new ability estimate. Conversely, if the examinee fails on the item, the adaptive test assumes that the examinee's ability is lower than the item's difficulty and the examinee's initial ability estimate is replaced with a lower ability estimate. In this case, the examinee is presented with an easier item. This process of presenting an item and re-estimating the examinee's ability based on his or her performance on each item is repeated several times. As this process proceeds, the estimates of the examinee's ability gradually stabilize.

In theory, the goal of an adaptive test is to narrow in on the examinee's ability and then present the examinee with a series of items that have the same difficulty as the examinee's ability. If the examinee's estimated ability were correct, the examinee would succeed 50% of the time on this series of items that match his or her ability. In reality, however, this final step is not possible, largely because it would be exceedingly difficult to develop enough items for every conceivable ability level. Instead, the fourth step applies a stop rule. When the stop rule is applied, a final estimate of the examinee's ability is made. In general, two types of stop rules have been used. The first ends the iterative process when the difference between the most recent ability estimate and the prior ability estimate is smaller than a predetermined number. The second stop rule ends the exam when the error associated with the most recent ability estimates reaches a predefined upper limit. In essence, the second stop rule recognizes that there will be error in the estimated ability and stops the testing process when the error decreases to an acceptable level.

ITEM GENERATION

Despite the advantages of computer adaptive testing, the large item banks required to generate reliable examinee scores across a wide range of ability is a serious obstacle to developing adaptive tests. Currently, the development of an item bank requires a substantial amount of effort. Typically, this item development process includes six steps.

- A test specification is developed which describes the content of the test and the appropriate item formats.
- A team of item writers produces a large set of items that meet the test specifications.
- A team of content and test experts review the pool of items and select a subset of items for possible use.
- This subset of items is piloted on a sample of students and item statistics are generated.
- Based on the item statistics, the pool of items is refined to meet the test specifications.
- A bias review committee reviews this reduced pool of items and removes items that are believed to discriminate against subsets of students.

The final set of items then form the test. For a test that contains 50 items, the development costs are affordable. But, for an adaptive test that requires 10 to 15 times the number of items, the development costs become prohibitive.

To decrease the cost of developing items, for either a paper-based or computer-based test, the Educational Testing Service has begun developing methods for computer-generated items. As an example, the Mathematics Test Creation Assistant tool automatically generates multiple questions based on item specifications entered by the test developer. The user defines each component of an item as a variable. For each variable, the user also enters constraints. This item definition then serves as a "parent" from which "children" or variants of the parent item are developed. Figure 6.2 displays the development of a mathematics item that could appear on the GRE.

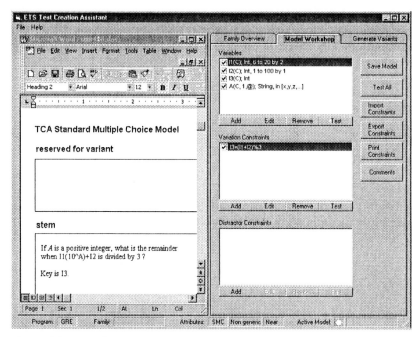

Figure 6.2.   Development of a GRE Mathematics Item

The left side of Figure 6.2 shows the Microsoft Word environment that test developers use to create a parent item. In the stem area, a typical math item is entered. But instead of using fixed terms, three variables are used. In the example depicted in Figure 6.2, three stem variables are represented as A, I1, and I2. The correct response is also represented as a variable (I3).

In the upper right portion of the screen, each variable is defined. For example, variable I3, which is the answer key, is defined as an integer, while I2 is defined as an integer that can range from 1 to 100 by units of one and variable A is defined as a string variable. The variable constraint box then provides the formula for the answer key: (I1+I2)/3. In the bottom left window, distractors can be created. As with portions of the item stem, the distractors can also be expressed as variables.

Based on the stem, the variable definition, the variable constraints, and the distractor definitions, item variants are created. Item variants fall into one of three categories: *close variants, medium variants,* and *far variants.* Close variants simply differ in the value of the variables. An example of a close variant in the above example is: "If z is a positive integer, what is the remainder when $6(10^z)$ is divided by 3? Answer key = 2."

Medium variants in some way differ in structure from the parent item. An example of a medium variant in the above example is: "What is the remainder when 10^{64} is divided by 11? Answer key = 0."

Far variants differ significantly from the parent item. An example of a far variant in the above example is: "When the positive integer n is divided by 9, the remainder is 7. What is the remainder when n+9 is divided by 9? Answer key = 7."

Once item variants are formed, the test developer can review and revise each variant. Those that are deemed acceptable are then forwarded to a pretest calibration process. This pretest calibration process provides initial estimates of item difficulty and other item characteristics used by the item response model.

In its current form, the Test Creation Assistant is capable of producing variants for several types of item formats, including multiple-choice, con-structed-response, and extended-response items. As of this writing, Educa-tional Testing Service (ETS) is using the Test Creation Assistant to develop mathematics items for the GRE, the Graduate Management Admission Test (GMAT), the SAT, and Praxis I. To ensure that a large percentage of close and medium variants of a single parent item are not placed in the same form of a test or in a single computer adaptive item pool, ETS has estab-lished quality control procedures.

Although this approach to item creation is in an early stage of use, ETS reports that it is helping to make the item creation process more efficient. Given the need for large item banks for computer adaptive tests, coupled with the need to replenish these item banks as items become overexposed, ETS is also exploring ways to use item generation to create "self-generating adaptive tests." If successful, this methodology would allow items to be gen-erated "on the fly" as an examinee is taking a test. Although this concept has not yet been put into practice, NAEP is considering using this "on the fly" item creation model in their mathematics assessment (NCES, 2003).[3]

COMPUTER-BASED ANALYSIS OF WRITING

Just as the process of developing large item banks is costly, the scoring of open-ended and essay responses traditionally has required considerable amounts of time and effort by people. To decrease the time and money required to score open-ended items, several efforts have been made to develop methods of using computers to analyze and score written responses.

Work on computer-based scoring dates back to the work of Ellis Page during the late 1960s. Since Page's (1966, 1968) pioneering efforts, four approaches to computer-based scoring have evolved and are being used to score student work both in the classroom and on large-scale testing pro-grams. These approaches include Project Essay Grading (PEG), Latent Semantic Analysis (LSA), e-Rater, and Bayesian Essay Test Scoring sYstem (BETSY). All four of these systems have been shown to provide reliable scores for various types of student writing (Burstein, 2001; Foltz, Gilliam, and Kendall, 2000; Page, 1995; Rudner & Liang, 2002). Below, each of these approaches is described briefly.

Project Essay Grading (PEG)

Ellis Page's PEG system, which was first introduced in 1966, is the oldest computer-grading product in use today. PEG began as a system that counted specific elements of a written passage, such as essay length, word length, and number of words and then examined the relationship between these numbers and the score awarded by a human reader. PEG then built a mathematical model that predicted an essay score based on these counts. Although this early system was not designed to imitate the criteria human graders use to score essays, scores awarded by PEG were highly correlated with human graders. Page's theory is that intrinsic variables (*trins*) such as grammar, diction, and fluency can be approximated (*proxes*) by observable variables such as essay length. Years of research and refinement of PEG have resulted in more complex models that close the gap between trins and proxes. The PEG system uses multiple regression techniques to predict the essay score (dependent variable) from independent variables (word length, number of prepositions, number of pronouns).

PEG is a useful tool for scoring essays based on the quality (i.e., English Standards) of writing. The major weakness of PEG is that it does not usually consider the content of the essay. Another potential drawback of the PEG system is that it does not offer diagnostic information and usually only offers a single holistic score.

Latent Semantic Analysis (LSA)

Latent Semantic Analysis compares the essay to be graded to calibration documents, which represent typical essays of each score. Each of the calibration essays is represented as a column in a matrix, and each row of the matrix represents a content term, which can be a word, a phrase, a sentence, or multiple sentences. The content terms are then compressed through factor analysis to produce a more manageable matrix. Each cell of the matrix is given a value that ranges from zero (the content term is completely absent) to one (the content term is fully present). The essay to be graded is given a score by averaging the scores of calibration documents most similar to the given essay. LSA requires content terms, weights of the content terms, and calibration documents to be identified prior to essay scoring. Depending on the essay topic, much of this information can be captured through analysis of textbooks or recent literature, instead of using a sample of essays. Because the LSA system produces a score for each of the content factors that are considered important in grading the essay, diagnostic information can be easily supplied to the essay writer. Although some quality of writing attributes may be included in the scoring model, the LSA system is best suited for awarding scores based on the content of an essay.

A major weakness of the LSA model is the amount of effort required to establish the model before grading essays (a minimum of 1,000 essays are recommended to calibrate LSA). It should also be noted that LSA is currently offered as a service rather than a stand-alone product, which makes it unattractive for classroom use.

e-Rater

Educational Testing System's e-Rater, which has been used since 1999 to score GMAT essays, combines the benefits of PEG and LSA. The three primary tools that e-Rater uses to score essays are:

- Syntactic variety, which counts the number of complement, subordinate, infinitive, and relative clauses as well as modal verbs such as "would" and "could" to determine a ratio of syntactic features per sentence and per essay.
- Discourse structure, which capitalizes on the benefits of PEG by using counts of 60 variables to determine quality of writing by searching for words that begin or develop an argument.
- Content analysis, which is similar to LSA because it creates indices to determine how similar the essay to be graded is to calibrated essays.

The above features are identified by having human readers score a sample of essays and are used to build a regression model that predicts essay score. The model is then pilot tested and eventually used to determine essay scores. The score is then converted to a score category by comparison to model essays. Although e-Rater has primarily been used to provide holistic essay scores, it can also be used for diagnostic purposes. Like LSA, e-rater requires large numbers of essays for calibration and is not currently available for use as a stand-alone product.

Bayesian Essay Test Scoring sYstem (BETSY)

The Bayesian Essay Test Scoring sYstem uses Bayesian logic to estimate the probability that an essay falls into each score category. Typically, the model begins by assuming that there is an equal chance of obtaining each score. Then a feature of the essay, such as use of a specific word or phrase, is examined and determined to be either present or not present. The probability of the essay falling into each score category is then updated using Bayes' Theorem. The next feature of the essay is examined and the score probabilities are updated again. This process is repeated for each individual feature or until a predefined stopping criterion is reached. Thus, unlike PEG, LSA, and e-Rater, BETSY examines features of an essay individually rather than collectively. Unlike the other models, BETSY has also been used to score responses for long essay items and short response items. As Rudner (2001) argues, the BETSY model captures the benefits of PEG, LSA, e-Rater, and more: "It can be employed on short essays, is simple to implement, can be applied to a wide range of content areas, can be used to yield diagnostic results, can be adapted to yield classifications on multiple skills, and is easy to explain to non-statisticians" (para. 14).

As noted earlier, all four of these automated scoring systems are being used today in classrooms and for larger testing programs to provide reliable scores. Like computer adaptive testing and item generations, however, the application of computers to score essays increases the efficiency of testing. Specifically, item generation increases the efficiency with which a test is developed, saving time otherwise needed by humans to create a large item bank. Computer adaptive testing increases the efficiency with which a stable, reliable score is generated for each examinee, saving the need to present examinees with items that are much too easy or too difficult. Like the scanner, automated essay scoring increases the speed with which essay and short answer items are scored, again saving the time of humans to read and score large number of written responses. As we will see in the next section, the Internet can also facilitate the efficiency with which tests are delivered, while also increasing access to information about the test prior to the actual testing time, and increasing access to test results once testing is completed.

COMPUTERS AND THE INTERNET

In its current form, the Internet alone does not add any value to testing. However, when coupled with the many ways in which computers are being applied to testing, the Internet enables computer-based testing to be conducted in a more efficient and potentially far-reaching manner. These efficiencies range from decreasing the cost of printing and shipping large numbers of paper-based tests or tests stored on disks, eliminating the need to scan paper-based tests or to aggregate results from multiple data disks, and returning results to multiple constituents instantly and simultaneously at minimal cost. In short, the Internet allows computer-based tests to be implemented in a more cost-efficient manner. The Internet also has potential to increase the utility of test information by collecting, disaggregating, and disseminating results in a timelier manner. Perhaps most important, the Internet has the potential to allow testing to occur any place and at any time. While a computer-based test could be delivered and installed on any computer in the world, the Internet dramatically simplifies this process and in turn makes it affordable.

Although still a relatively new technology, the speed at which the Internet has penetrated businesses, schools, and homes has increased the use of computer-based testing. As Bennett (2002) argues, the widespread and rapidly expanding access to the Internet makes Internet-based testing inevitable. In response to this rapidly emerging market, testing companies have already responded with a variety of products and services that several states are being to adopt. These services include producing online tests, providing online test preparation, and developing tools for presenting and analyzing test results online. Below I summarize recent development in each of these areas.

ONLINE TESTING

In the K–12 testing market, six companies have taken the lead in developing online testing products. Two of these companies, NCS Pearson and CBT Mcgraw Hill, are well established in the paper-based testing market. In response to growing interest in online testing, however, they have aggressively developed online testing products. Although smaller, Measured Progress has also secured several contracts for state testing programs and has begun developing computer-based tests for some its clients. Three other companies, EdVision, Northwest Evaluation Association, and Vantage Learning, are new to the testing market. While these three companies have less experience developing tests, they have considerably more experience in working with online technologies. In fact, during the course of researching this chapter, EdVision was purchased by Scantron Corporation, a leader in the test scanning industry. Despite these differences, the products and services provided by NCS Pearson, CBT McGraw Hill, and EdVision are remarkably similar in that they all develop online, linear tests. In essence, these companies are migrating paper-based tests to a computer format. Meanwhile, Northwest Evaluation Association has invested its resources in developing web-based adaptive tests and Vantage Learning has sought to create a new niche in the test industry, namely the scoring of essays.

As Table 6.1 displays, at least 12 states are actively exploring computer-based testing. In most cases, these states are developing or preparing to implement linear computer-based tests. But several states also began developing adaptive tests.[1] Two states, Indiana and Pennsylvania, are exploring the use of computer-based essay scoring for their state writing tests. Meanwhile, Massachusetts has contracted with Vantage Learning to pilot the use of computer-based scoring of writing as a diagnostic tool that teachers and students can use in preparation for the state writing test. Although it is too early to gauge the success of these programs, it is likely that other states will also begin transitioning their tests to a computer format over the next few years.

Table 6.1.   States Exploring Computer-Based Testing

State	CBT	CAT	Essay Scoring	Online	Implementation	Contractor
IN	Yes	Yes			2000	ETS
NC	Yes	Yes		Yes	2001	Internally developed
OR	Yes	Yes		Yes	2001	Vantage Learning
SD	Yes	Yes		Yes	2002	EdVISION
VA	Yes			Yes	2004	NCS Pearson, Inc. eMeasurement Services
PA	No	No	Yes			Vantage
GA	Yes			Yes	2003	NCS Pearson (eMeasurement: end-of-course); Riverside Publishing (CRCT)
KY	Yes			Yes		Currently using e-college
MN						
ID	Yes	Yes	Yes			Northwest Evaluation Association (NWEA)
UT	Yes			Yes		Measured Progress
MD	Yes	Yes		Yes		NCS Pearson

Online Test Preparation

Given the emphasis placed on student and school performance on state tests, it is not surprising that teachers are investing more time preparing students for these tests. A recent study released by the National Board on Educational Testing and Public Policy reports that approximately 50% of teachers nationwide spend 20 hours or more specifically preparing students for state tests. This practice is more common in states that make high stakes decisions about students and/or schools. More than 50% of all teachers in states that make high stakes decisions also report that they have students practice items that are similar to those expected to be on the test (Pedulla, Abrams, Madaus, Russell, Ramos, & Miao, 2003).

In response to this classroom practice, several companies have developed online test preparation tools. Perhaps the best-known online test preparation product is Homeroom.com, which was developed by Princeton Review. This web-based diagnostic tool contains more than 120,000 reading and math items that are aligned to various state standards, major classroom textbooks, and state tests. Through a three-step process, the system assesses students' strengths and weaknesses, relative to the state standards and state test, and provides remediation for areas of weakness. The system also provides practice tests and reports for state-mandated tests.

Similar to Princeton Review, Kaplan has also developed extensive test preparation services. In addition to its college and postgraduate test preparation, Kaplan recently launched K–12 Learning Services that provides preparation for standards-based, state-mandated assessments.

Beyond these two test-preparation giants, several smaller companies have emerged to provide services to schools and parents. In some cases, these services are delivered directly to students online. As an example, TestU first administers a diagnostic test to students online and then targets additional practice items to help students improve their weaknesses. In other cases, students come to centers at which computer-based tutorials are used. As an example, SCORE! Learning uses its computer-based Advantage Program and an intensive, single-subject Personal Academic Training Program to help students develop academic skills in core content areas. To date, 150 centers have opened nationwide and currently serve more than 100,000 students.

Taking a slightly different approach, ESylvan combines the Internet and a certified teacher to provide students with customized tutoring. In this system, students interact with a teacher via the Internet in an electronic workspace. In essence, the Internet is used to provide students with one-on-one tutoring without having to leave their home.

Although it is unclear just how many schools and families are investing in these various computer-based test preparation services, there is little doubt that the market is growing rapidly. In fact, some states have contracted with online services to help prepare students for state tests. As an example, in addition to contracting with Vantage Learning to pilot the use of their computer-scoring system to provide diagnostic feedback to students, Massachusetts has also contracted with Princeton Review's Homeroom.com to provide online tutoring for high school sophomores preparing for the state test. As described in the press release, "Students have 24-hour access to the web tutorial, which diagnoses their weaknesses in math and English and provides online tests and assignments to assist them" (Massachusetts Department of Education, 2002, para. 2). Similarly, Boston Public Schools has contracted with TestU to provide test preparation for sophomores taking the state test. Although it is unclear how effective these online test preparation programs are in improving student performance, the market has grown rapidly.

Online Test Items and Results

In an effort to provide teachers, students, and the public with information about state-mandated tests, several states have established web sites that contain items used during previous test administrations. In states like Virginia, Michigan, Oregon, and Massachusetts, entire test booklets are available online. In some cases, these released items are used by teachers to prepare students for future tests (Pedulla et al., 2003). In other cases, the items are used by critics to point out problems with the tests (Kurtz & Vaishnav, 2002). In a few cases, students have used the released items to review their performance and, in the process, have discovered errors in the scoring key (Vaishnav & Kurtz, 2002). Whereas ten years ago it was difficult to find detailed information about tests, the Internet is now being used to make detailed information about the test available to the public in an easy to access and efficient manner.

In addition to providing the actual test items online, the majority of states also use the Internet to report test results. In most cases, the Internet is used to deliver static reports that present descriptive test results. Typically, the results are aggregated at the state level, district level, and the school level. Many states also provide static reports that disaggregate results for specific subgroups of students including race/ethnicity, free/reduced lunch, and sex. As an example, Maryland provides the public access to a wide range of reports based on data collected as part of the Maryland School Performance Assessment Program. This data is reported at the state, local school-system, and school level. For each level (i.e., state, school-system, and school), reports are available summarizing student-level performance on each test given within each grade level, student participation rates, and demographics. In addition, the full data set can be downloaded directly on the Internet.

In two cases, Michigan and Pennsylvania, the reporting of state assessment results has been outsourced to Standard & Poor's School Evaluation Services. In addition to providing static reports, the School Evaluation Services provides information at the school level on spending, return on resources, the learning environment, financial environment, and demographics. Although it is unclear how this information is used by the public, it represents an attempt by states to both provide "independent insight" on the quality of schools and a fuller description of the inputs and outputs of the educational process. Like the state-run web sites, the School Evaluation Services also allow users to download the full data set to perform secondary analyses.

Finally, a few states have begun providing schools and districts with data analysis tools that enable school leaders to perform secondary analyses of their test data. Although still in the early stages of use, dataMetrics TestWiz.com is currently being used by Michigan and Massachusetts.

SUMMARY

Without question, considerable progress has occurred in applying computer-based technologies to testing. Computers are being used in several states to deliver both static and adaptive tests. Written responses are increasingly scored using computer-based algorithms. Information about the test, as well as actual results, is provided to consumers via the World Wide Web. In a few cases, computers are also being used to create test items. Given the growth in the test industry over the past 20 years and the projected growth over the next few years, these applications of computers to testing are helping to increase the efficiency of the assessment process. Specifically, item generation allows tests to be developed faster. The Internet allows tests to be delivered with less cost. Computer scoring of multiple-choice and essay responses occurs nearly instantly. And results are provided to consumers in a faster and arguably more informative manner. While these applications of computers to assessment do much to increase the efficiency of assessment, they do little to enhance the quality of information provided by assessments. As I explore in the next chapter, it is the enhancement of testing and assessment that will yield the most valuable impacts of technology on assessment.

NOTES

1. Those interested in a full discussion of computer-based testing are encouraged to read Mills et al. (2002), Drasgow and Olson-Buchanan (1999), as well as several articles by Randy Elliott Bennett (1998b, 1999b, 2001, 2002).

2. Over the past 30 years, item response theory has evolved into a diverse and complex field of study. The overview presented here just begins to touch upon the basic fundamentals. Those who are interested in learning more about item response theory are encouraged to read *Item Response Theory* (Hambelton, Swaminathan, & Rogers, 1991).

3. Those interested in a more detailed discussion of item generation are referred to Irvine and Kyllonen's (2002) *Item Generation for Test Development,*

which presents essays on several problems, procedures, and applications of item generation.

4.   It should be noted that the U.S. Department of Education has indicated that computer-adaptive tests do not meet the requirements of *No Child Left Behind.* As a result, states that began developing adaptive tests have since delayed further work in this area.

CHAPTER 7

DISRUPTIVE APPLICATIONS OF COMPUTER-BASED TECHNOLOGIES TO THE TECHNOLOGY OF TESTING

In 1783, Marquis Claude de Jouffroy d'Abbans navigated the *Pyroscaphe* against the current of the Saone River for 15 minutes. Although brief, this voyage was the first successful application of steam power to shipping. Some 40 years later, the *Savannah* completed its voyage from Georgia to Liverpool in 29 days, marking the first successful ocean crossing by a steam-propelled vessel. Although equipped with a steam engine and paddle-wheels, all but 85 hours of the *Savannah's* voyage was completed by sail rather than steam power (*Steamship*, 2001).

Like many innovations, the steam engine was layered on top of the existing technology of the time, namely sails. While this initial application of the steam engine allowed sailing vessels to make forward progress in the absence of wind, the added weight of the engine and fuel hampered speed when the ship was powered by wind. Eventually, as the power and stability of steam engines improved, sails were replaced entirely by this new source of power.

When considering the impact a new technology will have on existing technologies, it is important to distinguish between those technologies that sustain and those that disrupt current process and procedures (Chris-

Technology and Assessment: The Tale of Two Interpretations, pages 99–125
Copyright © 2006 by Information Age Publishing
All rights of reproduction in any form reserved.

tensen, 1997). *Sustaining technologies* are those that become integrated into current processes and procedures, and often allow them to become more efficient. As an example, the development of the cotton gin allowed cotton lint to be culled from its seeds more efficiently. Although this increased efficiency is believed to have made the farming of cotton more cost effective, it did not alter the technology of producing fabric from cotton plants.

In contrast, the introduction of a *disruptive technology* alters the current process and procedures, and eventually makes extinct those structures that do not adapt to the new technology. As an example, Bennett (2001) recounts the story of the demise of *Encyclopaedia Britannica*. Established in 1768, Encyclopaedia Britannica was the oldest encyclopedia in the English-speaking world. As Bennett describes:

> At its peak, Britannica was a 32-volume set of books costing well over $1,000. In 1993, Microsoft introduced Encarta on CD-ROM for under $100 and even though Britannica was much more comprehensive, the difference for most people wasn't worth an extra $900+. Initially, Britannica did not respond as it didn't take the threat from Encarta seriously. But when it did respond, it did so ineffectively because Britannica wouldn't fit on a single CD-ROM and because the company's large sales force wasn't suited to selling software. But, ultimately, Britannica wasn't ready to cannibalize its existing paper business to enter this new electronic one. (2001, Reinventing the Business, para. 4)

In the case of Britannica, CD-ROM and desktop computers combined to alter the way in which people sought information—no longer did they rely on paper-based books to seek information but instead acquired information through electronic sources. Initially clinging to the older paper-based process of providing information, Britannica lost a competitive edge. When it did attempt to employ the new technology, it did so without altering the underlying product it was attempting to sell. Within five years, Britannica's sales had decreased by 80% and the company was struggling to remain solvent.

COMPUTERS AND TESTING

As Madaus (2001) emphasized, testing is its own technology, with its own "body of special knowledge, skills, and procedures" (p. 1). As described in the previous chapters, computer-based technologies have penetrated the technology of testing. In most cases, however, computers have been applied in a variety of ways to help sustain the current technology of testing. Without question, these applications help to increase the validity of inferences based on tests and/or may increase the efficiency of testing. However, they do not fundamentally impact the technology of testing itself.

Even in the cases of adaptive testing and item generation, the psychometric principles and "rules" for test construction developed over the past 50 years are applied without significant alteration to determine which items are to be used in a given situation. Much like the cotton gin was layered on top of the technology of producing cloth from cotton, applications of technology to improve the validity and/or efficiency of testing are layered on top of the existing and long-established technology of testing.

Computer-based technologies, however, provide important opportunities to dramatically alter the technology of testing. Together, the ability of computers to present complex, multi-step problems that may incorporate several types of media, can have several different paths to reach a solution, can have multiple solutions, and can record the examinee's every action, creates opportunities to learn about students' knowledge, conceptual understanding, and cognitive development in ways that today's technology of testing cannot.

Over the past decade, the importance of testing in K–12 schools has exploded, yet interest in exploring new ways to apply computers to create new types of assessments has increased much more slowly. Perhaps the best examples of this interest are three published volumes that focus specifically on new forms of assessment that capitalize on the powers of computers. The first two—*Test Theory for a New Generation of Tests* (Frederisksen, Mislevy, & Bejar, 1993) and *Cognitively Diagnostic Assessment* (Nichols, Chipman, & Brennan, 1995)—present a variety of ideas and pioneering efforts to merge advances in cognitive science with computer-based technologies. The goal of these efforts is to develop tests that differ dramatically from today's primarily paper-based normative and summative tests. In an effort to increase research and development in this field, the National Research Council's (NRC) recent report (2001), *Knowing What Students Know: The Science and Design of Educational Assessment*, also describes some of the work performed to date and puts forth a call for more sustained efforts in this field. Beyond these three volumes, Mislevy (1993) and Bennett (1998a, 2001, 2002) have also been vocal advocates for reinventing assessment through the application of computers.

In the remainder of this chapter, I focus on six applications of computers to assessment which have the potential to enhance current approaches to student testing. These examples include the following:

- The efforts by ETS to use computer-based simulations to assess students' problem solving and science content knowledge.
- The development of a computer-based architecture exam that yields both summative and diagnostic information.
- Interactive Multi-media Exercises (IMMEX) that are designed to assess student problem-solving strategies.

- Computer-based simulations of surgical skills.
- Learning systems that have embedded diagnostic assessment.
- Diagnostically adaptive computer-based tests.

These applications are in different stages of development, with some in full use, some in the pilot stage, others in early stages of development, and still others are conceptual ideas that have not yet been applied. Together, these examples provide a look into the future of assessment. Before describing these applications in greater detail, I briefly summarize some of the shortcomings of the current approaches to assessment that these new approaches seek to overcome.

SHORTCOMINGS OF TODAY'S TESTS

Although the principles and procedures of the current technology of testing are well established, several shortcomings are apparent. Despite efforts to incorporate open-ended items into some tests, most test items result in binary information about a student—namely, did he or she answer them correctly or incorrectly? While scoring guides for some open-ended items focus on the procedures and cognitive process students use to solve problems, these items are dependent upon students' descriptions of their process, which are often incomplete and/or inaccurate reflections of the actual process of answering questions. As a result, these items provide indirect and crude insight into examinees' cognitive processes.

Similarly, while the educational community uses tests for a variety of purposes including diagnosing students' strengths and weaknesses; measuring achievement, aptitude, and ability; assessing the impact of instruction on student learning; and examining the quality of education students receive within a school, district, state or even country, test experts have long argued that the current technology of testing should be applied to meet a single purpose at a time. As Haney et al. (1993) maintain, the fundamental problem with using a single test or assessment for multiple purposes "is that such tests require ... fundamentally different characteristics" (p. 264). Nonetheless, many current testing programs attempt to use a single test or set of closely related tests to fulfill multiple purposes. As an example, the Massachusetts Comprehensive Assessment System (MCAS) uses results from 10th-grade English language arts and mathematics tests to: (a) make decisions about student competency and eligibility for graduation; (b) make decisions about the quality of education within individual schools; (c) identify exemplary educational programs; (d) assess the effectiveness of state and local interventions (such as tutoring); and (e) help teachers and schools diagnose student weaknesses. Despite including multiple item formats and requiring several hours to complete, the tests contain roughly 50 items that are completed by all students throughout the state. While performance on the same set of items helps reassure the public that decisions about student competency and graduation eligibility are based on the same information, this limited set of items attempts to assess such a broad domain that only a handful of items are used to measure the sub-domains. As a result, there is very little information available to usefully diagnose students' strengths and weaknesses. Moreover, the tests do not attempt to probe why students may have performed poorly within a given sub-domain. Similarly, by administering the same set of items to all students rather than spiraling item sets across sets of students, schools and districts are provided with very limited information about the strengths and weaknesses of their educational programs. In short, while tests like the MCAS ambitiously attempt to satisfy several purposes, they fail to adequately meet these needs.

Beyond the MCAS, several state-developed and commercial tests attempt to help teachers diagnose students' weaknesses. These tests, however, focus on specific content within a given domain, and often use multiple-choice formats to measure student performance within the several sub-domains. As a result, the diagnostic information provided to educators is typically limited to whether or not students tend to succeed or fail on items within a given sub-domain. While this information helps educators identify those sub-domains that may be in need of further instruction, these diagnostic tests tend to provide little or no information about *why* students may be struggling within a given sub-domain. Rather than diagnosing the misconceptions and/or specific skill sets that interfere with students' mastery of the sub-domain, most current diagnostic tests do not provide any more information than an achievement or mastery test.

Among other shortcomings of current testing practices is that most testing currently occurs outside of instruction. As a result, the amount of instructional time is decreased. Ironically, this problem is exacerbated in settings where tests are administered on a regular and frequent basis to help focus instruction and/or in settings that use a series of achievement tests to better measure the impact of instruction on student learning over time. With each test administration, regardless of whether the use is internal or external to the classroom, and whether it is teacher-developed or developed externally to the classroom, instructional time is decreased. While some educators argue that "embedded assessment" will better streamline the traditional instructional and assessment cycle, externally developed or mandated tests still diminish instructional time. (See Wilson and Sloane [2000] for an example of an embedded assessment system.)

Disruptive applications of computer-based technology to the technology of testing can address these shortcomings. The following examples attempt to tackle one or more of these shortcomings in a variety of ways.

NAEP SIMULATION

In response to the nearly universal presence of computers in schools and the rapidly increasing use of computers by students, the Educational Testing Service (ETS) is conducting a series of studies to explore uses of computers for the National Assessment of Educational Progress (NAEP). These studies focus on the use of computers to deliver and score assessments in the areas of mathematics, writing, and science. For mathematics and writing, the main research goal focuses on developing a better understanding of how computer delivery affects the measurement of students' mathematics and writing skills. In addition, ETS hopes to gain insight into the operational and logistical aspects of delivering NAEP online. In the area of writing, ETS is also studying the feasibility of using its e-Rater system to score students' written responses via computer. Thus, for mathematics and writing, the primary goals are to examine how computers can be used to more efficiently deliver and score tests, and how this delivery mechanism affects student performance.

ETS is using a different approach in science assessments, however, by exploring the feasibility of using computer-based tools and simulations to assess important emerging skills (Bennett & Persky, 2002). The primary goal of the Technology-Rich Environment project is to develop a set of modules to assess problem-solving skills. Computers are used to present multimedia tasks that cannot be delivered via paper and pencil. The first module, pilot tested during the spring of 2002, was designed to assess students' problem-solving abilities related to the uses and science of gas balloon flight. The module provided students with two work environments: a simulated World Wide Web and a tool that simulated the flight of a gas balloon. Students could use the simulated World Wide Web to search and analyze information related to gases, balloons, and flight. Students were also able to conduct experiments to answer "what-if" questions by using the gas balloon flight simulator. As an example, with the flight simulator, students could manipulate variables such as the amount of gas in the balloon and the payload of the balloon to explore how different variables affect the balloon's flight.

Through this module, two types of student ability were assessed. First, each student's ability to solve problems by searching for, accessing, and analyzing information available on the simulated World Wide Web was assessed by examining the strategies and types of information used to answer two questions about "scientific uses of large gas balloons." Second, the student's ability to perform experiments to develop an understanding of how mass and volume impact the flight of gas balloons is assessed using the computer simulation tool. For this problem set, students assemble data, interpret results, construct a table, display graphs, and draw conclusions, which they record through open-ended written responses. The module provides students with access to a glossary of science terms and science and computer help. Although students may learn while working on the problems, the modules are designed to assess examinees' skills and knowledge rather than to provide instruction. Moreover, the simulations are designed to be representative of the type of problems which computers are used to solve in educational and work environments. Most important, the tasks are designed to separate the several component skills required for success without requiring students to document their problem-solving strategies by describing these processes in writing.

Although ETS is still developing methods to assess student problem-solving skills that use data collected as students work on these two types of problems, both types of items represent cutting-edge efforts to use computers to assess skills that would be difficult to examine using paper-based tests. While still very much in the early stages of development, ETS hopes these two item models can be employed to assess problem-solving skills in other areas of science and social studies.[1]

ARCHITECTURE EXAM

In addition to exploring ways to use computers to enhance NAEP, ETS has also used computers to enhance assessment of architecture skill and knowledge. Architecture skill is complex and presents several challenges to assessment. Architecture combines a set of rules, many governed by laws of physics, with a set of design principles. Typically, an architectural project is produced over a period of several months, during which time the architect may relax some design principles in order to maximize others. While certain decisions made during this design process can be discretely categorized as correct or incorrect (e.g., whether seismic joints are used appropriately), the final design must be assessed on a continuum, based on the extent to which the design satisfies "the constraints of the design problem to a greater or lesser degree (Katz, Martinez, Sheehan, & Tatsuoka, 1998, p. 256). Given the amount of time generally required to produce a project coupled with the integration of discrete rules of physics and the flexible application of design principles, it is difficult to imagine how a traditional paper-based, multiple-choice test can adequately assess this complex domain.

During the mid-1990s, researchers at ETS began exploring the use of short performance-based tasks to assess architectural skill. During the task, examinees are presented with a series of figural items and asked to construct their responses by manipulating the figural material to produce a representation that meets specified conditions. Given the time that would be required for examinees to produce responses by hand combined with the time and money required for humans to score such hand-produced responses, the figural items are delivered on the computer. Using computer-based tools similar to those the examinees work with on a daily basis, they manipulate the figural depictions to produce their responses. Each item, then, consists of a stem that describes what the examinee is to attempt to accomplish, a figure, and a set of tools for drawing or manipulating the figure. As Katz et al. (1998) describe, one item:

> ...requires examinees to move the structures at the bottom of the screen (library, parking lot, and playground) onto the provided site. Examinees must abide by explicit constraints stated in the item stem [Prepare a site plan that preserves all existing trees] as well as the implicit constraints that architects associate with libraries, parking lots, and playgrounds (e.g., a playground should not be adjacent to a parking lot; a parking lot must have street access). (p. 255)

To score student responses, Tatsuoka's (1983) Rule Space methodology is employed. Unlike item response theory which can yield the same proficiency estimate for two examinees whose response patterns differ radically, rule space methodology decomposes item responses into attributes. Each attribute represents a dimension of knowledge or process demanded by the item. Based on a cognitive model of the skills and knowledge required by the domain being assessed, the attributes assessed are defined *a priori*. In this way, rule space methodology does not generate the attributes, but rather generates information about an examinee's proficiency for each of the attributes. Thus, unlike item response theory, which requires items to measure a single dimension, rule space methodology enables the assessment of multiple dimensions simultaneously. As an example, Katz et al. (1998) write:

> Consider an item that can be described in terms of four attributes. If an examinee answers this item correctly, we would infer that the examinee has mastered all four attributes. If an examinee answers this item incorrectly, however, we could only say he or she has not mastered some combination of one, two, three, or all four of the attributes. Thus, for an item with four attributes, there are 2^4-1 latent states that can account for an incorrect answer. (p. 257)

Rule space methodology is able to address this combinatorial problem by treating each attribute response pattern as a series of correct and incorrect responses. This series of responses indicates whether the examinee's response represents mastery or non-mastery of each attribute. The response patterns are then analyzed across multiple items and each examinee's response patterns are classified as belonging to a latent knowledge state.[2]

As noted earlier, the first step in developing an assessment that employs the rule space methodology is to define the attributes that form the cognitive domain. The attributes required by each item must then be defined. It is this step that is crucial to effectively apply the rule space methodology to a cognitive assessment since failing to assign an attribute to an item or assigning an attribute to an item that does not require that attribute may result in inaccurate estimates of the examinee's proficiencies. Through analyses of the examinee response patterns across all test items, both an estimate of an examinee's overall proficiency and an estimate of the examinee's proficiency on each attribute are provided.

By providing information about the several cognitive attributes required for success in a complex cognitive domain, the application of rule space methodology allows for a richer and potentially more useful diagnostic assessment of examinees' proficiencies.

INTERACTIVE MULTI-MEDIA EXERCISES (IMMEX)

Like the Architecture Exam, Vendlinski and Stevens (2000) employ methods for analyzing complex patterns that differs dramatically from methods based on item response theory. Again, unlike item response theory, which will assign the same test score to two examinees who have very different response patterns, IMMEX employs artificial neural networks (ANN) to analyze the steps an examinee takes when solving a complex problem. This analysis results in a classification of an examinee's problem solving strategy. Based on an analysis of different problem solving strategies, insight is gained into an examinee's understanding of the tested subject area.

To date, Vendlinski and Stevens have used IMMEX to assess student understanding in several areas of science and with examinees who have ranged in age from fifth graders to medical school students. The IMMEX system is web-based and begins by posing a problem for students to solve. Students are then offered a variety of tools and resources that they can use as they work on the problem. As students work through the problem, their every action is recorded. This record of actions is then processed by the artificial neural network to classify the student's problem-solving strategy.

Initially, IMMEX was used to assess student problem-solving skills within a given subject area for the purpose of classifying the student's current state of understanding. More recently, however, the system has been used to inform instruction and to track students' progress over time, as they work on a series of problems related to a given subject area. As an example of the latter application, Vendlinski and Stevens (2002) have begun to provide evidence that IMMEX can identify changes in student problem-solving strategies over time. In this example, students work on a problem related to hazardous materials (Hazmat). The Hazmat problem begins by informing students that there has been an earthquake that has caused a number of chemicals to fall off of shelves and become mixed up. Some of the chemicals are hazardous, and all the labels are missing. Students are asked to help identify the spilled chemicals. To do so, students may consult the stockroom inventory, perform three physical tests and eight chemical tests, and consult any of the eight library reference materials. In total, there are 57 unknown substances, five of which students are asked to identify. Again, as students work to solve each case, all of the tests they conduct and the information they consult are recorded. It is this sequence of actions taken by each student that is used to analyze and classify student problem solving strategies. Recognizing that there is no one correct way to solve these large and open-ended problems and that insight into student understanding can be gleaned from the strategy they employ, rather than employing a deterministic model of student performance, IMMEX uses artificial neural networks to identify groups of similar performances in the data.

The neural network analysis occurs in two-stages. First, clusters of similar performances are identified, based on the information students viewed. The system is then presented with a student performance and a cluster of performances that the individual performance is expected to represent. As the authors describe:

> Generally, the particular feature(s) of the performances in individual clusters that make them similar are easily discerned. For example, it is common for students to attempt to identify the unknown in a *Hazmat* case with just one test. Thus, a common cluster contains student performances with just this one test. Other clusters are more complex. In order to understand what these clusters represent we used a technique called *mock performance analysis*. In mock performance analysis, we create a performance that represents those features thought to describe each cluster. Then each of these mock performances is fed into the appropriately trained artificial neural networks. By adding to and subtracting from each mock performance, the features of each performance that cause the neural net to cluster them together are identified…We term each of the resulting cluster descriptive a *strategy* (Vendlinski & Stevens, 2002, p. 8).

Each strategy, then, can be interpreted as representing different stages of development in understanding the given content area. For the Hazmat case, three general families of strategies were revealed—*limited, efficient,* and *prolific.* For the set of limited strategies, students generally collected too little information to reach a conclusion about a given chemical. For prolific strategies, more information than was required is collected before attempting to identify the chemical. For efficient strategies, the appropriate amount of information is collected. Note that the classification of students into these families of strategies occurs regardless of whether they correctly identify each chemical.

Information from the Hazmat case is returned to teachers who are then able to intervene with those students who employ limited and prolific strategies. Through the presentation of additional problems, Hazmat tracks changes in student strategies over time. In this way, IMMEX functions both as a diagnostic assessment system and as a method of measuring changes in student learning over time.

SURGICAL SIMULATION

The United States Army is often credited with sparking the growth of large-scale standardized testing. With the onset of World War I and the need to quickly assess and assign recruits to various positions believed to require different levels of intelligence, the Army administered the Army Alpha and Beta intelligence tests to more than 1.75 million recruits (Gould, 1996). Soon thereafter, school systems began using standardized achievement tests to evaluate program effectiveness (Madaus, Stufflebeam, & Scriven, 1993). Since then, testing has grown into a billion-dollar industry (Clarke, Madaus, Horn, & Ramos, 2001).

Given the initial merit and stimulus the U.S. Military gave to the standardized testing industry, it is fitting that it is now playing a major role in reshaping future assessment methodologies. In response to a 1998 report issued by the General Accounting Office that underscored the need to provide military medical personnel with trauma care training that reflected the injuries encountered during wartime, the U.S. Army Medical Research and Material Command (USAMRMC) and the Advanced Technology Research Center (TATRC) has launched several initiatives involving medical simulations. While the main purpose of these initiatives is to develop medical and surgical simulators to efficiently and more effectively train Army medics, these simulators are providing unique opportunities to assess kinesthetic, content knowledge, and medical decision-making skills.

Working collaboratively, the Technology and Assessment Study Collaborative (inTASC) at Boston College and the Center for the Integration of Medicine and Innovative Therapy (CIMIT) are applying computer-based technologies to assess several aspects of medic training and proficiency. For example, CIMIT has developed a chest tube and surgical airway simulator. The simulator is intended to train medics how to alleviate three conditions commonly caused by chest trauma, namely tension pneumothorax (collapsing lung with trapped air under pressure), hemothorax (collapsed lung with blood in the chest cavity), and hemopneumothorax (blood and air in the chest cavity). All three conditions are life threatening if not alleviated in a relatively short period of time. As part of the learning system, medic recruits first interact with a web-based tutorial that provides information on basic first aid, detailed descriptions of these three conditions, protocols and video demonstrations of the procedures required to alleviate these conditions, and detailed descriptions of common complications and appropriate counteractions. As part of this component of the learning system, opportunities for recruits to demonstrate the acquisition of the basic knowledge through traditional multiple-choice items are being incorporated. When mastery of this information is not demonstrated, recruits are presented with additional information to help them master the content. While this component of the learning system does not expand upon the current technology of testing, the actual simulator does.

Upon demonstrating mastery of the content knowledge, recruits are introduced to the simulator. The simulator combines a sophisticated mannequin (see Figure 7.1) that contains flesh-like tissue, bonelike ribs, and pockets of blood-like liquid with a computer that contains an exact digital model of the mannequin with the addition of internal organs. In addition, all surgical tools employed for these procedures are connected to tracking devices that record all movements made with the device inside and outside of the chest cavity. By combining the instrument tracking with the simulated model of the mannequin's internal organs, the simulator is able to record the amount of time it takes to perform each task required for a given procedure, while also monitoring all movements of the instruments in three-dimensional space. Based on these recorded movements, it is then possible to calculate factors that can impact the success of the procedure such as the speed with which instruments enter the cavity, their angle of entry, and their depth of entry. In addition, it is possible to examine factors

Figure 7.1.   CIMIT Chest Tube Trauma Mannequin (also known as VIRGIL).

such as acceleration and deceleration and changes in the direction and angle of movement. Using the recorded movements, the simulator is also able to reproduce the procedure on screen and show the relationship between surgical tools, ribs, and key organs that could be harmed.

As a training tool, the simulator provides several benefits. Whereas medics typically practice these procedures on animals and do so only a couple of times, procedures can be performed repeatedly on the simulator (without harm to animals). In addition, since the mannequin is a reproduction (both externally and internally) of a real person and has tissue and bone properties very close to real flesh and bones, the training more accurately reflects procedures that will likely be performed in the field. Finally, the portability of the mannequin allows training to occur just about anywhere (even on a helicopter en route to a battlefield).

From an assessment perspective, the simulator enables unique approaches to diagnostics and mastery testing. As the simulator provides opportunities for the recruit to practice new procedures or introduces new complications, the system can identify tendencies such as inserting an instrument at a dangerously steep or flat angle or inserting instruments too deeply. This information can then be shared with the recruit and the instructor.

The simulator also has potential to compare the skill of the recruits with those of masters. These comparisons can be made at the macro or the micro level. At the macro level, the enhanced-reality reproductions of the recruits can be layered on top of the reproduction of an expert allowing the recruit to visually compare the "track" of their performance with that of the expert. Through this macro comparison, important differences in technique may become apparent. On subsequent attempts, the recruit can then adjust his or her technique until it reflects that of the expert. As an example, Figure 7.2 depicts the motion trajectories of novice, trainee, and experienced surgeons performing a simulated sinus surgery (note that this example is not from the chest tube simulator). As expertise increases, random motion decreases and movements become more precise and focused on each of the four specific areas of work.

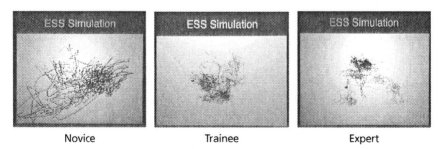

Novice   Trainee   Expert

Figure 7.2.   Motion trajectories of novice, trainee. and experienced surgeons. (Images taken from Satava, 2001)

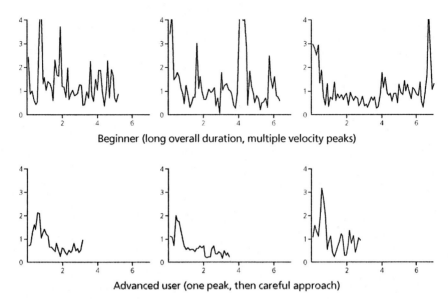

Figure 7.3.   Results of time and velocity tracking of novice and expert surgeons. (Images taken from Satava, 2001)

At the micro level, individual metrics such as changes in velocity, angle of insertion, or depth of insertion, can be compared between the recruit and experts. As an example, Figure 7.3 compares both the amount of time required to complete a task and the velocity of movements while performing the task for advanced and beginning surgeons. In all three trials, the advanced surgeon completed the task in about half the time. In addition, the advanced surgeon executed the tasks with one initial burst of speed and then deliberately slowed down whereas the beginner made several bursts of speed and inefficiently narrowed in on the target.

Whether focusing on the macro or micro images of performance, comparisons between the performance of the recruits and experts may be a useful way to assess mastery. In addition, by examining how many practice sessions are required before a recruit's performance reflects that of an expert, it is possible to identify recruits who seem to posses innate kinesthetic surgical skills and/or those who are rapid learners—recruits that could be very valuable to the Army when training time is cut short by military engagement.

By presenting recruits with scenarios that involve a range of complications and then examining how each recruit responds, the learning system provides opportunities to examine how well the candidate is able to integrate his or her content and conceptual knowledge with his or her kinesthetic skills. The realism of the scenario could be further enhanced by placing the chest tube simulator in a simulated war environment or by introducing the scenario after extended physical exercise, sleep deprivation, or both. The recruit's ability to respond to complications and conduct the necessary physical movements can be examined in a real-life context. Finally, by providing the recruit access to reference materials that might be available in the field (either during initial training or during future training), the recruit's ability to rapidly access and apply information to resolve a problem could also be assessed.

K–12 LEARNING ENVIRONMENTS

At first brush, medical simulators may seem far removed from K–12 education. However, the approaches used to collect a diverse set of information about recruits and the challenge of figuring out how to make use of this set of information is directly applicable to learning systems currently in place and under development for K–12 schools.

For the past decade, national leaders have emphasized the importance of preparing students to compete in an increasingly technological world. Pointing to low performance in mathematics and science as compared to other industrialized nations, leaders have called for increased attention on student learning in these areas. As just one example, President Bush states that, "Quality education is a cornerstone of America's future and my Administration, and the knowledge-based workplace of the 21st century requires that our students excel at the highest levels in math and science" (The White House, 2001).

In mathematics and science, the ability to reason and develop an understanding of complex concepts is crucial. To aid in developing reasoning skills and conceptual understanding, research shows that feedback is an important component of the instructional process (Barron, Schwartz, Vye, Moore, Petrosino, Zech & Bransford, 1998; Bereiter & Scardamalia, 1989; Johnson & Johnson, 1975; Slavin, 1987a,b). Moreover, research suggests that feedback that focuses both on the "correctness of a student's answer" and on the underlying causes of error has larger positive impacts on student learning as compared to feedback that focuses solely on "correctness" (Azevedo & Bernard, 1995a,b). Moreover, the closer the proximity between feedback and the development of a misconception, the more feedback motivates students, helps them improve their reasoning, and corrects misconceptions (Sivin-Kachala & Bialo, 1994).

A separate line of research also demonstrates that the development of higher-order reasoning skills and conceptual understanding requires that students have opportunities to work on complex, extended problems related to the reasoning and concepts of interest. Since computer-based technologies can be interactive (Greenfield & Cocking, 1996), it is possible to create environments in which students learn by doing, continually refine their understanding, and build new knowledge (Barron et al., 1998; Bereiter & Scardamalia, 1993; Schwartz, Lin, Brophy, & Bransford, 1999). Since the early 1980s, researchers have developed computer-based learning systems that enable students to explore complex concepts and develop reasoning skills through active exploration. Examples in this arena include applications of Logo to develop students' reasoning through programming and debugging (Klahr & Carver, 1988), development of intelligent tutors for algebra and geometry (Anderson, Corbett, Koedinger, & Pelletier, 1995), and for genetics (Hickey, Kindfield, & Horwitz, 1999), and, most recently, the development of Interactive Multimedia Exercises (IMMEX) to examine decisions made as students work on problems in a variety of subject areas (Vendlinski & Steven, 2000).

Although these computer-based learning tools have been used in a relatively small number of schools, research to date indicates that their use often has a positive impact on student learning (see National Research Council, 2001; Anderson et al., 1995). In most cases, these systems provide students with multiple opportunities to practice and develop skills and knowledge. In addition, the systems provide feedback to students about their success and reasons for failure. In all cases, the feedback is based on student responses to what are effectively multiple-choice or correct/incorrect short-answer items that require students to enter their numerical answer for a given problem. At times, this feedback simply informs the student whether his or her responses were correct or incorrect. At other times, the feedback results in the presentation of additional information and/or activities designed to enhance a student's understanding of a given concept. In the second case, instruction becomes adaptive and is tailored to the instructional needs of each student.

Research, however, indicates that metacognition and the articulation of ideas and thought processes aid the development of reasoning skills and conceptual understanding (see National Research Council, 2000, for a review of this research). Some computer-based learning systems provide opportunities for students to describe their thinking process, provide support for students' solutions, and ask students to consider how sure they are of their thinking. But unlike responses to multiple-choice items, responses to these open-ended questions are not used by the learning systems to assess and provide feedback to students. Instead, responses are often recorded in a data file that can be accessed by a teacher who may then use the information to provide formative feedback to students. In most cases, however, teachers access this information after the instructional period has ended. As a result, any feedback that is provided has lost much of its instructional efficacy.

One example of this type of learning system is BioLogica. Developed by the Concord Consortium, BioLogica helps students learn key concepts in genetics and develop scientific reasoning skills. The system is intended to help 8th-, 9th- and 10th-grade students learn about genetics through guided exploration. In its current form, BioLogica comprises 13 modules, each of which focuses on a different and increasingly more complex aspect of genetics. In most cases, the modules begin by asking students to explore a specific topic by manipulating genetic traits of a fictitious species of dragons. As an example, Figure 7.4 depicts the first exploration students encounter in the second module. In this exploration, students manipulate the dragon's chromosomes to determine how many different ways they can produce a dragon with horns. As each module progresses, new concepts are revealed through guided exploration. For example, the first set of explorations during lesson two culminate by asking students to describe how traits are produced in dragons (Figure 7.5). At times, the learning system presents textual or graphical information to explain concepts and provides students with access to various tools and pieces of information via menu selections. In addition, the system often asks students to demonstrate their understanding through written responses to specific open-ended questions, multiple-choice questions, and, most often, by modifying different aspects

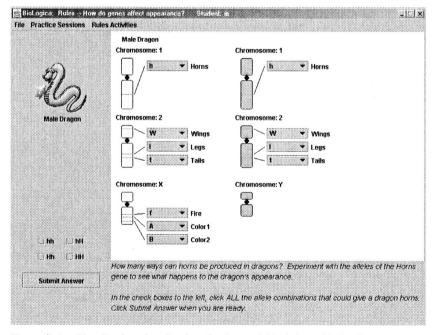

Figure 7.4.   First Exploration During the Second Module of BioLogica.

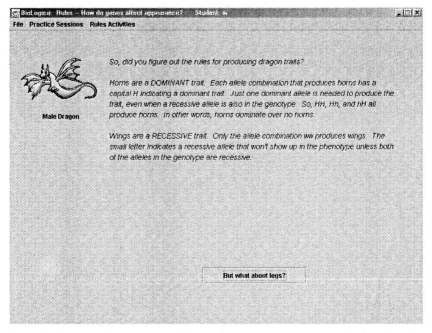

Figure 7.5.   Generalizing from guided explorations to rules of genetics in BioLogica.

of genetic codes to create dragons with specific traits or to determine how a trait suddenly appeared in a generation of dragons. Throughout the students' use of BioLogica, all interactions with the system are recorded.

From an instructional perspective, BioLogica allows students to explore a complex topic via a variety of media, and enables teachers to work individually or with small groups of students as questions arise. From an assessment perspective, the learning system provides a number of opportunities to assess student learning. Beyond examining students' understanding via their responses to the multiple-choice and open-ended questions, the guided explorations and the problems posed to students present opportunities to:

- Examine students' conceptual understanding by examining their written responses to prompts, the tools and information they opt to use, the amount of time required to solve problems, the type of strategies they employ (e.g., randomly changing chromosomes versus making initial changes on the appropriate chromosomes), as well as their success with the problem.
- Compare the students' pattern of interactions with those of "experts."
- Probe apparent misconceptions by presenting additional problems that focus on the specific misconception.

Currently, BioLogica uses students' responses to multiple-choice questions and their success on extended tasks to tailor the subsequent information and tasks presented to students. Students' responses to open-ended prompts, however, are not used by the system to adapt instruction. Instead, student responses are recorded in a log file that can be accessed by their teacher.

Advances in computer-based scoring of writing, however, provide opportunities to analyze and provide feedback to students based on their responses to open-ended questions embedded in a learning system. Work on computer scoring of writing began in the 1960s with the work of Ellis Page (1966, 1968). During the 1990s, rapid advances in the strategies and algorithms used led to the development of four distinct approaches, all of which have demonstrated high levels of score reliability (Burstein, 2001; Page, 1995; Foltz et al., 2000; Rudner & Liang, 2002). Although the development of these methods has been aimed at scoring extended essay questions, recent work by Rudner and Liang (2002) indicates that at least one of these methods can be used to reliably score responses to short-answer responses.

As an example of how automated essay scoring can be used for short answer items, part of BioLogica's eighth module asks students to produce a baby dragon that does not have horns from two parents that do have horns. For dragons, horns are a dominant trait, and one of the parents has the dominant trait on both of its chromosomes. Students are given an opportunity to examine the chromosomes of both parents and to make changes to their chromosomes, if needed. Students are also given opportunities to perform meiosis with both parents to create four gametes. Students can examine the chromosomes of the resulting gametes and are asked to select one gamete for each parent for fertilization. After selecting the two gametes, but before actually performing fertilization, students are asked how sure they are that their selection will result in a baby without horns and to describe why they feel that way. Beyond providing an opportunity for students to reflect on their thinking, responses to this prompt provide opportunities to examine several aspects of a student's understanding of genetics. As an example, a student may confuse recessive and dominant genes, believing that crossing an "H" and "H" rather than an "h" and "h" will produce a dragon without horns. Such a response could occur for at least three reasons:

1. The student could have simply confused the terms, but understood the concept.
2. The student might have confused the representation of the dominant and recessive genes, believing an "H" is recessive and an "h" is dominant.

   3. The student could have misunderstood the concept.

To provide insight into the first potential cause, BioLogica would prompt the student to define recessive and dominant genes and then analyze his or her response using automated essay scoring. If it is evident that the student does not understand the definition of the terms, BioLogica would return him or her to a previous module that focused on developing an understanding of the terms or a short explanation of the terms might be provided. If it is evident that the student does understand the definitions of the terms, BioLogica would explore the second potential reason by presenting the student with two chromosomes and asking him or her to click on the chromosomes which contain the dominant trait. If the student is unsuccessful, BioLogica would return him or her to the module that focused on the representation of dominant and recessive traits or might present supplemental information or activities to help develop this understanding. If, however, the student is successful in selecting the chromosome containing the dominant trait, BioLogica would allow the two selected gametes to be crossed. If the crossing results in a horned baby, BioLogica would ask the student why his or her selection was unsuccessful. The response would be examined to see if the student recognizes his or her error. If so, the student would be given a second opportunity to cross the two dragons. If not, the student would be presented with additional activities that develop an understanding of how to pass a recessive trait onto offspring.

In addition, insight into students' learning styles might be gained by beginning modules and sub-modules in different ways. For example, a module might begin with a textual explanation of a concept followed by an opportunity to demonstrate understanding. If understanding is not demonstrated, subsequent instruction might employ a guided exploration of the same concept. If understanding is still not demonstrated, a visual presentation of the concept might follow. Across multiple concepts, the order of presentation could be altered and the efficiency with which the student mastered the concept recorded. After several iterations, the system might identify the preferred order of instructional strategy and utilize that order for that student during subsequent modules.

Finally, and perhaps most important, since the learning system provides multiple opportunities for students to demonstrate conceptual understanding, the need to administer a separate test on the material mastered could be eliminated. Moreover, since records could be sent electronically to any location, it would be possible to maintain a database that indicates which students have mastered each concept. This information could be used by the teacher to identify common misconceptions and help inform instruction. In addition, this information could assess achievement at the student level or at a higher level of aggregation. While there might not be much value in recording achievement data at an aggregate level for a single learning system, the value would increase rapidly as more learning systems are used within a school, district, and state. And, again, if this information proves to be redundant with information provided by on-demand, external tests, the need for external standardized tests might be eliminated.

DIAGNOSTICALLY ADAPTIVE ASSESSMENTS

Computer adaptive tests provide a more efficient method of assessing student ability within a given domain. As described in greater detail in the previous chapter, this efficiency results from tailoring the items presented to an examinee so that they provide the maximum information about that examinee's ability. It has been shown that a well-designed adaptive test can provide a more accurate estimate of an examinee's ability in about half the amount of time required by a comparable paper-based test. Yet, despite its efficiency, the resulting ability estimate does not provide any information about why a student with a low ability estimate performs poorly in the given domain.

It is possible, however, to extend current approaches to adaptive testing to provide diagnostic information for low-performing students. One approach to providing more instructionally useful information is to employ a multi-staged and multilevel assessment strategy. During the first stage, traditional adaptive testing techniques are used to estimate student ability. For students whose ability is estimated to be below a given level of proficiency, an adaptive strategy is used to present students with items designed to diagnose the misconceptions and/or lacking skills that contribute to their low performance. In this way, the test would first adapt items to efficiently assess student ability level within the domain. For those students performing below a predetermined level of proficiency, the test would adapt items to diagnose the reason or reasons for low performance.

Recognizing that items within a given domain often cluster to form sub-domains or item classes and that difficulty differs among item classes, the multilevel aspect of this assessment model uses both item-level and class-level difficulties to estimate examinee ability. Much like hierarchical linear modeling capitalizes on the relationships within groups to yield more accurate estimates of the relationships between independent and dependent variables, the multilevel approach could provide ability estimates for each sub-domain as well as an overall domain-level estimate. The sub-domain estimates, then, could be used for two purposes. First, within the context of a single test administration, proficiency thresholds could be set for each sub-domain.

Examinees that perform below a given sub-domain proficiency level would be presented with the diagnostic adaptive portion of the test within that sub-domain. Second, across test administrations, changes in student achievement within each of the sub-domains could be examined. While one would expect the difficulty of items within a sub-domain to remain unchanged relative to each item forming the sub-domain, the sub-domain difficulty may shift relative to other sub-domains. Analysis of shifts in sub-domain difficulties would enable educational programs to monitor the effects of instructional programs on the several components of a domain.

In essence, this multistage, multilevel assessment model builds on what Mislevy (1993) terms tectonic plate models:

> In tectonic plate geological models, points within a given land mass, or plate, maintain their relative positions, but the plates move with respect to one another. In tectonic plate psychometric models, items tapping the same set of skills maintain their difficulties relative to one another, but the difficulties of the *groups* of items change with respect to other groups as learners acquire new skills or concepts. (p. 30)

The combination of being able to detect shifts in performance on items that belong to a sub-domain and being able to adaptively probe causes of low performance in these sub-domains produces an assessment model that can provide diagnostic information at multiple levels. At the student level, information provided by the adaptive probing for misconceptions that may contribute to low performance may allow teachers and/or tutoring systems to focus instruction on these misconceptions. At the classroom or school level, the detection of shifts in performance for specific sub-domains may allow teachers and schools to identify strengths and weaknesses in their instructional strategies and programs. Although this model has not yet been fully developed, the information provided at both levels would represent an important extension of current applications of item response theory that produce a single domain-level estimate of the examinee's ability.

MOVING FROM VIRTUAL POSSIBILITIES TO REALITY

While the possibilities for enhancing current approaches to assessment are enticing, several challenges must first be overcome. These challenges fall into three broad categories—technical, political, and practical.

Technical Challenges

The first major challenge involves identifying which pieces of information collected by these systems is most useful for a given purpose and how to combine this information so that it is interpretable. This is not an easy challenge to overcome. Unlike a traditional multiple-choice test that may contain 50 to 100 pieces of binary information, the amount of data produced by these systems can span several pages and include the amount of time between actions; quantity of changes made before a solution was found; materials and tools accessed; textual responses; and long lists of items clicked, alterations made, or items moved. While current psychometric models should not be abandoned altogether, new models will need to be created to make use of these multiple pieces of information.

Given the potential to map actions, whether they are physical, in the case of surgical simulators, or cognitive, in the case of K–12 learning systems, methods of analyzing graphical representations of processes should also be explored. Already, Vendlinski and Stevens (2000) have developed a set of IMMEX programs, each of which captures a users path, displays the map graphically, and allows teachers and students to visually compare maps generated at different times. To help automate and standardize these comparisons, recent advances in biometrics may be applicable to assessment in education. As an example, advances in image recognition now make it possible to quickly identify people by comparing video images of their faces with digital photographs stored in large databases. Adapting this technology to compare the paths of learners and experts may prove a useful way to assess level of expertise.

If comparisons between learners and experts are to be made, a significant investment must also be made in capturing the strategies and processes that experts employ. While this may be a relatively easy task in the case of physical skills such as those employed during surgery, it is a significantly greater challenge for K–12 learning systems. This challenge is compounded at lower grade levels for which the definition of "expertise" may be radically different than for high school students. While settling on an appropriate definition of expertise may be more political than empirical, acceptable definitions will need to be reached before such comparisons will be broadly embraced.

Much work will also be needed to validate the decisions made as students work with such learning systems. This is particularly true for decisions about academic achievement. While these systems have the potential to greatly reduce or eliminate external testing, these radical changes will not occur unless it can be demonstrated that the information gleaned from these systems are redundant with information provided by external tests. Moreover, given the current climate of high-stakes testing, it will be necessary to develop methods of verifying the identity of the student working with the learning system.

Political Challenges

Currently, political and educational leaders strongly embrace large-scale and high-stakes testing, and educational accountability appears to be the top priority shaping our educational system. Despite calls for the incorporation of multiple measures into these school accountability systems, political and educational leaders appear deaf to these calls. One reason for the resistance to broaden the types of measures (be they grades, teachers' judgments, portfolios or work samples, or "performance-based" tests) likely relates to a belief that standardized tests provide more objective, reliable and accurate measures of student achievement. In part, the failure to expand the measures used for accountability purposes results from the failure to convince leaders of the utility and validity of these other measures. Although several years of research, development, validation, and dissemination will be required before integrated learning and assessment systems could be widely available, efforts should begin now to familiarize political and educational leaders with these methods of assessment. To increase buy-in, roles in the development process should also be created for political and educational leaders.

Additionally, efforts are needed to help leaders see the potential role computer-based technology can play in expanding notions of accountability. As Haney and Razcek (1994) argue, current notions of accountability in education are narrowly defined as examining the performance of schools via changes in their test scores. Under this definition, the iterative process of reflecting on programs and strategies, providing accounts of the successes and shortcomings of those programs, and setting goals in response to those shortcomings is, at best, an informal and secondary component of school accountability. While computer-based learning and assessment systems have the potential to make information provided by current achievement tests redundant and thus eliminate the need for such external tests, computer-based technologies could also be applied today to disrupt current notions of school accountability by providing a forum for schools to account for their practices and to learn from the practices of other schools. Rather than simply transferring achievement testing from paper to a web-based delivery system (as is currently occurring in Virginia, Oregon, Georgia, and South Dakota), the Internet could be used to collect information about classroom performance (e.g., electronic portfolios or work samples), more closely scrutinize the reliability of scores given to such work, return data from multiple measures in more useful formats, share information and student work with a wider base of constituents, and provide a forum for schools to account for their programs and strategies. Investing now in developing web-based accountability systems that broaden the definition of educational accountability will better set the stage for replacing external, state-mandated achievement tests with assessments that are integrated into learning systems.

Practical Challenges

If these disruptive approaches to assessment are to become a regular practice within schools, learning systems like BioLogica must be developed across a wide range of topic areas. Anticipating the potential growth of these types of learning systems, the Concord Consortium has developed a scripting language that allows users to easily create new modules for current learning systems or develop new learning systems. In a sense, this scripting language is analogous to HTML in that it has the potential to standardize learning systems and would allow learning systems to interact with one another. Not only will this scripting language be useful for those who want to develop new learning systems, it also provides an easy way to alter current systems so that assessment components can be added or modified.

The high initial costs required to develop a learning system and the need to have the system used by students so that psychometricians have sufficient data to conduct the technical work required to develop appropriate psychometric models poses a major obstacle to the development of such learning systems. As an example, not long ago, the National Board on Educational Testing and Public Policy worked with a coalition of schools, political and educational leaders, and Internet-based database developers to develop a proposal to design a comprehensive web-based accountability system that builds on Massachusetts' current MCAS assessments. While the proposal dedicated substantial resources to piloting and validating the system, the high costs associated with developing database engines and interfaces resulted in a research and development budget that was too large to be attractive to those who could provide funding. The same obstacle exists for learning and assessment systems. One strategy is to focus first on those systems that are already in use or already have funding to support development. By collaborating with the developers of these existing systems, the resources required to support the development and validation of new approaches to assessment are greatly reduced. In addition, by starting with those systems that are already in use in schools, we have access to sets of data that are more immediately available. For example, BioLogica is currently used by some 10,000 students across the nation. In addition, because it is delivered via the Web, its modules can be easily updated and student data can be sent to a central database. Rather than investing two to three years in developing a learning system, we can work with the highest quality systems that are currently in use or will soon be in use. This provides opportunities to begin immediately to explore some of the technical challenges outlined above.

A third practical challenge involves tapping expertise from a range of fields. As the NRC's (2001) *Knowing What Students Know* notes, collaboration among cognitive scientists, assessment experts, and content experts is needed to better inform the development of new approaches to assessment. In addition, input from instructional leaders and developers of technology also is needed to better anticipate how these systems might be used within classrooms, and how emerging computer-based technologies might impact these systems. Finally, political and educational leaders must be brought into the research and development process to better assure that these systems will be accepted as a valid means of measuring student achievement.

Clearly, there is a tremendous amount of work that must be performed before these learning systems can adequately meet assessment needs. As the tools students use as they learn become more sophisticated, there are opportunities to acquire a more detailed understanding of how and what students learn. Without question, as current and future computer-based technologies are used regularly in the classroom, they will continue to pressure changes in testing. While small-scale studies may be required to initially demonstrate the need to incorporate these technologies into testing, the primary responsibility for examining and implementing changes falls on the testing programs themselves. Similarly, given the financial rewards the testing industry will realize, it is likely that it will continue to take on the challenge of developing ways to apply computer-based technologies to increase the efficiency of testing. However, given the potential of computer-based technologies to seriously disrupt the current technology of testing, it is unlikely that the testing industry itself will invest in researching and developing disruptive uses of computer-based technology. Given the positive impact integrated learning and assessment systems could have on teaching and learning, coupled with the vast amount of technical work that must be accomplished to develop these new methodologies, national education and political leaders need to follow the military's lead by investing now in developing applications of computer-based technology that have potential to dramatically alter the technology of testing and assessment. Without such investments by the federal government, it is likely that first generation applications of computers to testing will continue to increase the efficiency of current testing practices while the development of second and third generation computer-based tests will proceed slowly. As I explore in the next several chapters, this need for national leadership to help support the advancement of computer-based testing parallels the need for national leadership to support comprehensive research on effective applications of computers to instruction and learning.

NOTES

1. For more information, on the Technology-Rich Environment project see National Center for Education Statistics (2003) and Bennett and Persky (2002).
2. See Tatsuoka (1991) and Varandi and Tatsuoka (1989) for a detailed presentation of the algorithms used to classify response patterns.

CHAPTER 8

THE ROLE OF TECHNOLOGY
IN EDUCATIONAL REFORM

During the past 20 years, the power of computers has grown at an astonishing rate. Computers that only presented text in black and white are now capable of running full motion video complete with stereo sound. Whereas early desktop computers only accessed a limited amount of information stored on a floppy disk, internal hard drives are now capable of storing vast libraries. Applications that required arcane keyboard codes to perform a limited number of tasks can now perform hundreds of tasks through voice commands. Information that once was transferred by physically exchanging floppy disks can now be sent across a room through an infrared beam or accessed almost immediately by hundreds of people across the world via the Internet.

Amazingly, this increased power has come at little additional cost to consumers. The relatively low cost combined with increased power has led to the profusion of computers in the work place and in homes (for data on this growth, see Newburger, 2001). Although schools have been slower to acquire computers, the presence and use of educational technologies are increasing rapidly (Zandvliet & Farragher, 1997). While schools had one computer for every 125 students in 1983, they had one for every nine students in 1995, 1 for every six students in 1998, and one for every 4.2 students in 2001 (Glennan & Melmed, 1996; Market Data Retrieval, 1999, 2001). Today, some states, such as South Dakota, report a student:computer ratio of 2:1 (Bennett, 2002). And in the fall of 2002, Maine officially

Technology and Assessment: The Tale of Two Interpretations, pages 127–135
Copyright © 2006 by Information Age Publishing
All rights of reproduction in any form reserved.

launched the first phase of its Learning Technology Initiative which provides a laptop for every seventh grader and their teacher (Maine Learning Technology Initiative, 2002). Since then, several more states and large districts have introduced similar 1:1 laptop programs, albeit on a smaller scale.

Together, the growing presence of computers in and out of schools and the increased power of computers have sparked the development of a wide variety of software. Some of this software is targeted specifically for educational settings and is designed to impact student learning. Other software, originally designed to meet specific business and consumer needs, has been adapted to enhance instruction, communication, and productivity within schools. This profusion of software has allowed schools to put computers to use in increasingly diverse ways. A national survey of teachers in 1998 shows that 50% of K–12 teachers had students use word processors, 36% had them use CD ROMs, and 29% had them use the World Wide Web (Becker, 1999). More recent national data indicates that 75% of elementary school-aged students and 85% of middle and high school-aged students use a computer in school (U.S. Department of Commerce, 2002). Although it is unclear how often students actually use computers in schools, this more recent data suggests that computers have become a learning tool employed by the vast majority of students.

In reality, however, computers are more than just tools: Computers are toolboxes that contain many different software applications or tools. When districts decide to invest in computers, they do so not because of any one tool, but to make use of a variety of tools. Some of these computer-based tools are designed to have a direct impact on students, others are intended to increase productivity, while others indirectly support teaching and learning outside of the classroom. Naturally, as new tools have been developed and as educators have gained experience working with these tools, the way in which computers fit into the educational process has shifted over the past two decades.

COMPUTERS AND THE EDUCATIONAL PROCESS

Airasian (1997) suggests that the prevailing conception of education is that of a process that helps change students in desirable ways (see also Popham, 1988; Tyler, 1949). To define the ways in which teachers are expected to help students change, schools develop a curriculum. The curriculum describes the skills and knowledge students are expected to learn in school. To help students develop the skills and knowledge described by the curriculum, teachers employ a variety of instructional strategies.

In this model of education, teaching and learning begins with a curriculum that is delivered through instruction. Airasian further divides the instructional process into three interrelated components: Planning instruction, delivering instruction, and assessing student outcomes. Teachers refer to the curriculum during the planning phase to determine what they are to teach, and then select instructional methods they believe will best help foster desired student changes. These methods are then applied while delivering instruction. During and following the delivery of instruction, teachers assess students to determine whether they have mastered the desired curriculum goals (Airasian, 1997). Figure 8.1 depicts the relationships between curriculum and the three parts of the instructional process.

Within this educational process, computer-based tools play three primary roles. These roles include (a) defining aspects of the curriculum, (b) providing instructional tools, and (c) supporting productivity and communications.

When schools first acquired computers, their primary impact was felt at the curriculum level. To prepare students for computer-related jobs, the curriculum was expanded to include goals related to computer programming and development of business-related skills such as keyboarding, use of spreadsheets and databases, and related workplace productivity skills (Fisher, Dwyer, & Yocam, 1996). In this way, computer-based tools enter the model of education primarily at the curriculum level. These new curricular goals then drive instruction. And during instruction computers are used to help students reach specific computer-related curricular goals.

During the past decade, however, many observers have argued that simply making computers part of the curriculum fails to capitalize on the instructional powers of computers. As deGraaf, Ridout and Riehl (1993) describe, "Rather than computing and technology as a new subject which will take its place alongside mathematics, reading, social studies, language arts, and science as curriculum subjects...some educators believe that the computer should be viewed as a tool which should act invisibly in all curriculum areas" (p. 850). From this perspective, computer-based tools are viewed as instruc-

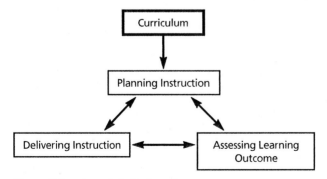

Figure 8.1.   A model of education.

tional tools that teachers use to help students obtain curricular goals in language arts, mathematics, science, social studies, and other subject areas. In the model of education depicted in Figure 8.1, this concept of computer-based tools affects the planning and delivery of instruction. During instruction, teachers select and use computer-based tools that they believe will help students develop subject area curricular goals.

As this concept of technology as a tool takes hold in schools, it is becoming clear that pedagogy alone does not lead to effective use of technology. Unless students have developed the essential computer-related skills that enable them to use instructional technology to meet specific subject area curricular goals, the impact of computer-based instructional tools is limited. To develop these skills, technology skills are once again becoming a part of the curriculum. The re-emergence of technology in the curriculum is reflected in the technology standards developed by the International Society for Technology in Education (ISTE). But unlike technology curriculum a decade ago, the ISTE standards connect technology with the broader curriculum (International Society for Technology in Education, 2000).

In addition to having an impact upon curriculum and instruction, computer-related tools are also used by teachers and administrators to support communication and productivity outside of the classroom. While planning instruction, teachers might use web-browsers to access information over the Internet or develop worksheets or other instructional materials using a word processor. To communicate with parents, teachers might use email or create newsletters using word processors or graphic layout software. And to develop individual education plans, teachers might access students' records through a database program and correspond with counselors via email. Rather than fitting neatly into any one part of the model of education, the use of computer-based tools to support communication and productivity surrounds the model.

But beyond using discrete computer-related tools to meet specific needs—whether those needs are defined as a component of the curriculum, an instructional tool, or a tool used for professional activities outside of the classroom—some observers believe technology can be an important tool that fosters educational reform.

TECHNOLOGY AS AN EDUCATIONAL REFORM STRATEGY

In the preface to *Technology and Educational Reform*, Means (1994) wrote:

> ...the authors of the chapters in Technology and Education Reform suggest that technology does have the potential to support education reform and that there have been changes both in the political climate and in people's

understanding of instructional technology and its implementation that provide grounds for optimism. Specifically, the political will to rethink the entire educational system and the basic organization of schools is combined with renewed emphasis on teaching advanced skills to all students. At the same time, schools are increasingly using technology as a tool to support student and teacher inquiry rather than as a substitute lecturer or workbook...

Teachers who rethink their curricula, replacing short pieces of didactic instruction on separate topics in discrete disciplines with multidisciplinary projects in which students tackle meaningful, complex tasks over extended periods of time, are establishing the prerequisites that will allow them to apply technology meaningfully to support student work. In classrooms where such meaningful education goes on, technology can amplify students' skills and make students' tasks more authentic—that is, more like real-life tasks. Students will approach their tasks with the same tools and access to information available to practitioners in the world beyond the schoolhouse. Students will engage in high-level planning and problem solving as they choose technological tools appropriate to their tasks and apply these tools in flexible ways. At the same time, as teachers become comfortable with technology, it can inspire them to think of new projects and activities and can raise their expectations for their students. (Means, 1994, pp. xi–xii)

Several of the ideas captured by Means (1994) defined the model of school reform developed and implemented by Co-NECT starting in 1992 (Russell & Haney, 1997b). As one of eight "break-the-mold" school reform designs funded by New American Schools, the Co-NECT model emphasized the development of students' higher-order skills through their work on extended, multidisciplinary projects. To provide teachers and students more flexibility to engage in project-based learning, the Co-NECT model restructured the organization of students from specific grade levels into clusters composed of students across grade levels. To provide students access to current information, multiple media, and experts beyond the school walls, the Co-NECT model placed heavy emphasis on the use of computers in all curricular areas (Russell & Haney, 1997b). Consistent with Mean's view, the Co-NECT model did not intend for technology to be a reform in and of itself. Rather, technology served as a hub that helped hold together several aspects of a broad school reform effort. Technology enhanced communication among teachers, the school leader, and outside experts who facilitated the school reform effort. Through the school network, students and teachers could access their work from any computer in the school and thus were no longer tied to a single computer located within a single classroom, enabling flexible grouping of students and teachers. Through the Internet, students and teachers could access content and expertise unavailable within the school, enriching the project-based work performed by students. Through word processors, hypermedia authoring tools, a digital video and music studio, and digital drawing and photograph programs, students developed a wider range of communication skills. Finally, by allowing students to work together or independently to select the tools and resources used throughout the course of a given project, students had multiple opportunities to develop problem-solving, strategic planning, and cooperative learning skills.

Similarly, the Apple Classrooms of Tomorrow (ACOT) project placed large numbers of computers directly into classrooms. Launched in 1985 and extending for more than a decade, the project aimed "to find useful ways to support students' learning with a wide variety of digital tools" (Fisher et al., 1996, p. xiv). While the ways in which computer-based technologies were used varied widely across classrooms, the goal was consistent—to expand the ways in which teaching occurs in the classroom and the types of skills and knowledge students develop. In many cases, the access to and use of computer-based technologies led to a restructuring in the way classrooms were physically arranged and the ways in which students and teachers interacted with each other.

More recently, technology-inspired reform efforts have emphasized new skills and knowledge believed to be important for the modern workplace. These reform efforts focus on "21st Century Skills" and were first kindled by a report issued by the Labor Secretary's Commission on Achieving Necessary Skills (SCANS) in 1991. Formally titled, *What Work Requires of Schools*, the report identified several skills needed by students to succeed in the workplace. These skills included:

- Basic skills: reading, writing, listening, speaking, and the ability to perform arithmetic and mathematical operations.
- Cognitive skills: creative thinking, decision-making, problem-solving, visualization, knowing how to learn, and reasoning.
- Personal qualities: responsibility, positive self-esteem, sociability, self-management and integrity.
- Workplace skills: being able to identify, organize, plan and allocate resources, working with others, acquiring and using information, understanding complex interrelationships, and working with a variety of technologies.

This initial set of skills has since been refined by organizations like the CEO Forum (2001a), the International Society for Technology in Education (2000), and the North Central Regional Educational Laboratory (Lemke, 2002). As described by Lemke, the 21st Century Skills are currently defined as:

1. Digital-age Literacy including:
   (a) basic, scientific, mathematical, and technological literacies,

     (b) visual and information literacies,

     (c) cultural literacy and global awareness.

2. Inventive Thinking including:

     (a) adaptability/ability to manage complexity,

     (b) curiosity, creativity, and risk taking,

     (c) higher-order thinking and sound reasoning.

3. Effective Communication including:

     (a) teaming, collaboration and interpersonal skills,

     (b) personal and social responsibility,

     (c) interactive communication.

4. High Productivity including:

     (a) ability to prioritize, plan and manage for results,

     (b) effective use of real-world tools,

     (c) relevant, high-quality products.

While it is still unclear whether these 21st-Century Skills will be widely embraced by schools, politicians and the general public, recent emphasis on the importance of addressing these skills in K–12 schools reflects the merging of early efforts to place technology into the curriculum and later efforts to use technology as a tool to reform teaching and learning. That is, by establishing formal standards that are intended to become a component of instruction, technology is placed directly into the curriculum. But, by including standards that are best met through extended collaborative projects, the establishment of these standards also encourages teachers to employ instructional practices that include more student-centered activities. In this way, more recent technology standards attempt to fit into existing curriculums while also promoting the reform of traditional teacher-centered instructional practices.

INCREASING INVESTMENT IN AND QUESTIONS ABOUT TECHNOLOGY IN SCHOOLS

To provide teachers and students access to technology in schools, investments in educational technologies by the federal government have increased dramatically from zero in 1994 to $785 million in 2001 (see Figure 8.2). On top of this, state and local educational agencies have spent an additional $10 billion. In California alone, the Digital High School Educational Technology Grant Program allocated $1 billion to support educational technology (Schiff & Lewis, 1999).

Given these massive investments in educational technologies, it is not surprising that many observers are questioning whether computers are hav-

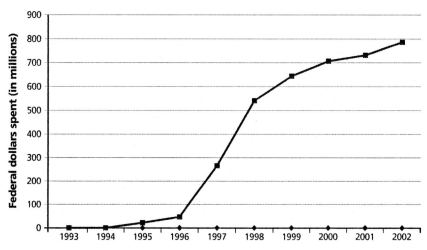

Figure 8.2.　Federal dollars spent on educational technology 1993–2002.

ing a positive impact on education. Over the past few years, a series of books have been published that question the value and impact of computers in schools (Cuban, 2001; Healy, 1999; Oppenheimer, 2003; Stoll, 1999). Similarly, numerous editorials and articles in newspapers and magazines have questioned this same issue. As just a few examples, headlines have read:

> "It Just Doesn't Compute: How the Big Push to Put Computers in Schools Can Actually Harm Kids"—*The Toronto Star,* September 6, 1998.
>
> "Misplaced Emphasis on Computers in Schools"—*The Record,* May 14, 1999.
>
> "Putting Internet in Classrooms Wastes Education Resources"—*Arizona Republic,* June 3, 1999.
>
> "Educators Pondering Pitfall of Computers"—*Start Tribune,* April 11, 1998.
>
> "The Computer Delusion"—*Atlantic Monthly,* July 1997.
>
> "Some Educators Question Value of School Computers"—*Boston Globe,* May 9, 1999.
>
> "The Joys of Not Being Wired"—*Palm Beach Post,* April 24, 1999.
>
> "Reckless Computer Use Takes Byte Out of Education"—*USA Today,* May 7, 1999.

Concern about the return on investments in technology has become so heightened that it spurred the U.S. Department of Education to hold a conference during the summer of 2000 that focused exclusively on evaluating the effectiveness of technology. As noted in the conference summary report, "Parents and teachers, school boards and administrators, governors and state legislatures, and Congress all want to know if investments in technology are providing a return in student achievement. Indeed, if resources are to be expended on technology, it is becoming a political, economic, and public policy necessity to demonstrate its vital effectiveness" (McNabb, Hawkes, & Rouk, 1999).

Although a large body of research on educational technology exists, recent concerns about the impact of technology has shifted the focus of research from understanding how technology can change teaching and how to support these changes to a narrower focus on how technology is impacting student learning as measured by standardized test scores. However, as described earlier, in many cases the tests used to measure student learning forbid students from using the computer-based tools they use in the classroom while developing skills and knowledge. In other cases, the tests do not measure the skills and knowledge students develop while using technology. As a result, test scores may not provide adequate information to address the impacts of technology use on student learning. It is for this reason that many researchers who have been examining educational technology argue that new, technology-appropriate assessment tools are needed (Baker et al., 1996; Means et al., 2001; Russell & Haney, 2000).

The following chapters examine the evolution of educational technology and efforts to examine these new technologies. Specifically, Chapter 9 documents a pattern of excitement and resistance that has accompanied the introduction of a variety of educational technologies over the past 150 years. Chapter 10 then examines the approaches used to examine the impact of many of these educational technologies and in the process traces the rise, fall, and re-emergence of large-scale experimental designs as the acid test for the effectiveness of a given educational technology. Chapter 11 focuses on some of the challenges posed by employing large-scale randomized studies to examine the effect of computer-based technology on teaching and learning and describes several alternative approaches that hold promise for understanding and supporting educational uses of computer-based technologies.

CHAPTER 9

A BRIEF HISTORY OF TECHNOLOGY IN EDUCATION

Today, most people associate "educational technology" with computers and the Internet. In America's primary and secondary schools, however, educational technology encompasses much more than computers and has roots that extend back several centuries.

The first American schools were one-room cabins, the mission of which was to produce literate and moral citizens. Students attended school for between one and six months a year and there were few educational tools available. But as increasing numbers of American communities were settled, the education system became more firmly established. To aid the learning process, educational technologies, such as slates, hornbooks, blackboards, and books were introduced.

Although technologies like the blackboard and books are now taken for granted and are assumed to be part of every student's educational experience, these technologies were viewed as radical and revolutionary teaching and learning tools when they were first introduced. Over time, a variety of technologies such as film, radio, television, teaching machines, microcomputers and the Internet have been introduced to schools, each sparking controversy about its appropriateness for schooling and effectiveness as a teaching and learning tool.

Technology and Assessment: The Tale of Two Interpretations, pages 137–152
Copyright © 2006 by Information Age Publishing
All rights of reproduction in any form reserved.

To help place the current debate over the role and effects of computer-based technologies in today's K–12 schools, this chapter traces the history of educational technology from the 1600s to the present time.

THE HORNBOOK AND PRINTED BOOKS

Johannes Gutenberg began building a primitive version of the printing press in 1436 and the first Gutenberg Bible was printed in 1455 (de la Mare, 1997). Nearly two centuries later Stephen Dayne brought the first printing press used in the United States (Rubinstein, 1999). However, since they were expensive and were not readily available, books were not commonly used in the early years of American schooling.

In lieu of printed books, American settlers improvised with a device known as the hornbook. Adopted from England, the hornbook was one of the first forms of educational technology used to aid in teaching reading in American schools. A hornbook was "a small, wooden, paddle-shaped instrument. A sheet of paper, with the alphabet, numerals, the Lord's Prayer, and other reading matter printed on it was pasted upon the blade and the entire implement was covered with sheets of transparent horn" (Good & Teller, 1973, p. 28). The hornbook was a crude, low-cost solution to the American settler's problem of how to teach children to read without having books available. Although it was useful at the time, the hornbook became obsolete as the cost of printing decreased and texts became more widely available.

Perhaps the most popular early printed book was the *New England Primer*. Introduced to schools in 1690, the *New England Primer* was intended to make learning to read more interesting for children. "*The New England Primer* contained the twenty-four letters of the alphabet, each letter being illustrated with a drawing and a verse to impress it on the child's mind. The primer also contained various lessons and admonitions for youth, the Lord's Prayer, and the Ten Commandments" (Gutek, 1986, p. 10). Historian Paul Leicester Ford estimates that 3 million copies of the *New England Primer* were printed (Gutek, 1986).

The next generation of written texts included Webster's first spelling book, followed by the McGuffy Readers. The evolution of these primitive textbooks allowed teachers to follow a predefined sequence of lesson plans that taught students how to read and write. In this way, early books served as a tool that began to standardize the content to which students were exposed.

THE SANDBOX

In 1806, the Lancastrian methodology of schooling was introduced in New York City and with this new method of teaching came a new form of educational technology. Lancaster's method of education was appealing because a large number of students could be educated for a low cost. This method employed a master teacher as well as "monitors" (more advanced students) to teach large classes of students. The monitors, who had been trained by the master teacher taught groups of approximately twenty students a skill, such as writing. Students would use a sandbox on their desk to practice the alphabet: "White sand overlaid the box and the children traced the letters of the alphabet with their fingers in the sand, the black surface showing through in the form of the letter traced...After the children had made each of the letters, the monitor smoothed the sand with a flat iron and a new letter was presented" (Gutek, 1986, p. 62).

Lancaster chose sandboxes because they were the most economically affordable form of technology available at the time. But by the 1830s, doubts about the effectiveness of the Lancastrian system surfaced. With the decline of this teaching method, the use of monitors and sandboxes ended. Later the sandboxes would be replaced by individual slates. Although they were more expensive, slates allowed students to practice their writing skills more easily. Erasing chalk from a slate was quicker and cleaner than ironing the surface of the sandbox.

THE BLACKBOARD

While individual slates were used in classrooms during the early 1800s, it was not until 1841 that the classroom chalkboard was first introduced. Shortly thereafter, Horace Mann began encouraging communities to buy chalkboards for their classrooms. By the late 1800s, the chalkboard had become a permanent fixture in most classrooms.

As with many forms of educational technology, learning how to integrate the chalkboard into classroom instruction was not an easy task. As Shade (2001) explains, "When first introduced, the chalkboard went unused for many years until teachers realized that it could be used for whole group instruction. They had to change their thinking from individual slates to classroom slates" (p. 2).

Similar to more modern forms of educational technology, the chalkboard also received praise from community leaders. As an example, Josiah Bumstead, a Springfield Massachusetts councilman, said, "The inventor or introducer of the blackboard deserves to be ranked among the best contributors to learning and science, if not among the greatest benefactors of mankind" (Daniel, 2000, p. 1). Thinking of the blackboard as a revolutionary form of educational technology seems counterintuitive. But it is one of the few types of media that has survived the test of time and is still regularly used in classrooms today.

FILM

During the next several decades, the American educational system expanded and became more developed. The price of producing paper and printing books also dropped to levels that enabled paper to replace slates and allowed each child to have his or her own books. But just as books were becoming widely available to students, a new form of educational technology began to emerge, namely film.

The kinetoscope, which is now known as the motion picture, was invented in 1889. Over the next decade, film equipment was developed and refined. And in 1902, Charles Urban of London began exhibiting the first educational films. Among these films were "slow-motion, microscopic, and undersea views" and "such subjects as the growth of plants and the emergence of the butterfly from the chrysalis" (Saettler, 1990, p. 96). In 1911, Thomas Edison also contributed to the use of film in the classroom by producing a series on the American Revolution.

With the rapid growth of American schools, both in terms of the number of schools and the quantity of students attending those schools, there was a pressing need to provide standard, high-quality instruction to large numbers of students. At the time, some proponents believed that using film in classrooms met this important educational need. As an example, Thomas Edison proclaimed, "Books will soon be obsolete in the schools. Scholars will soon be instructed through the eye. It is possible to touch every branch of human knowledge with the motion picture" (Saettler, 1990, p. 98).

In 1910, enthusiasm for educational films led Rochester New York's Board of Education to adopt education films for instructional use. Many other public school systems soon followed Rochester's lead and by 1931 "twenty-five states had units in their departments of education devoted to films and related media" (Cuban, 1986, p. 12). Edison's prophecy and the public school support for educational film spawned a new and quickly growing industry in America, namely educational film.

As early as 1910, more than 1,000 film titles were catalogued in George Kleine's *Catalogue of Educational Motion Pictures.* In 1923 Frank Freeman classified the existing educational films into the following four categories: "(1) the dramatic, either fictional or historical; (2) the anthropological or sociological, differing from the dramatic in that it is not primarily based on a narrative or story; (3) the industrial or commercial, which show the processes of modern industry and commerce; and (4) the scientific, which may be classified into subgroups corresponding to the individual sciences, such as earth science, nature study, etc." (Saettler, 1990, p. 97).

Despite the explosion of educational films, conflict emerged between the commercial interests and the educational interests of the film industry.

Concerns about the financial bottom line led the film industry to develop educational films which some critics claimed lacked content and were more theatrical in nature. In addition, teachers often were not asked for input and guidance in making educational films. As a result, the films frequently did not meet teachers' needs. Then, in the late 1920s, sound film was introduced.

Although the ability to include sound was a step forward for the film industry, it also contributed to the demise of educational filming. Requiring new and expensive equipment, production of educational sound films became an expensive endeavor. At a time when commercial filming was struggling and educators were questioning the merit of film in classrooms, strong advocacy for educational sound films was lacking.

Although film continued to be widely used by the government for armed forces training, agricultural demonstrations, and public relations, the impact of film in the classroom was minimal. As Cuban (1986) described, "film took up a bare fraction of the instructional day. As a new classroom tool, film may have entered the teacher's repertoire, but, for any number of reasons, teachers used it hardly at all" (p. 17). According to Cuban, the main reasons for the limited instructional use of film included "teachers' lack of skills in using equipment and film, cost of films, equipment, and upkeep, inaccessibility of equipment when it is needed and finding and fitting the right film to the class" (p. 18).

THE TYPEWRITER

An often overlooked form of educational technology, the typewriter is the one form of mechanical technology that has penetrated and been used by large numbers of students over several decades. This use, however, has generally been limited to "business" classes that focus specifically on teaching students how to type. While typewriters were present in most high schools into the 1990s, they have been absent from the majority of classrooms and not used widely throughout a student's educational experience. However, there are close parallels between the typewriter and more modern forms of computer-based technologies.

The first functioning typewriter was marketed and sold by the Remington Arms Company in 1873. Years of refinement and use in the business world followed this initial product launch before typewriters were introduced to schools in the 1920s. Soon thereafter, Ben Wood and Frank Freeman (1932) conducted a large-scale experiment to develop an understanding of how typewriters might be used in early elementary classrooms. Occurring between 1929 through 1931, Wood and Freeman's experiment was similar to many studies of computers conducted during the late 1980s and the 1990s in that the stated purpose of Wood and Freeman's investigation was "to study the nature and extent of the educational influences of the portable typewriter when used as a part of the regular classroom equipment in the kindergarten and elementary school grades" (p. 1). In other words, rather than focusing narrowly on how the use of typewriters affected the writing skills of young children, Wood and Freeman were primarily interested in how instructional practices and classroom ecology changed. For this reason, Wood and Freeman's study examined how the typewriter could be integrated into the curriculum and the impacts that it had on teaching and learning.

Almost 15,000 students from eight public school districts and five private schools participated in the experiment. Treatment and control groups were formed in order to study the differences in student learning. Data that was analyzed included achievement test gains, student writing samples, teacher questionnaires, classroom observations, and student letters about why they like typewriting.

Based upon their study, Wood and Freeman (1932) concluded that there were three important reasons for using the typewriter in schools: "to teach students skills that they will use later in life for personal or professional reasons and to enable students to better learn English, spelling, arithmetic, geography, history, etc., and to develop those attitudes and habits which constitute so important a part of the aims of elementary school education" (p. 179).

Even though Wood and Freeman (1932) found evidence that typewriters could be used in early elementary classrooms, and this use had a positive impact on student learning, their recommendation to place typewriters in all early elementary classrooms was never implemented. In part, the high cost required for such large numbers of typewriters was not feasible, particularly when the nation was struggling with a major economic depression. Instead of being directly placed and used in classrooms as a writing tool, typewriters were used to prepare students for the business world by teaching high school students the professional skill of typewriting.

RADIO

Radio entered the educational system in the early 1920s. Like the early days of film, radio was heralded as a tool that would revolutionize classroom teaching. Similar to the proclamations of Thomas Edison regarding film, William Levenson, the author of *Teaching Through Radio*, predicted, "The time may come when a portable radio receiver will be as common in the classroom as is the blackboard. Radio instruction will be integrated into school life as an accepted educational medium" (Cuban, 1986, p. 24).

In 1923 Haaren High School in New York City became the first public school to use the radio in classroom teaching. Following a decision by the Radio Division of the U.S. Department of Commerce to license time from commercial stations to broadcast educational lessons, many more schools and districts bought equipment and made plans to use the radio in classrooms. Falling equipment prices in the 1930s further increased interest in the instructional use of radio.

Typically, educational radio programs lasted between 30–60 minutes and were broadcasted a few times a week. This limited amount of broadcast time "destined radio usage to be viewed, at best, as a supplement to teacher instruction" (Cuban, 1986, p. 22). Nonetheless, a wide range of radio lessons were readily available to teachers. "There were broadcasts for elementary school listeners and for secondary-school students. There were dramatic re-creations of American history, challenging interpretations of American folk music, delightful dramatizations of children's stories and legends. There were, in short, a variety and a wealth of curricular material on the air" (Woelfel & Tyler, 1945, p. 42).

Two survey studies conducted in 1941, one in Ohio and one in California, found that the majority of schools had radio receivers. Moreover, the amount of radio hardware available to teachers in the 1930s and 1940s exceeded the amount of film hardware available at the height of film use.

Higher education was also impacted by the invention of the radio. Some colleges and universities established their own radio stations for instructional use. Ohio State University first began broadcasting weather reports in 1912. But the radio was not used for instructional use in higher education until the 1920s, when "schools of the air" were formed. These radio-based schools partnered with a local radio station, developed curriculum, created lesson leaflets, produced educational programs, established a weekly schedule for broadcasts, trained staff, and ultimately executed the concept of "schools of the air."

Educational technology zealots initially dreamed of the radio replacing both schools and teachers. But by the end of the 1940s, funding and educators' enthusiasm for radio use diminished significantly. Saettler identified problems with equipment and support as two factors that limited instructional use of radio. In addition, Saettler (1990) found that schools "fail to use (the radio) properly or integrate its programming with the school curriculum" (p. 197).

Similar to problems encountered by educational films, another factor that contributed to the downfall of educational radio was the struggle between commercial stations and educators. A 1925 decision by Herbert Hoover, who was then Secretary of Commerce, to leave radio in the hands of American business, instead of having it controlled by the government made efforts to keep educational radio alive exceedingly difficult. Unable to conduct a unified fight to maintain a presence on radio stations, educational interests in radio were overpowered by the commercial radio stations united fight against educational radio. "The networks maintained that allocating frequencies for educational broadcasting would only disrupt a successful system of broadcasting that had just begun to function well" (Saettler, 1990, p. 203). As a result, educational radio languished as the big business of commercial radio boomed.

By the end of the 1940s, technology proponents had given up on educational radio and instead began focusing on the use of television in schools, which was perceived to be the ultimate combination of audio and visual technology.

TELEVISION

Although it wasn't until the 1950s and 1960s that instructional television reached its peak, the first documented use of closed circuit television was in Los Angeles public schools and at the State University of Iowa in 1939. While the popularity of instructional television was rising between 1939 and the 1950s, the overall United States educational system was facing harsh criticism. Alleged evidence of the ailing educational system culminated with Russia's launch of Sputnik in 1957. Fear that the Russians had surpassed the United States in science and technology led to educational reform efforts. Instructional television was viewed as one way to gain ground in the fight to stay ahead in technology. In response, financial support for instructional television poured in from many government and industry sources. The Ford Foundation alone "expended more than $300 million for the national educational television movement" (Saettler, 1990, p. 372).

Funding was provided for several types of instructional television applications. Similar to the introduction of film, some administrators and government officials hypothesized that television could provide students with a better education at a lower cost. To this end, a few school systems, such as Hagerstown Maryland and American Samoa, attempted to substitute a large portion of teacher-led classroom time with educational television programming. The primary reason for the infusion of television in these communities was the lack of certified teachers. In most schools, however, instructional television served a supplemental role and was used minimally. Cuban estimates that by 1975 primary-grade students spent on average only five hours a week learning through instructional television (Cuban, 1986, p. 32).

During the 1960s the television industry underwent a major transformation. In 1965, a Carnegie Corporation Commission recommended that "the federal government establish an independent, nonprofit Corporation for Public Television that would receive money from the government and other sources and distribute these funds to individual stations and independent production centers" (Saettler, 1990, p. 377).

Essentially putting into effect the Carnegie Corporation recommendations, the Public Broadcasting Act was passed in 1967. Two years later, the Corporation for Public Broadcasting was established and in 1970 the Public Broadcasting Service was created to act as a distribution point and to manage the interconnection between stations. All of these events in the public television industry would appear to set the stage for tremendous success of instructional television. However, some critics believe the end result hurt instructional television more than it helped. For example, Bronson criticized the way that the CPB handled instructional television, stating that it "indicates a questionable bureaucratic concern with directing social change rather than in promoting the development of educational broadcasting" (Saettler, 1990, p. 384).

Although several early studies showed benefits of television over teacher instruction, later reports revealed that support for instructional television had diminished significantly. One source of this lack of support was from teachers. Typically, implementations of instructional television did not consider teacher needs or views. Cuban (1986) describes how, rather than consulting teachers, "television was hurled at teachers" (p. 36).

Interest in educational applications of televisions were revived in 1989 when a private, for profit company began marketing an educational channel directly to schools. As Saettler (1990) describes, "Whittle Communications assembled a board of twelve educators and public figures to provide advice and direction for Channel One, a satellite-received news programming venture aimed at elementary schools" (p. 533). As an incentive to broadcast Channel One to students, Whittle Communications offered schools up to $50,000 of free televisions and video equipment and 1,000 hours of educational programming in exchange for a guarantee that students would watch 12 minutes of daily news programs which includes two minutes of paid commercials each day. Channel One has since changed its focus from elementary schools to middle and high schools, but maintains the same business plan. Despite the fact that California and New York banned Channel One, by 1993, more than 8 million students nationwide watched Channel One's programming daily (Barry, 1994, p. 103). Channel One, however, has faced strong opposition. As Saettler (1990) states, "All critics agree that the classroom should not become another market to exploit" (p. 534). Channel One is yet another example of the tension, and perhaps incompatibility, between corporate America and the educational system.

TEACHING MACHINES AND PROGRAMMED INSTRUCTION

In the 1960s, behavioral psychology contributed to the educational technology field by introducing "teaching machines." Reminiscent of *The Turk*, an 18th century "computer" that wore a turban and played chess (Standage, 2002), teaching machines were intended to teach students through thoughtfully programmed instruction.

The premise behind teaching machines was that objectives must be defined in advance and the extent to which these objectives are achieved must be measured. Students operated the machines themselves and followed instructions on a screen similar to a television. Typically, individual student cubicles were set up to block the noise made by the machines. This format minimized the amount of interaction among students and between students and the teacher.

Books accompanied the teaching machines and functioned in an adaptive fashion, so that if a student did not understand a concept, the student was directed to a section that further explained it. If the student exhibited mastery of the concept, he or she was directed to the next topic. Teachers were able to program the teaching machines based on their desired curricular goals while students worked at their own pace through the lesson plans. But once programmed, it was the machine that directed students to the appropriate lesson, either in books or on the machine.

When using programmed instruction, students were first presented with material in successively more difficulty steps. The student was then asked to answer a question about the material. Some questions were multiple choice, while others used a fill in the blank format. The program then compared the student's answer with the correct answer. Positive reinforcement was given to students who responded correctly while the proper response was provided to students who answered incorrectly. Skinner believed that all students should be administered the same set of questions, and students should be able to answer 95% of the questions correctly.

Later in the life cycle of teaching machines and programmed instruction, branching algorithms and adaptive tests were developed to tailor the material and questions to an individual student's needs. In general, evaluations of programmed instruction in the classroom showed that although implementation was difficult, the combination of teacher instruction and programmed instruction was more effective than either method used in isolation.

Skinner described the key characteristic of teaching machines and programmed instruction as "the arrangement of materials so that the student could make correct responses and receive reinforcement when correct responses were made" (Saettler, 1990, p. 294). This statement points to one of the major sources of conflict in the use of teaching machines. Too often teachers and administrators found themselves caught up in the excitement of using technology and neglected what many people now recognize as the more important component—the program of instruction. Students were sometimes bored with the level of instruction, and other times, they found ways to cheat the system and bypass lessons (p. 303).

Skinner introduced programmed instruction at Harvard University in 1957. A year later, Evans used the programmed instruction concept in books at the University of Pennsylvania. The first use of programmed instruction in an elementary school was in 1957 at the Mystic School in Winchester, Massachusetts. In general, though, teaching machines and programmed instruction were not widely used in public school classrooms or in higher education.

The popularity of teaching machines and programmed instruction followed the familiar cycle of most other forms of educational technology. In the late 1950s many people in the educational technology community expressed praise for this new tool: "In its short history this area of teaching technology has had a remarkably widespread effect on all forms of teaching" (Kay, Dodd, & Sime, 1968, p. 1). However, teaching machines and instructional programming never reached the stage of widespread use and in the late 1960s, even the strongest proponents were backing down from their initial claims. Skinner once said, ". . . unfortunately, much of the technology has lost contact with its basic science. Teaching machines are widely misunderstood" (Saettler, 1990, p. 303).

COMPUTERS

The research in the 1950s and 1960s on programmed instruction laid the foundation for the development of more advanced learning systems. Computers were first used in education in the 1960s in a way that was intended to individualize instruction. This method became known as computer assisted instruction (CAI).

CAI was intended to teach students a specific content area. Initially, the only difference between CAI and teaching machines was the type of technology used to deliver the material. Drill and practice techniques were common. "The student was asked to make simple responses, fill in the blanks, choose among a restricted set of alternatives, or supply a missing word or phrase. If the response was wrong, the machine would assume control, flash the word 'wrong' and generate another problem. If the response was correct, additional material would be presented" (Saettler, 1990, p. 307).

The first generation of CAI programs used mainframe computers, was very expensive, and did not achieve the expected benefits of improving education through computer-based individualized instruction. However, this initial introduction of computers in schools spawned interest in a variety of other computer-based applications.

In the late 1970s the cost and availability of microcomputers reached a level at which it was more practical to place computers in K–12 schools. For a variety of reasons, parents, industry leaders, and government officials put pressure on school districts and principals to introduce computers into the schools. One reason for this computer enthusiasm was the fear that the United States was continuing to fall behind other world powers in terms of technology (C. Hunter, 1998), and teaching students to learn how to use computers seemed like one solution to this problem.

Another reason for the external pressure to use computers in schools was the perceived need to teach children job-related skills. In the late 1970s and early 1980s, the importance of computers in the business world increased rapidly. As a result, teaching students how to use computers provided them with real-world skills and helped them become more competitive in the job market.

Finally, it was argued that computers would make the educational process more efficient. Many computer advocates argued that a more refined version of the mainframe computer-assisted instruction would allow larger class sizes and, therefore, there would be a need for fewer teachers, since students would be able to rely on the computer for a significant portion of their learning.

Depending upon one's perspective, the use of computers in schools differed significantly. For example, if the goal was to teach students how to use a computer so that they could obtain work skills, schools would introduce computer literacy classes into the curriculum. If the goal was to improve instructional efficiency, the computer was used as a tool to teach students the predetermined content. Finally, some people argued that the main benefit of using a computer in the classroom was to improve students' problem-solving skills. This debate over how computers should be used in schools still exists today and is strikingly similar to the differences between Wood and Freeman's rational for placing typewriters in elementary classrooms in the late 1920s versus the use of typewriters in business classes to teach discrete typewriting skills in order to prepare students for the workplace.

But no matter what the intended uses were, computers entered schools in large numbers during the early 1980s. Cuban (1986) references a survey that found an increase of 100,000 computers in schools over the year and a half between fall 1980 and spring 1982. Between 1982 and 1984, that number grew to 325,000 computers. By 1988, there were an estimated 3 million computers in schools (Saettler, 1990, p. 457).

Much of this growth can be attributed to corporate donations, which companies made in an effort to gain an edge in the educational computing market. Throughout the 1980s, IBM, Apple Computer, Hewlett-Packard, and Tandy all donated substantial numbers of computers to public schools. In elementary schools, these computers were generally used for repetitive drilling of specific content. In high schools, computers were generally used to teach students computer skills.

By the end of the 1980s, computers came under heavy scrutiny. Government leaders, parents, and school administrators wanted evidence of the effectiveness of using computers in schools. Instead of detailing benefits, researchers revealed a list of obstacles to the use of computers in classrooms. Similar to the problems identified with film, teachers felt that they were generally excluded from the development of instructional software and that the commercially available software generally did not meet their needs. Specifically, teachers felt that many of the available software packages did not engage students, and teachers felt that the drill and practice format was not an effective use of students' time. Again similar to film, teachers also did not have the time or expertise to develop their own computer-based instructional materials. Finally, technical problems further frustrated teachers. All of these problems contributed to low usage. Saettler estimates that, on average, in the late 1980s, a typical student used a computer for less than 30 minutes a week.

In contrast to the 1980s, the 1990s was a decade of new ideas and innovations for computer use in classrooms. With the introduction of color monitors and graphical user interfaces, more interactive and interesting content-based software packages were developed by companies like Tom Snyder Productions. In addition, simulations, intelligent tutors and cognitive-based learning tools such as DIAGNOSER (Minstrell, Stimpson, & Hunt, 1992) or the Algebra Cognitive Tutor (Anderson et al., 1995) began to show promise for improving classroom learning. Schools also began to understand the benefit of helping teachers determine how to integrate computers into their curriculum. While these advances did not correct all the obstacles to computer use identified by teachers during the late 1980s, they reignited interest in instructional uses of computers.

INTELLIGENT TUTORING

The field of cognitive science has exploded over the past decade and computer applications have emerged to take advantage of this new knowledge of how the brain works. Merging the fields of education and cognitive science has proven to be difficult. As Bruer (1998) describes, "Truly new results in neuroscience, rarely mentioned in the brain and education literature, point to the brain's lifelong capacity to reshape itself in response to experience. The challenge for educators is to develop learning environments and practices that can exploit the brain's lifelong plasticity" (p. 9). One practical application of lessons learned from programmed instruction and new information about how the brain works came in the 1990s in the form of intelligent tutoring.

For the past decade, Carnegie Mellon has been developing cognitive tools. Carnegie Mellon's first major tool, called the Practical Algebra Tutor (PAT), strives to improve students' algebra skills and contains "a psychological model of the cognitive processes behind successful and near-successful student performance" (Koedinger, Anderson, Hadley & Mark, 1997, p. 32).

PAT is computer-based, uses real-world problems, and allows students to use several tools to solve a given problem. One example of a PAT problem is to determine which car rental company should be used on a vacation, given differing cost and terms of agreement information. Feedback is given to the student while he or she is solving the problem, allowing student misconceptions to be addressed while the student is still engaged with the problem.

PAT uses model tracing to track a student's progress throughout a problem and knowledge tracing to track a student's progress in a series of problems. A Bayesian model, which estimates whether a student possesses a certain skill or knowledge of a particular subject, is used to highlight each student's strengths and weaknesses. This information is then used to choose the next problem to be administered and to pace students.

The PAT program was first pilot tested in 1993 in three Pittsburgh high schools. Since then, the intelligent tutoring tools have been expanded to include a fully developed series of products (Algebra I, Geometry, Algebra II, Integrated Math Series and Quantitative Literacy) that are being used throughout the country. Through a series of studies conducted over the past decade (see Corbet, 2002 for a review of this research), evidence suggests that a diverse population of students "including mainstream, non-mainstream, gifted, minority, ESL and inclusive education students all benefit" from the use of the Cognitive Tutor® curricula (Carnegie Learning, 2002, para. 1).

Similarly, researchers at the Concord Consortium have been working on an intelligent tutoring device that focuses on genetics and scientific reasoning skills. The system is intended to help eighth-, ninth-, and tenth-grade students learn about genetics through guided exploration. Most often, the system introduces students to new concepts by asking students to explore a specific topic through manipulation of genetic traits of a fictitious species of dragon. As students work with the system, new concepts are revealed through guided exploration. For example, the first set of explorations during one lesson culminate by asking students to describe how traits are produced in dragons. At times, the learning system presents textual or graphical information to explain concepts and provides students with access to various tools and pieces of information via menu selections. In addition, the system often asks students to demonstrate their understanding through written responses to specific questions, multiple-choice questions, and, most often, the modification of different aspects of genetic codes to create dragons with specific traits or to determine how a trait suddenly appears in a generation of dragons. From an instructional perspective, Biologica enables students to explore a complex topic via a variety of media and enables teachers to work individually or with small groups of students as questions arise.

Although these tools are being used in a relatively small number of classrooms, they show tremendous promise for using technology as a tool that assists students and teachers in both identifying and correcting misconceptions in a timely manner.

THE INTERNET

Today, the Internet is one of the more popular forms of educational technology used in classrooms. Although some college level courses can be taken online, often without any student-teacher interaction, this type of use is just beginning to penetrate K–12 public schools, particularly at the high school level. As an example, the Virtual High School (VHS) was launched in the late 1990s. Since then, VHS has grown and served approximately 3,000 students in more than 150 schools with 134 online courses in 2001. Similarly, the Florida Virtual School provides free, online instruction to 6,900 students enrolled in 65 Florida county school systems.

In addition to online courses, there are a variety of ways that the Internet is being used in classrooms. A 2002 study by the American Institutes for Research found that students use the Internet for school in the following five ways: as a virtual textbook and reference library, as a virtual tutor and study shortcut, as a virtual study group, as a virtual guidance counselor, and as a virtual locker/backpack and notebook (Levin & Arafeh, 2002, p. iii). Teachers also integrate Internet-based activities into their lessons. In some cases, teachers will use data or simulations available on the Internet to demonstrate a concept or work through a problem with the whole class. With the rapid increase in Applets (mini-applications that are available on the Internet), teachers have access to powerful tools that enable easy manipulation of data and displays information in a manner that often makes it easier for students to visualize concepts.

As one example, the Technology and Assessment Study Collaborative has developed a set of applets that focus on specific statistical concepts (www.bc.edu/research/intasc/tools.shtml). These tools enable teachers and students to generate scatterplots that meet specific conditions (e.g., a correlation between two variables of .65 with 200 cases). The correlation applet also allows the user to move individual data points around within the scatterplot and then see how this change in a single data point affects the correlation. In addition, the applet allows the user to manipulate a "line of best fit" by clicking and dragging it on the screen. As the line is moved, the error of prediction is updated automatically, enabling the user to visually explore how changes in the line affect the accuracy of the prediction. Applets developed by other organizations allow teachers to model scientific principles such as plate tectonics and sound waves by manipulating data and then visually displaying the effects.

Teachers also direct students to use the Internet to find and explore information related to a specific topic of study. As an example, many upper elementary and middle school teachers have students perform web-quests. In some cases, web-quests take the form of problems that require students to find and apply information to solve. As an example, a teacher might present a problem in which an animal that lives in Australia has decided to relocate to one of three areas within the United States. Students are then asked to use the Internet to find specific information about the animal and about each area of the United States and to then use this information to write a recommendation to the animal that includes data to support the recommendation. In other cases, web-quests take a more mundane form in which students are given a list of factual questions and are asked to use the Internet to find the answers.

While there are many more examples of computer-based tools that are used in today's classrooms, there is no question that computers are the most recent technology that has penetrated the American educational system. However, an important question that remains largely unanswered focuses on how computer use in schools is affecting teaching and learning. Chapter 10 examines several complications that arise as researchers endeavor to answer this seemingly simple yet deceptively complex question.

RESEARCH ON EDUCATIONAL TECHNOLOGY

As the educational technologies described in Chapter Nine were introduced to schools, they sparked a surge of excitement about the possibilities of educational improvements that might follow. Throughout the 20th century, this initial interest has been followed by efforts to examine the educational impact of these technologies. In this chapter, I describe how the questions addressed by educational technology researchers have expanded over the past 80 years. In the sections that follow, I summarize efforts to study educational technologies prior to the desktop computer. I then discuss challenges that desktop computers present to research and describe strategies that researchers have employed to overcome these challenges.

RESEARCH ON FILM AND EDUCATIONAL TECHNOLOGY: 1910–1980

Although formal schooling in the United States dates back several centuries, the first formal research in education was not conducted until 1887 when Joseph Rice began to study the effect of different methods of teaching spelling (Madaus & O'Dwyer, 1999). Thirty years later, the first large-scale study of an educational technology was initiated. Designed to measure the effects of silent film in schools, the 1922 Freeman Commonwealth

Technology and Assessment: The Tale of Two Interpretations, pages 153–177
Copyright © 2006 by Information Age Publishing
153

study focused on eight school systems in Chicago and involved more than 5,000 students (Saettler, 1990).

Since the Freeman Commonwealth study, research on film, typewriters, radio, television and learning machines has focused on four categories of research questions. Initially, the questions focused on how many teachers were using a given technology, how often, and to what effect on student learning. Recognizing that answers to the third question often varied widely within and between studies, researchers expanded their focus from pure learning outcome measures (e.g., differences in test scores) to documenting changes in teaching and learning processes within the classroom. During the 1930s and 1940s, these efforts focused on changes in student attitudes, participation, and engagement in classroom discussions. With the introduction of learning machines in the 1950s and 1960s, researchers began to focus more closely on the learning process in an effort to better understand how learning machines could fit into this process and make it more efficient.

To address these four categories of questions, research on these 20th century educational technologies generally employed four methods, including (a) survey research, (b) quasi-experiments, (c) mixed methods, and (d) case studies. Below, I describe these methods and provide examples of research that employed each method.

Survey Research

Surveys were used to collect information about how often teachers used a given technology in the classroom. The first major survey of teachers was conducted by the Eastman Kodak Company in 1923. This survey was designed to document the extent to which teachers were using the educational films available at the time and investigated the size of the market for these films. Based on the results of this survey, Eastman Kodak decided to produce a set of 60 of educational films.

In 1933, the National Elementary Principal's Association also surveyed teachers about their instructional use of silent films. The survey was administered in 366 schools and showed that silent films were used in 52% of the schools. This survey was repeated on a larger scale in 1946 and 1954. Based on the survey results, Cuban (1986) concluded that, although most schools had collections of films, teachers used films infrequently as part of their instruction.

During the 1920s and 1930s, survey research was also conducted on educational uses of radio. These surveys focused on radio usage and opinions regarding ways in which radio listening "furthers the objectives of education" (Woelfel & Tyler, 1945, p. 23). While this survey research documented the extent to which radio and film were being used, it provided little insight into the effects these technologies had on student learning. In addition, the radio and the film surveys were not designed to help researchers understand the challenges that teachers encountered when using the technology and could not explain why usage was low.

Quasi-Experiments

Quasi-experiments designed to measure the impact of educational technology on student learning were popular during the 1920s and 1930s. In many cases, these studies were very large by today's standards and included more than 10,000 students. The largest of these studies were conducted by Ben Wood of Columbia and Frank Freeman of the University of Chicago. Freeman conducted the first of these experiments in 1922. Funded by the Commonwealth Fund of New York and by the Society for Visual Education, the study found that film could be useful in the classroom for certain subject areas, specifically for delivering content that involved motion.

Six years later, Wood and Freeman (1929) collaborated to study the series of 60 films produced by the Eastman Kodak Company. This experiment focused on students in grades 4–9 and was conducted in schools in twelve cities, with almost 11,000 students and 1,200 teachers. As part of the study, a set of films, textbooks and specific lesson plans were developed which teachers in the experimental group were to follow. Teachers in the control classes were asked to teach similar lessons, using any tool except film. Tests that focused on the content of the lessons were administered to all students before and after each set of lessons. Wood and Freeman found that the experimental group significantly outperformed the control group.

Wood and Freeman collaborated again in 1929 to investigate the usefulness of the typewriter in schools. Pre- and posttests, teacher surveys and student letters were all used to collect information about the impacts of using typewriters in schools. More than 1,800 students in eight cities participated in the experiment. But classes were not randomly assigned to treatment and control groups. Instead "the superintendents designated certain schools to serve as Experimental, and other schools to serve as control schools" (Wood & Freeman, 1932, p. 6). This experiment spanned two years and researchers found that student writing improved and that both teachers and students had a positive attitude toward using typewriters in school.

Although research studies in the 1920s and 1930s most often used experimental strategies and were relatively large in scale, there were several problems with the way that these experimental techniques were employed. Typical experimental studies first assigned students to experimental and control groups, then the experimental group was exposed to the educational technology media. All students were given tests before and after exposure to the educational technology. Differences in test scores between the groups were intended to show the effects of the treatment, which was usually exposure to educational technology. But random assignment of students to experimental and control groups was most often not possible. As a result, it was difficult to assess the extent to which the process of selecting classrooms might have biased results. Cuban (1986) also raises concerns about the extent to which socioeconomic status was controlled for when selecting classrooms and schools for the experimental and control groups. It was also difficult to control the implementation of the treatment to ensure standardization between treatment and control groups. In addition, many of the outcome measures used to examine changes in student learning were "home grown" and lacked evidence of validity and reliability. Saettler (1990) identifies another problem with experimental studies on film by stating that much of the film's effectiveness is based on the quality of the individual film, not on film as a form of educational technology. Therefore, the results of the 30 documented experiments on film in the 1930s vary drastically in terms of the quality and application of the individual film. As a result, the findings of each study cannot be generalized to other films. Finally, Cuban (1986) raised concerns that researchers too often mistook correlational findings as cause-and-effect relationships. This concern may be warranted given that when random assignment was possible and tests were well constructed, it was found that there were not significant differences between the technology-based teaching and the teaching in the controlled classroom.

Although research on television focused on "social, psychological, and instructional effects of broadcast television in less formal environments" (Seels, Berry, Fullerton, & Horn, 1996, p. 304), the vast majority of research on the use of television in classrooms also employed experimental techniques to examine impacts on learning outcomes. Most of the early television research that studied effects of television on student performance had methodological problems similar to the film and radio studies and usually found no significant difference in student learning. "In approximately four hundred quantitative studies in which television instruction was compared to conventional instruction[it was found] that students in some cases will learn more, and in some, less" (Saettler, 1990, p. 426).

Similarly, one line of research on learning machines also relied heavily on quasi-experimental designs. As an example, the first major field study involving learning machines was conducted in Roanoke, Virginia. The Carnegie Foundation funded this work, and the machines and programs were developed through collaboration between Encyclopedia Britannica Films and Hollins College. More than 900 ninth-grade students participated in the field study research. Three groups of students were formed: students who were only taught by programmed instruction, students who were only taught by a teacher, and students who were taught using a combination of traditional teachers instruction and programmed instruction. The results were mixed and the study did not control for extraneous variables.

Mixed Methods

In addition to the methodological shortcomings of the experimental designs used to study film, radio, typewriters, and television, experimental designs provided little insight into why these technologies may or may not have an impact on student learning. In essence, these studies treated classroom instruction as a "black box" into which a technology is placed and an outcome is or is not produced. In an effort to develop an understanding of both the outcome and the reasons for the outcome, some researchers used a combination of measures collected before and after instruction, as well as data collected during instruction.

As an example, in 1927, researchers at Yale initiated a study that examined the effects of sound films on student learning in 15 seventh-grade history classes. In addition to measuring student learning through tests, surveys were used to collect information about students' attitudes. Classroom observations also occurred in eight of the classrooms to collect information about how student engagement was affected by films. During the observations, trained observers counted the number of students who raised their hand in response to a question and recorded the student responses. To examine effects on retention of knowledge, follow up tests were administered three to six months after the experimental film lessons were given. Results from the experiment showed that by using sound film, student learning and class participation increased. Although this experiment was on a relatively small scale compared to the Wood and Freeman study, it was one of the first studies on educational technology that combined three sources of data to examine impact on both learning and behaviors in the classroom.

Like the Yale study, a series of studies which became known as the Payne Fund Studies also focused on a variety of effects of film on learning. These areas included information, attitudes, emotions, health, and conduct (Saettler, 1990). Both the Yale and Payne Fund Studies, however, were rare examples of research on film that combined multiple methods to examine multiple effects. As Hoban and Van Ormer report in their 1950 review of research on film conducted between 1918 and 1950, most studies employed quasi-experimental designs in which teaching with films was compared to traditional teaching and student learning as measured by a content-specific test was the primary outcome measure (Spencer, 1999).

Case Studies

Although experimental designs were used to examine the effect of teaching machines in some classrooms, a separate line of research relied heavily on small case studies to develop an understanding of how teaching machines support the learning process. As Saettler (1990) describes, these case studies were conducted outside of the classroom in a laboratory setting and focused on individual students rather than classrooms of students. These case studies examined such factors as pace of learning, the role of reinforcement, size of increments of instruction, and immediate feedback. Unlike experimental designs that were intended to examine the average impact of teaching machines on student learning, case studies were employed to develop an understanding of the learning process and to design teaching machines that would maximize learning.

In the late 1960s and early 1970s, television research experienced a similar shift in focus from average effects to identifying "individual variables, media characteristics and the interaction between viewer characteristics and television effects" (Seels et al., 1996, p. 306). Cognitive scientists played a large role in this change of direction in educational technology research. This shift caused research to be less focused on the outcomes of what students learn from the media and more focused on the process of how students learn from the media. The technique most commonly used in these studies is called aptitude-treatment interaction (ATI) research which attempted to match student characteristics with mode of teaching in order to identify how different types of students could best learn. In essence, aspects of the media were being studied in relation to the learning environment, instead of just studying the specific media itself. This type of research was revolutionary in combining the fields of psychology with scientific research. But in 1977, Cronbach and Snow, who were the primary experts developing the ATI methodology admitted that their findings on similar studies were inconsistent (Martinez, 2002, p. 2). The complexity of relationships between individual student learning styles and aspects of learning media was difficult to model in research.

THE DESKTOP COMPUTER

The introduction of the desktop computer to the classroom greatly expanded the role educational technology could play in the classroom.

Whereas film, radio, and television were controlled by the teacher, desktop computers allowed students to access and be in direct control of multiple types of media. Although students were in direct contact with learning systems, this contact generally occurred outside of the classroom in a laboratory setting. With desktop computers, tutorial and computer-assisted learning systems were brought directly into the classroom. Similarly, desktop computers brought word processors directly into the classroom and provided students with a wealth of additional productivity and information tools. In addition, whereas film, radio, television, typewriters (briefly), and learning systems were placed into schools in order to support discrete areas of an existing curriculum without any pretense of affecting the actual process of teaching and learning, some educational reformers saw desktop computers and the Internet as a vehicle for reforming the educational process.

The wide variety of ways in which computers are used in schools coupled with the rapid pace of change in the capabilities of computers greatly expanded the range of research questions posed about technology and presented several challenges to the assessment of their educational impact. Below, I describe some of these challenges and then examine the variety of methods researchers have employed in an effort to overcome these challenges. As an aid to discussing the challenges to studying technology, I use a study released by Angrist and Lavy (2001) which garnered significant attention in the press as an example of research that falls short of meeting these several challenges. This study, titled "New Evidence on Classroom Computers and Pupil Learning" uses test scores collected from a large sample of Israeli students to assess the impact of a national program that placed computers in schools at a ratio of 1 computer for every 10 students. The test data was collected from students in the schools that received these computers and in those that did not. In addition, the Mathematics and Hebrew tests were administered at the end of the year in which the majority of the computer schools received their new computers.

Computers are Toolboxes

Despite their many uses, policy makers, the general public and some researchers often focus their questions about educational technology on the measurable impact of computers on student learning. As an example, Angrist and Lavy (2001) attempted to estimate "the impact of computerization on both the instructional use of computers and pupil achievement" (p. 1). This question implies that a computer is a single or discrete tool, the impact of which can be measured and summarized in a universal manner. Computers, however, are toolboxes that contain many different software applications or tools. When schools invest in computers, they generally do so not because of any one tool, but to make use of a variety of tools. Although teachers or students may only work with one tool at a time, over the course of the school year teachers and students use a variety of different computer-based tools. Some of these tools are designed to have a direct impact on student learning, others are intended to increase productivity, while others indirectly support teaching and learning outside of the classroom. Thus, one challenge to assessing the educational impact of computers is shifting the focus from the computer to the specific uses of the computer. Rather than asking how have computers impacted education, the focus should be on how a specific use or combination of uses of computers have affected a specific aspect or aspects of education.

Aligning Outcome Measures with Instructional Uses of Computers

Aligning outcome measures with the aspects of learning a computer-based tool is believed to affect presents a major challenge. In many cases, researchers use existing measures, like standardized tests, to assess the impact of computers on student learning. This strategy was at the heart of Angrist and Lavy (2001) study, which used student test scores on Israel's national Hebrew and Mathematics standardized tests as the outcome measure for the impact of computers on student learning. While standardized test scores can be useful for comparing performance or changes in performance across large samples of students, the domain tested by most standardized tests is defined broadly. As an example, the National Assessment of Educational Progress 8th Grade Mathematics test includes items from several sub-domains, including number sense, probability and statistics, algebra, and geometry. Similarly, off-the-shelf tests like the Iowa Test of Basic Skills tests cover a domain broadly.

In many classrooms, however, a computer-based tool is used to develop knowledge and skill in a single area of the curriculum. As just one example, an evaluation of a Massachusetts school district revealed that most third- and fourth-grade teachers in this district use computers as a part of their mathematics instruction to help students develop spatial reasoning skills (Russell, 2000). However, on the state's fourth grade test (MCAS), only two of the 39 released items relate to spatial reasoning. For this reason, it would be tenuous, at best, for this district to use changes in MCAS total scores to examine the impact of computer use on students' math achievement.

Similarly, most mathematics tests include items that test students' mathematical problem solving skills. Typically, these items take the form of word problems for which students must define a function that represents the relationship described, plug in the appropriate numbers, and perform accurate computations. While it is important for students to develop these mathematical problem-solving skills, these skills are not what advocates of computer use envision when they discuss the potential impacts of computers on students' problem solving skills.

Problem solving with computers is more than just decoding text to define functions. As Dwyer (1996) describes, when developing problem-solving skills with computers, "students are encouraged to critically assess data, to discover relationships and patterns, to compare and contrast, to transform information into something new" (p. 18). To help students assimilate, organize, and present their learning, some teachers have students use HyperCard and other multimedia tools.

After studying HyperCard use in a small set of ACOT classrooms, Tierney (1996) concluded:

> Technology appears to have increased the likelihood of students' being able to pursue multiple lines of thought and entertain different perspectives. Ideas were no longer treated as unidimensional and sequential; the technology allowed students to embed ideas within other ideas, as well as pursue other forms of multilayering and interconnecting ideas. Students began spending a great deal of time considering layout, that is, how the issues that they were wrestling with might be explored across an array of still pictures, video segments, text segments, and sound clips. (p. 176)

These findings are echoed by teachers in other schools. After studying technology use across classrooms in one school district, Russell (2000) wrote:

> In addition to exposing students to a larger body of information related to the topic of study, creating HyperStudio stacks also requires students to more carefully plan how they integrate and present this information. As one teacher explains, "First they do the research and identify what it is they want to include in their stack. They then create a flow chart that depicts how the pieces fit together. They sketch their stack on paper and then begin putting it into the computer." Through this process, students develop their planning skills and learn to anticipate how information will be received by their audience. (p. 11)

Despite the skill development enabled by HyperCard and other multimedia authoring tools, students who develop complex, high quality products using HyperCard do not necessarily perform well on current tests. While studying the impact of computers on student learning in the Apple Classrooms of Tomorrow project, Baker et al. (1996) found that "...a sizeable portion of students who used HyperCard well to express their understanding of principles, themes, facts, and relationships were so-so or worse performers judged by more traditional forms of testing" (p. 198). Over the past decade these and similar findings have led proponents of computer use in schools to conclude that technology enables students to develop new competencies, "some of which were not being captured by traditional assessment measures" (Fisher et al., 1996, p. 5).

In short, when examining the impact of technology on student learning, it is critical that the outcome measure or measures actually assess the types of learning that may occur, and that those measures are sensitive enough to detect potential changes in learning.

Specifying Computer Use

A third major challenge to researching the impact of computers in schools is to place the specific uses of computers within the context of the educational process. As described earlier, Airasian (1997) suggests that the prevailing conception of education is that of a process that helps change students in desirable ways (see also Popham, 1988; Tyler, 1949). In this model of education, teaching and learning begins with a curriculum that is delivered through instruction. Airasian further divides the instructional process into three interrelated components: Planning Instruction, Delivering Instruction, and Assessing Learning Outcomes. Teachers refer to the curriculum during the planning phase to determine what they are to teach, and then select instructional methods they believe will best help foster desired pupil changes. These methods are then applied while delivering instruction. During and following the delivery of instruction, teachers assess students to determine whether they have mastered the desired curriculum goals (Airasian, 1997). As Figure 10.1 depicts, within this model of education, computer-based tools play three primary roles which include (a) defining aspects of the curriculum, (b) providing instructional tools, and (c) supporting productivity and communications.

As Figure 10.1 depicts, there are multiple entry points for computer-based tools into the model of education. At the highest level, computer-based tools may lead to the creation of new curricular goals. In this way, computer-based tools may help define what it is students are expected to know and be able to do. Within the classroom, computer-based tools may be used during instruction to help students develop skills related to subject-area curriculum. That is, computer-based tools are used to help students develop skills and knowledge defined by the curriculum. Surrounding the model, computer-based tools help teachers be more productive by supporting communications, access to information, and the development of instructional materials.

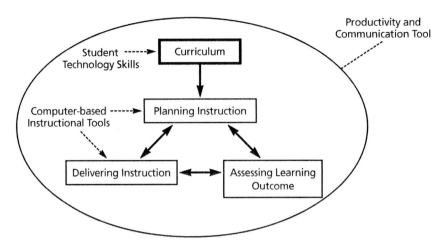

Figure 10.1.   How computer-based tools fit into the model of education.

At first brush, it might appear relatively easy to determine how a computer-based tool fits into the educational process. Yet, when schools acquire computers, school leaders are often unclear what they expect technology to do within their schools (Herman, 1994; Russell, 2001). As Rockman's (2000) observations of technology evaluation planning sessions reflect, educators express outcomes in general terms when asked to describe the desired impact of technology upon students. They state that technology will improve thinking skills, authentic learning, collaboration, and that it will help students become independent learners, good problem solvers, and active participants in the new economy. However, when asked how specific computer-based tools affect these desired outcomes, educators are unclear.

The lack of specificity is also evident in the way many researchers define computer use. As an example, Angrist and Lavy (2001) presented teachers with the following survey questions:

Which of the following do you use when teaching?
    Xeroxed worksheets
    Instructional booklet
    Games
    Computer software or instructional computer programs
    TV programs
    Other audio-visual materials

For each item, teachers responded:
    not at all
    sometimes
    frequently
    almost always

Each teacher's response to how often "computer software or instructional computer programs" served as the measure of instructional use of computers for Mathematics or Hebrew.

While it may be reasonable to infer that a teacher who indicates that they use computer software or instructional computer programs "frequently" employs different instructional practices than the teacher who responds "not at all," this single item does not provide sufficient information about how, when, why, or who is actually using the computers. As a result, a teacher who uses PowerPoint several times a week to present information that otherwise would be presented using an overhead projector will appear to use a computer more than the teacher who has students work for thirty minutes twice a week on a mathematics tutorial. Similarly, this measure of computer use makes this second teacher appear the same as a third teacher who might also have students use a computer twice a week for 30 minutes to collect data, create spreadsheets, and create graphs to explore relationships in the data. Finally, the teacher who uses computers daily outside of class to create worksheets or record grades might appear to be the most frequent computer user. As Bebell, Russell, and O'Dwyer (2004) demonstrate, teachers' use of computers is not unidimensional. For this reason, a single or even small set of survey items often provide inadequate measures of computer use.

Essential Conditions for Implementation

Once the use of a computer-based tool is placed within the educational process and a specific measure of this use is developed, a fourth challenge is to identify the conditions that must be established before meaningful effects can reasonably occur. Depending upon the computer-based tool, these enabling conditions might include: (a) providing access to equipment, software and other physical infrastructure such as the Internet or servers; (b) professional development; (c) time for teachers to learn how to use the tool; (d) time for teachers to work with other teachers or curriculum technology specialists to develop lessons that incorporate the computer-based tool into instruction; (e) time for students to develop the essential skills to make use of the tool; and (f) sufficient time for teachers to improve these lessons. Unless the conditions believed necessary for successful use of the computer-based tool are provided and it is established that the tool is actually being used, it is premature to examine the impact the tool has on the intended outcome.

When examining the impact of a computer-based tool, it is also important to consider the extent to which the tool is readily accessible to students and teachers, and used by a critical mass of students, teachers or both. As an example, Angrist and Lavy (2001) assume that the installation of computers at a ratio of 10 students per computer provided sufficient access to the computer-based tools. Moreover, they assume that the mere installation of computers led to use by students. Recent research, however, suggests that the ratio of students to computer-based tools has a large impact on the extent to which the tools are used. In their study of Alpha-Smarts in the fourth-grade classrooms, Russell, Bebell, Cowan and Corbelli (2003) found that use of AlphaSmarts for writing increased noticeably when the ratio of students to AlphaSmarts was increased from about 3:1 to 1:1. Interestingly, this increased use was largest in the classrooms taught by teachers who employed less constructivist instructional practices and were initially less comfortable having students work with AlphaSmarts and computers. Beyond increasing the amount of student use of AlphaSmarts for writing, the increased ratio also decreased the amount of time teachers spent managing student use of the technology and increased the amount of time they spent working directly with students on their writing. Given the complex relationship between presence, access, use, and a teacher's role in the classroom, simply establishing that technology is present is not sufficient for measuring how often and in what ways a computer-based tool is used. Without understanding how and how often a tool is used, it is difficult to assess the impact of that tool on the intended outcome.

Shifting Goals and Rapid Evolution

Although schools purchase technology to enhance teaching and learning, when a piece of technology is first introduced, schools are often unsure how to use the technology in order to have an impact upon teaching and learning. It is not until teachers have had multiple opportunities to work with the new technology that they begin to develop a sense of how to use the technology or how it can have an impact upon teaching and learning. At the same time, new technologies are continually emerging and being added to the program. As a technology program matures, new possibilities for instruction and learning constantly emerge (Baker et al., 1998). As Herman (1994) explains, this makes "the goals of technology [programs] and technology's potential effects on students into moving targets; evaluators may carefully set their sights on evaluating the achievement of one goal, only to find that changes in teacher expectations about technology or in technical capabilities have led to substantial modifications in a desired outcome" (p. 150).

The time required for teachers and students to become acquainted to teaching and learning with a new computer-based tool, however, may result in an initial decrease in efficiency and productivity. But, as teachers and students become accustomed to working with the tool and learn how to integrate it with their other teaching and learning strategies, efficiency and productivity increase. For this reason, it is important to provide sufficient time for teachers and students to become accustomed to working with the new technology before assessing its educational value. Too often, however, studies like Angrist and Lavy's (2001) attempt to measure impacts during the first year of implementation and draw conclusions about the impacts based on data collected over a short period of time. While such studies provide insight into the initial affects of a new computer-based tool, they miss any long term effects (positive or negative) that may result.

GENERAL STRATEGIES FOR EVALUATING TECHNOLOGY PROGRAMS

To date, the research community has recommended several strategies that researchers might employ to overcome some of these challenges. To capture the wide variety of impacts technology can have on teaching and learning, multiple measures are recommended. "These should include traditional experimental and quasi-experimental designs and include such methods as paper surveys, email/web-based surveys, informal and in-depth interviews, focus group interviews, classroom observations and document analysis" (Heinecke, Blasi, Milman, & Washington, 1999). In addition, Bodilly and Mitchell (1997) recommend that data collection focus on a wide variety of outcomes including test scores, dropout rates, discipline referrals, homework assignments, college applications, and entry into the workplace.

Given the difficulty some districts have in defining specific goals for technology use, Knott (1993) suggests that researchers and evaluators set aside goals-based approaches to investigating computer-based educational technology and instead adopt Scirven's (1972) concept of goals-free evaluation. Rather than comparing the effects of technology programs to stated goals, a goals-free approach compares outcomes to the needs of those who are impacted by the intervention. From Knott's (1993) perspective, "According to most of the America 2000 and other educational reform literature, attempts at reformation should be unrestrained and unrestrictive in order to ensure that no viable solution is missed" (pp. 803–804). To protect against missing an effect "simply because it was not included in the stated goal" (p. 804), Knott advocates a goals-free approach to technology evaluation.

While it is important to focus on outcomes, pre-specified or otherwise, Baker (1999) and Herman (1994) urge that implementation be examined along with impact. As Herman describes, teachers often adapt computer-based tools to their instruction in different ways. These adaptations lead to various levels of implementation. Before outcomes can be attributed to the use of a computer-based tool, an understanding and documentation of implementation is needed (Heinecke et al., 1999).

To capture the full impact of technology on teaching and learning, Goldman-Segal (1998) suggests that the researchers consider both the effects with and the effects of technology. Summarizing the thoughts of Salomon, Perkins, and Globerson (1991), Goldmann-Segal (1998) distinguishes between "effects with" and "effects of" in this way: "*Effects with* occur when people work with technologies—the technology becomes a partner that can do things people cannot, whereas *effects of* occur when 'cognitive residue' can be used after we stop working with a technology" (p. 52, italics in the original).

With this distinction, changes in student learning, both in traditional subject areas and in the acquisition of computer competencies, represent desired effects of technology. Changes in how schools function and in instructional and learning practices are effects with technology. Since both "effects of" and "effects with" influence a school's decision to acquire educational technology, both types of effects should be considered during the research process.

Finally, as McNabb et al. (1999) note, "Standardized test scores have become the accepted measure with which policymakers and the public gauge the benefits of educational investments" (p. 4). However, there is growing evidence that standardized test scores do not provide valid measures of the types of learning impacted by computer-based tools (see Russell & Plati, 2000 for a review of some of this evidence). Although some researchers advocate the development of new assessment instruments (Means et al., 2001; Russell, 2002), others suggest that other methods for examining student learning be employed (Heinecke et al., 1999). In either case, it is clear that research on technology must reach beyond current standardized test scores to examine the impact computer-based tools have on student learning.

Collectively, the research community is urging technology research to employ a variety of data-collection methods to examine both the implementation and the intended and unintended consequences of technology on a variety of areas of schooling.

RESEARCH METHODS AND THE DESKTOP COMPUTER

Just as the introduction of the desktop computer sparked an explosion in the ways in which computers were used in schools, the methods used to examine the impact of computers in schools has also expanded. As described earlier, surveys and quasi-experimental designs that focused almost exclusively on learning outcomes measured by pre- and posttests were the two methods most often used to assess the use and impact of film, typewriters, television, and early computers. In general, research conducted on these early instructional technologies focused on two questions: (a) how extensively is a given technology being used; and (b) how is a given technology impacting student learning. While these two questions are asked often of desktop computers in schools, the power and flexibility of today's computer-based tools have led to several additional questions which range in focus from impact on specific sub-populations of students to impacts on instructional practices and classroom culture and to the factors that influence teacher and student use of computer-based tools.

In general, research on computer-based technologies in schools has evolved into two lines of research. The first focuses on the development and effects of computer-based tools on student learning. The second line of research examines effects with technology and attempts to document conditions that support uses of technology that have potential to alter pedagogical practices and school culture. Within each of these lines of research, a variety of methodologies have been employed. While there is not room here to examine the vast body of research that has been conducted since the introduction of the desktop computer, common questions and methodologies employed within each line of research are summarized below.

Development and *Effects of* Computer-Based Tools

As personal computers penetrated K–12 schools, researchers have explored a wide variety of ways to use computers to support the learning process. In some cases, these uses focus on productivity tools, such as word processors, hypermedia authoring software, or spreadsheets. In other cases, this research has focused on software designed to help students develop an understanding of specific topics. And in still other cases, the focus has been on information and data collection tools, such CD ROM-based encyclopedias, the Internet, science probes, or Global Positioning System (GPS). Despite the wide variety of computer-based tools that have been examined, this line of research is united by a focus on how a tool can be used to increase student learning in a relatively specific area.

In general, this line of research can be divided into two phases. During the first phase, case studies that often include close collaboration between the researcher and a limited number of classroom teachers are performed to explore ways to use a specific tool to help students develop a specific set of skills and knowledge. For example, in an effort to help seven- and eight-year-olds develop a better understanding of line graphs, McFarlane, Friedler, Warwick, and Chaplain (1995) undertook a small-scale study that examined the use of probes to collect data and accompanying software to graph data. This research occurred in a small number of elementary class-rooms, in which the researchers worked with the teachers to use the probes and software. The study reported the experience of introducing the new technology into the classroom and also included a comparison of pre- and posttest results to examine changes in student learning.

Similarly, Ramirez and Althouse (1995) developed and examined the Palm Beach County Geographic Information System (GIS) Project which employed ArcView software to help students examine various environmen-tal issues. The project involved ten teachers from six high schools who received training on the software and then worked with the researchers to develop a two-semester curriculum that employed the software. Each teacher then implemented his or her curriculum and the ways in which the software was used within each curriculum to help students develop an understanding of environmental sciences was examined. Like these two examples, the primary purpose of research conducted during this first phase is to develop an understanding of *how* a given computer-based tool or set of tools can be used to help students develop skills and knowledge.

In many cases, these first phase studies are followed by more formal efforts to examine the *effect of* a given tool on student learning. As an exam-ple, research conducted during the mid-1980s initially addressed the ques-tion, "Can word processors be used to help students develop writing skills?" Following initial investigations which documented that students could use word processors in school, more than 200 studies have been conducted to examine the effects of using word processors on the quantity and quality of student writing. (See Cochran-Smith, Paris & Kahn, 1991; Bangert-Drowns, 1993; Goldberg, Russell, & Cook, 2002 for a review of these studies.) Simi-larly, following the development and piloting of several different com-puter-based tutorials, a large number of studies have examined the effects of these tutorials on student learning (Kulik, 1994).

Typically, a combination of qualitative methods, including observations, interviews, and examination of work products, are used during phase-one studies. While some studies conducted when a new technology is intro-duced to a classroom also include formal measures of student learning, the primary focus on these early studies is to explore the utility and practicality of using the technology. Once it has been demonstrated that the technol-ogy can be used to support learning, the focus shifts to examining the mea-surable effects on student learning. In many cases, measures of student learning are collected before and after the technology is used and changes in scores are used to assess the impact on student learning. In some cases, pre- and post-measures are collected in classrooms that use the technology and in classrooms that do not. However, as is documented later in this chapter, these studies often employ convenience samples as opposed to randomly selected or randomly assigned groups. In the vast majority of cases, these comparative studies involve relatively small numbers of classrooms or students.

Essential Conditions and *Effects With* Technology

Beyond affecting discrete skills and knowledge, some advocates of technology in schools believe that the use of computer-based technologies has the potential to affect the process of education. To this end, a substantial body of research has examined a variety of ways in which the use of technology alters the types of skills and knowledge students develop while working with computers, pedagogical practices employed by teachers, and changes in classroom and school culture. In an effort to spur such changes, this line of research has also examined the conditions that support or inhibit uses of technology that can lead to such changes.

In general, research that focuses on *effects with* technology and the conditions that support such effects, has relied primarily on case studies and, to a lesser degree, survey research. In some cases, this research has placed substantial amounts of technology into classrooms and then examined how instructional practices and classroom culture have changed in response to the presence and use of technology. Perhaps the best example of this research strategy is the Apple Classrooms of Tomorrow (ACOT) project, which conducted research over several years in a small number of schools that were equipped with then-state-of-the-art computer-technologies. Through a series of case studies involving interviews, observations and analyses of student work, researchers documented changes in the types of learning students developed, interactions between students and teachers, and changes in pedagogical practices (Fisher et al., 1996).

In other cases, researchers examine classrooms that contain technology purchased by the school or district (as opposed to being placed in the classroom by the researchers or an outside agency). As an example, Schofield (1995) examined computer use in a large urban high school for two years. Initially, her primary research question focused on the effect of computer use on students and on classroom social processes. To address this question, she conducted an extensive case study involving classroom observations and repeated interviews with students and teachers. As her research progressed, Schofield discovered that while computer use did indeed affect classroom culture, contextual factors also had important effects on how computers were used. As she writes in her conclusion, "things as varied as the name given to a computer course, the physical location of the computers within a room, or the extent to which students are allowed or encouraged to assist each other while working on the computers can have their own impact" (p. 226). This finding led to a dual focus on how computers affect student learning and how these effects are moderated by contextual factors, many of which can be altered by teachers and schools in order to increase the effects computer use have on teaching and learning.

In still other cases, researchers develop a model for change that intentionally alters conditions in hopes of increasing various types of computer use and pedagogical practices. As an example, Hunter's (1998) Vanguard for Learning Project was based on a model of change that included teachers working together in small teams to develop projects that integrated technology into the curriculum over an extended period of time. To support these teacher teams, access to technology, content, and assessment experts was provided both in person and via electronic communications. In addition, teachers were equipped with technology that met the needs of their specific project and had easy access to technical support. Finally, efforts were made to involve the school community in the technology projects by tapping local expertise and by creating projects to help solve local problems. The research team worked with a small number of schools in a single district to implement the reform model and then examined the effects of the model on technology use, teaching practices, school and community culture, and, in some cases, on student learning. Thus, the model employed by the Vanguard for Learning Project sought to create several conditions believed to be essential for supporting instructional uses of computers. Among these conditions were teacher collaboration, community involvement, access to technology that met teachers' needs, technical support, and access to expertise.

Conditions that influence the use of technology have also been examined via survey research. Perhaps the best-known example is the Teaching, Learning and Computing (TLC) survey study conducted by Becker and his colleagues in 1998 (Becker, 1999; Ravitz, Wong, & Becker, 1998, 1999). The TLC study involved a nationally representative sample of teachers and focused on both the extent to which teachers use various technologies and the factors that influence these uses. Among the factors Becker found that moderate instructional uses of technology were teachers' pedagogical beliefs, beliefs about technology, technology skills, professional development history, educational background, access to technology, use of technology outside of school, principal support, and school culture. Although this line of research does not provide direct evidence of how technology use impacts students and their learning, it provides insight into the factors schools can alter in order to increase instructional uses of technology believed to impact student learning. In addition, this survey research compliments and, in many cases, validates findings from case studies.

Together, research that focuses on effects of and effects with technology provide a complex picture of the conditions required to support instructional uses of technology, the different types of changes in practices and culture that can arise through different uses of technology, and the resulting impacts on student learning.

RESEARCH ON COMPUTERS AND WRITING, READING, AND SCIENCE

To develop a fuller understanding of the types of questions researchers have sought to answer and the methods used to address these questions, it is useful to examine research that has focused on the use of computers within specific subject areas. To this end, a sample of studies were selected and then used to summarize the range of research questions and methodologies used to examine technology in schools over the past decade. More specifically, the studies summarized below focus on computers and, science, reading, or writing. Studies that focus on writing were included in a meta-analysis on computers and writing conducted by Goldberg, Russell, and Cook (2002). For this meta-analysis, 103 research articles that appeared to focus on the effects of computers on writing were found. Of these, 38 were not original research, but instead presented theoretical uses of computers for writing or were summaries of previous research. Thus, the summary presented here focuses on 65 writing articles

The studies that focus on science and reading were found by searching the Educational Resources Information Center (ERIC) database using the following keywords: [subject] and computers; [subject] and instruction and research; and [subject] and technology (where subject was science or reading). This search resulted in 98 articles related to reading and 25 articles that focused on science.

The summary presented below focuses on two issues: (a) the range of research questions examined, and (b) the range of methodologies employed. To be clear, this summary is based on a small sample of studies and is not intended to represent all of the research conducted over the past decade. For the reading and science studies, several characteristic of each study were classified, as indicated in Table 10.1.

For the writing studies, the classification system employed by Goldberg, Russell, and Cook (2002) was used. Among several additional characteristics, this classification system included: Random Assignment, Pre/Post design, standardized writing conditions, length of intervention, sample size, grade level, measure of prior keyboarding skill, and intervening factors such as feedback, collaboration, peer-editing, type of hardware used, etc.

Table 10.1.   Study Characteristics

Random Assignment	Whether participants were randomly assigned to groups
Sample Size	Number of participants
Number of Classrooms	Number of classrooms from which participants were selected
Number of Schools	Number of schools from which participants were selected
Number of Districts	Number of districts from which participants were selected
Grade Levels	Grade level of participants
Formal Learning Outcome	Whether or not a formal outcome measure of learning was employed (e.g., standardized test, grades, common writing assignment, etc.)
Attitudinal Methods	Whether or not a measure of student or teacher attitude was employed
Quantitative Methods	Whether or not quantitative methods were used to analyze data
Qualitative Methods	Whether or not qualitative methods were used to analyze data
Length of Intervention	Amount of time during which the use of a specific technology was examined

Reading and Computers

An initial search of ERIC resulted in 98 studies related to reading and computers. From these 98 studies, a sample of 50 was randomly selected and each study was reviewed. Of those 50 selected studies, 19 were excluded because they either were not research-based or did not apply to our topic: Using technology to teach reading to students in Grades K–12.

Across the 31 studies, research questions generally focused on three aspects of computers and reading: (a) improvement in reading achievement, (b) increasing student interest in reading, and (c) assisting students with special needs or underdeveloped reading skills.

Of the 31 studies that qualified for our review, 27 collected data directly from students, 4 collected data from teachers, and 2 collected data from both students and teachers. Sample sizes varied widely from six students to a national sample of students in Grades 4 and 8 (employing National Assessment of Educational Process [NAEP] data). Nonetheless, 19 of the 31 studies (61%) focused on samples of less than 100 students. Most of the studies (58%) also did not randomly assign students to treatment groups.

With respect to the number of classrooms, schools and districts that participated in the research, ten studies did not specify any information about the number of classrooms. Six of the studies occurred in one classroom, five occurred in two or three classrooms, while two occurred in more than ten classrooms. Of the 27 studies that indicated the number of participating schools, 16 (59%) occurred in a single school, five (19%) occurred in two schools, and three occurred in more than 10 schools. Similarly, the vast majority of the studies (81%) occurred in a single district.

Although several reports did not include information on specific grades, 26 of the projects conducted research in Grades K–8, with seven studies occurring in fifth grade and five studies in third and fourth grade. Only seven studies targeted "high school," "secondary school," or Grades 9–12.

Seventy-one percent of the studies employed quantitative methods with 61% including formal measures of student learning. Forty-two percent of the studies employed qualitative methods, which generally included classroom observations and interviews of teachers, students, or both. Thirteen percent employed a combination of quantitative and qualitative methods. Only two of the studies that employed qualitative methods also collected information about student learning while 69% of the studies employing qualitative methods included an attitudinal measure. Of the 31 studies, only 3 included both a formal learning outcome measure and an attitudinal measure, and only one included both measures and employed both quantitative and qualitative methods. The most frequent length of research was 3 years (7 studies), followed by 1 year (6 studies).

In summary, most research projects used a quasi-experimental design to focus on a small sample of students in one elementary school classroom with the goal to improve learning.

Science and Computers

A search of ERIC resulted in 25 research articles related to science and computers. After reviewing each article, three were found to be conceptual papers or summaries of prior research.

Across the 22 studies, research questions generally focused on 4 aspects of computers and science: (a) improvement in science achievement; (b) enhancing instruction through the use of technology; (c) improving students' attitudes toward science; and (d) teachers' attitudes toward using technology during science instruction.

Of the 22 studies that qualified for this review, 68% collected data directly from students, 36% collected data from teachers, and 9% collected data from both students and teachers. Several studies also collected data from principals or other administrators. Sample sizes varied widely from 5 to 670, although 54% used a sample less than 50. Only 4 (18%) of the studies randomly selected or assigned students to groups.

Of the 16 studies that included information about the number of classrooms that participated, four (25%) occurred in a single classroom and two occurred in more than 10 classrooms. Similarly, of the 19 studies that included information about the number of schools, 42% occurred in one school and 37% occurred in two schools. Three studies occurred in more than one district and most of the studies focused on students in middle and high schools.

With regard to methods used, 73% collected attitudinal measures, 45% collected formal measures of student learning, and 18% collected both attitudinal and learning measures. Sixty-three percent of the studies employed quantitative methods, 55% used qualitative methods, and 18% used a combination of quantitative and qualitative methods. Two of the studies employed both quantitative and qualitative methods and collected both attitudinal and learning measures. Of the 16 studies that reported the length of intervention, only one lasted for more than 1 year and eight (50%) lasted for 6 months or less.

In summary, the research was typically quasi-experimental, focusing on small samples of students in one district and one grade who were not randomly assigned. Research centered on the upper elementary/middle school years, and researchers employed attitudinal measures that were either quantitative or qualitative.

Writing and Computers

A search of ERIC and similar databases resulted in 65 research articles related to writing and computers. After reviewing each article, twenty-one were found to be conceptual papers, instructional practice plans, or summaries of prior research.

Across the forty-four remaining studies, research questions generally focused on five aspects of computers and writing: (a) improvement in quality of writing, (b) increase in quantity of writing, (c) transformation of the writing process from linear to iterative, (d) transformation of the writing process from an independent or isolated process to a social process, and (e) improving students attitudes and motivation toward writing.

Of the 44 studies that qualified for this review, 42 (96%) collected data directly from students while 2 collected data from both students and teachers. Sample sizes varied widely from 2 to 152, although 75% used a sample less than 50. Only six of the studies (14%) randomly selected or assigned students to groups.

Of the 44 studies, nineteen (43%) occurred in multiple classrooms and the remaining twenty-four were single classroom studies. Similarly, 3 of the 44 studies were conducted in two schools, while the remaining 41 were single-school studies. All studies were single-district and more than half of the studies focused on students in middle and high schools.

With regard to methods used, all 44 studies collected formal measures of student outcomes, nine of which (21%) collected both attitudinal and learning measures. Seventy-three percent of the studies employed quantitative methods, 11% used qualitative methods, and 21% used a combination of quantitative and qualitative methods. Seven (16%) of the 44 studies lasted for a year or more and eleven (25%) lasted for six weeks or less.

In summary, the research was quasi-experimental, focusing on small samples of students in one district and one grade who were not randomly assigned. Research centered on the upper elementary and middle school years, and researchers employed attitudinal measures that were either quantitative or qualitative.

Across the sample of reading, science and writing studies summarized above, four patterns emerge:

1. The majority of studies are small-scale and short in duration.

2. Few studies employ multiple methods of data collection.

3. Few studies include sufficient numbers of classrooms and/or schools to examine relationships between implementation and outcomes.

4. Learning outcomes usually focus on custom-made measures that have not been as well validated as accepted standardized or state-level tests.

SUMMARY

As noted above, the studies selected from ERIC includes only a fraction of the research on computer-based tools conducted since the infusion of desktop computers into schools. Beyond the body of research summarized above, there have been a number of large-scale research efforts undertaken by several researchers. As described, Becker (Becker, 1999; Ravitz et al., 1998, 1999) and his colleagues have employed survey methods to collect information from a nationally representative sample of teachers about their uses of computers in school and the factors that influence those uses. The Apple Classroom of Tomorrow project (Fisher et al., 1996) sponsored several studies, both qualitative and quantitative, that focused on the ways in which teachers use computers in the classroom, the factors that influence these uses, and the impacts they appear to have on student learning. Similarly, Means and her colleagues have conducted several case studies that focus on the uses of computers in the classroom and have developed methods for examining how uses of computers impact collaboration and student research skills (Means et al., 2001). And researchers like Wenglinski (1998), Ravitz et al. (2002), Angrist and Lavy (2001), and Mann, Shakeshaft, Becker, and Kottkamp (1999) have employed statewide and national samples of students, to examine the impact computer use has on student learning, as measured by standardized tests.

In short, the variety of questions researchers have attempted to address with respect to technology in schools and the methods used to explore these questions has expanded greatly from the predominantly quasi-experimental and large-scale survey methods used prior to desktop computers. While there have been some large-scale efforts to examine effects on student learning (Angrist & Lavy, 2001; Mann et al., 1999; Ravitz et al., 2002; Wenglinski, 1998), to document the extent to which teachers use computers, and to explore the factors that influence these uses (Becker, 1999), there have been many more small scale efforts that focus on use by a small number of teachers and students in a limited number of classrooms. As the summaries above demonstrate, in the vast majority of cases, a single methodology (either qualitative or quantitative) is employed. In most cases, these studies occur during the initial implementation phase or last for a year or less. As Goldberg, Russell, and Cook's (2002) meta-analysis of writing reports, methodologies and results are also too often presented in a manner that make it difficult to replicate studies or to fully interpret the results. And, perhaps most important, although a substantial amount of research on technology in schools has been conducted since the infusion of the desktop computer, it has generally been conducted and presented in an uncoordinated manner. Thus, while a substantial body of research on technology in schools has accumulated since the first desktop computers were placed in schools, the quality and scope of the research have varied widely.

As is explored in Chapter 11, several researchers have recently shared these concerns and have offered strategies that hold promise to overcome some of the shortcomings of past research on educational technology.

CHAPTER 11

PROMISING APPROACHES
TO ASSESSING TECHNOLOGY

As discussed in the previous chapter, over the past two decades there has been a considerable amount of research on educational technology. In fact, a search of the Educational Resources Information Clearinghouse (ERIC) shows that more than 23,000 articles have been indexed with the keyword "educational technology" since 1996 alone. This research has focused on a wide range of issues which, among others, include the use and effect of specific software; issues related to access and use; the need for and effect of professional development on teachers' comfort, skill, and use of educational technology; the relationship between pedagogy and use of computers; effects of computer use on classroom culture; enabling conditions for the use of computers; uses of the Internet for teaching and learning; and ways to use emerging tools such as Palm Pilots and science probes for instructional purposes.

Just as the research questions have varied widely in focus, so too have the methods used to address these questions varied. In a few cases, experimental designs have been employed to examine the effects of a specific technology on student learning. More often, quasi-experimental designs have been employed. In other cases, carefully designed case studies have been conducted to examine issues of implementation and effects on teaching and classroom culture. In still other cases, well-designed representative samples of teachers have been surveyed to describe the current state of

Technology and Assessment: The Tale of Two Interpretations, pages 179–203
Copyright © 2006 by Information Age Publishing

access and use of technology. And in a few cases, meta-analyses have been conducted to help summarize findings from across multiple studies.

In too many cases, however, researchers have depended upon anecdotal evidence and opinions regarding the effects of and satisfaction with specific types of technology or professional development programs. As Baker and Herman (2000) state, "The great preponderance of technology evaluation studies to date depend upon relatively weak survey measures of implementation—one-item scales, for instance, that rely on the self-report of members of user groups" (p. 7). Without question, several well-designed, rigorous research studies that focus on various aspects of technology in schools have been conducted. But these high- quality studies represent a small minority of the research conducted to date.

Given the abundance of research but the paucity of high-quality studies, it is no surprise that the Bush administration and the federal government have called for "scientifically-based evidence" and have embraced randomized experimental designs as the "gold standard" (Thomas, 2002). In this chapter, I explore the feasibility and value of employing randomized experiments for research related to educational technology. I then present several alternatives and promising approaches to assessing technology that are designed to overcome some of the challenges described in the previous chapter. The purpose of this chapter is not to argue that one method is better than another. Rather, the goal is to help readers better understand the challenges to technology assessment and the strategies that hold promise to provide more useful information about the conditions that enable specific uses of technology and the impacts of these uses.

RANDOMIZED EXPERIMENTS

Despite a sentiment among many educational researchers that randomized experimental designs are impractical or inappropriate for educational research (Cronbach, 1982; Cronbach et al., 1980; Guba & Lincoln, 1982; Stake, 1967), Cook (2000) argues that large-scale randomized experiments have already been conducted and are used to shape policy and practice. As a few examples, Cook includes:

- A study on the effect of class size on student achievement that was conducted across the state of Tennessee (Finn & Achilles, 1990; Mosteller, Light & Sachs, 1996).
- Two studies on the effect of vouchers (Peterson, Greene, Howell, & McCready, 1998; Witte, 1998).
- Two experiments on the effect of school-based management (Cook et al., 1999; Cook, Hunt, & Murphy, 1999).

- Several studies on the effect of various curriculum programs on student health, violent behavior and use of tobacco, drugs, and alcohol (Connell, Turner & Mason, 1985; Cook, Anson & Walchli, 1993; Durlak & Wells, 1997; Peters & McMahon, 1996; St. Pierre, Cook, & Straw, 1981).

Yet, despite these examples, Cook concedes that randomized experiments are rare in education. As evidence, Cook references research performed by Nave, Meich, and Mosteller (1999) that reveals that less than 1% of the dissertations archived in ERIC employed random assignment.

There are several reasons why randomized experiments are not performed more often in educational research, in general, and educational technology, specifically. First, it is difficult to convince schools and districts to participate in a randomized experiment in which some participants will benefit by receiving different treatments or types of technology which are believed to be beneficial.

Second, once a classroom, school, or district is assigned to a treatment group, it can be difficult to prevent the participant from either dropping out of the study or learning about and adopting an alternative treatment. As an example, Cook (2000) describes how a principal whose school was assigned to the control group in a randomized experiment learned about and liked the treatment so much that he tried to implement it in his school. As a result, the study design was contaminated.

Third, it is difficult to develop an understanding of why a treatment works in one setting and not in another. In such cases when a fuller understanding has not been developed as to why the treatment works in some settings and not in others, policymakers are apt to apply the findings across all settings without also seeking to establish the conditions that enable the treatment to be applied successfully. As an example, Cook (2000) describes how policymakers in California attempted to apply the findings from the Tennessee Class-Size study by mandating smaller class sizes without considering the extent to which qualified teachers and adequate classrooms were available to teach students in these new, smaller classes. The product of this decision was a mixture of successful and unsuccessful impacts. Of course, through careful planning and additional data collection a randomized experiment can also shed light on the conditions that affect implementation. And, since the treatment is assigned randomly across settings, there is potential to learn more about implementation issues than typically occurs when a treatment is assigned to a volunteer group that is fully receptive, and in some cases, already prepared to implement the treatment.

Fourth, the length of time required to implement many educational treatments, whether they be whole school reforms or adaptations of new technologies and accompanying pedagogical practices, makes it difficult to sustain the integrity of an experimental design. As an example, approximately 20% of the schools participating in the Tennessee class size study had either switched group membership on their own or dropped out entirely from the study within three years (Finn & Achilles, 1990). But, the problems associated with longevity are not specific to randomized experimental designs. As Baker and Herman (2000) state, studies of technology in schools have "rarely taken a longitudinal view of outcomes" (p. 11). While differential dropout rates over time may present added challenges to a randomized experimental design, the relatively short time frame of most educational research is problematic across all methodologies.

Fifth, and perhaps most important, randomized experimental designs are not appropriate for all research questions. This point is particularly true for educational technology which often goes (or at least should go) through several stages of development before being adopted on a large scale. From my perspective, these stages of development include:

1. Identifying a need and developing a prototype.
2. Testing and refining the prototype.
3. Demonstrating a proof of concept.
4. Identifying the enabling conditions.
5. Developing a professional development program to help teachers learn how to use the new technology.
6. Demonstrating the efficacy of the new technology and accompanying professional development.

Clearly, randomized experimental designs would serve little purpose for the first two steps. While an experimental design could be used when demonstrating a proof of concept, this use would be inefficient given the enabling conditions that are often required for technology to be used effectively in schools. To avoid finding a lack of impact due to the absence of enabling conditions, it makes sense to conduct research intended to demonstrate a proof of concept in settings in which the enabling conditions are likely to exist.

Just as it is inappropriate to employ a randomized design when identifying a need and developing a prototype, it is unclear how the development of teacher training would benefit from such a design. But, like the technology itself, once developed, randomized experiments may be helpful in demonstrating the efficacy of the professional development program.

Clearly, the most appropriate use of a randomized experimental design occurs when demonstrating the efficacy of a new technology. Through such a design, it is possible to examine the efficacy of the new technology in relation to the effect that is likely to have occurred in the absence of the technology. But, as Cook (2000) argues, randomized experiments may also be helpful in identifying the conditions that enable effective use of the new technology. By first forming a theory regarding the enabling conditions, measuring the extent to which the key conditions are absent or present in the intended participants, and then using this information to stratify participants during the random assignment process, it is possible to compare and contrast effects across various conditions. This sentiment is shared by Culp, Honey, and Spielvogel (2000):

> [W]e certainly conceded the value of incremental knowledge-building through systematic, controlled study of well-defined interactions with particular technologies. The mistake lies not in conducting this research, but on relying on it exclusively, or even primarily, to guide effective decision-making about investment in and implementation of technology in working educational environments. (p. 7)

Thus, while randomized experiments add little, if any value, to the initial phases of research on a new technology, there are advantages to this methodology during the later phases of research.

While this may not be appropriate for all research questions, I believe that randomized experimental designs do have an important role to play in technology research. This is particularly true for mature and stable technologies for which careful research conducted over an extended period of time is likely to inform decisions about the adoption of that technology. Although Baker and Herman (2000) create the impression that the majority of educational technologies have a short shelf-life, many educational technologies used today have remained relatively stable over the past decade. As a few examples, the basic look, feel, and function of word processors has not changed since the first Graphical User Interface (GUI) versions were introduced in the later 1980s. Similarly, spreadsheets, databases, web browsers and email have remained remarkably stable since GUI versions were introduced. Without question, new features have been added to these software applications, but their basic form and function have remained unchanged. Similarly, the ways in which people access and work on networks has experienced little change. Most popular educational software has also been revised only slightly since its introduction. And, while devices like Palm Pilots were introduced more recently and their functions have been increased, the way in which a user interacts with these devices has remained stable since their introduction. There is no doubt that new technologies will continue to be developed and introduced to schools. But once unveiled, it is likely that these new technologies will remain relatively stable. And, rather than replacing existing technologies, it is likely that these new technologies will coexist with the existing technologies for several years. Take, for example, laptop computers. Although laptop computers have been available for more than a decade, they have just begun to enter schools in meaningful numbers over the past two to three years. And, as they enter schools, most schools purchase a combination of desktops and laptops. Thus, while new technologies are being developed at a faster pace than at any other time in history, once introduced most educational applications of a given technology have a substantial shelf life. For this reason, the rapid pace of developing and introducing new technologies does not eliminate the need for and utility of studies that have a longer time horizon.

In short, there is neither something inherent in the process of education nor special about educational technology that prevents the use of randomized experiments to examine specific aspects of technology. Yet, like any research methodology, randomized experimental designs should only be used when they are appropriate for the given research question and when sufficient control over the conditions is likely to exist. Although some federal officials have created the impression that randomized experiments are the gold standard and that alternatives to random assignment are fallible, I agree with Cook (2000) that such assertions are "silly" (p. 8). Moreover, I agree with Cook that "premature experimentation is a real danger. There is little point evaluating educational reforms that are theoretically muddled or that are not implementable by ordinary school personnel" (p. 31). Recognizing the multiple stages through which research on technology passes as a specific use or set of uses of a computer-based tool is developed, I instead favor a medical model to technology research.

Initially, some readers will find the support of a medical model contradictory because the medical model is often equated with randomized experiments. While randomized experiments play an important role in the final stages of medical research, significantly more time and energy are expended before a randomized experiment is conducted. Although the specific steps vary, the pattern is similar across scientific and medical research endeavors that begin with a theory that is tested in a small setting. Intervening factors are then identified and an understanding of the relationship between these factors and the new treatment is developed. The treatment is then tested in a laboratory setting, usually using animals. If successful and repeatable, a randomized trial using humans is then conducted.

Clearly, this approach is not directly transferable to education since it is not possible to develop an initial understanding of the factors that might interact with the treatment using anything other than humans: It is not possible to develop an understanding of the relationship between access to word processors, keyboarding skills, pedagogy, and effects of word processors on writing skills using mice or monkeys. But, just as medical research conducts a series of small-scale studies to develop an understanding of the interactions between a small set of variables, technology researchers conduct similar studies in carefully selected classrooms to develop an initial understanding of the enabling conditions and the potential impacts of the technology. Once an initial understanding of these conditions and potential impacts is developed, it is then reasonable to examine the extent to which the initial findings generalize across settings and compare with "traditional" treatments. It is here that randomized experiments can play an important role in technology research.

BEYOND RANDOMIZED EXPERIMENTS

Despite the attraction to and utility of well developed and appropriately applied randomized experiments, there are several other methods that have tremendous potential to provide valuable information about educational technology. These approaches fall into two general categories: (1) New Approaches to Assessing Student Learning; and (2) Statistical methodologies and research designs. Within the first category, I describe two emerging approaches to assessing student learning (project based assessment and web-based assessment of digital literacy skills). Within the second category, I describe three potentially useful methodologies, including multilevel analysis of technology in schools, meta-analysis for synthesizing findings from multiple studies, and a systems approach to studying technology.

Project-Based Assessment Model

As described in the previous chapter, a major challenge to assessing the impact of technology on student learning is identifying learning measures that are aligned with and sensitive to the types of learning that may occur when students work with computers. Although it is attractive to use existing measures of learning such as standardized tests to examine the impact of technology on learning, standardized tests are often not well aligned with the learning that occurs with computers. Recall Russell (2000) found that, although upper elementary school teachers used computers to develop students' spatial reasoning skills, there were only two items on the state test related to spatial reasoning.

A second problem associated with using standardized tests to examine impacts of technology on learning is that in the vast majority of cases, standardized tests do not allow students to use computers when working on the test. In general, this is done to create standard test administration conditions—and since some students do not know how to use a word processor, are less comfortable keyboarding, or simply do not have easy access to computers, pen-and-pencil is the preferred method for standardizing the administration conditions. This decision not to allow students to write with computers has led to severe underestimates of the writing skills of students accustomed to writing with computers (Russell, 1999; Russell & Haney, 1997a; Russell & Plati, 2001).

As Becker and Lovitts (2000) argue:

> ...the assessment setting for standardized tests defines away any possible utility of computer-based tools and resources by preventing their use during the assessment situation. What is being tested, then, is whether the use of computers in learning has any residue that carries over to intellectual challenges students may face without being able to call upon technology tools or resources. In Salomon et al.'s (1991) terms, norm-referenced outcome measurements test the effects "*of technology*" rather than the effects "*with technology.*" (p. 8)

In other words, tests used to assess the impact of technology on student learning, but which do not allow students to use the technology during testing which they use during learning, are effectively measuring the cognitive residue of the skills acquired while learning with the technology. Given that students will increasingly be using computer-based tools once they enter the workplace, the focus on cognitive residue or transferability of skills developed on a computer to skills demonstrated on paper seems short-sighted. Since much of the reported benefits of learning with computers result from the "*effects with*" computers—that is "the enhancement of learning and performance capacity provided by knowledgeable access to and use of computer tools and resources" (Becker & Lovitts, 2000, p. 8)—use of paper-based standardized measures designed to measure the effects of computers may create a misleading portrait of the impact of computers on students learning.

In an attempt to overcome this shortcoming of standardized tests, Becker and Lovitts (2000) propose a new approach to assessing the impact of computers on learning: Project-Based Assessments (PBA). In essence, there are three aspects of a PBA that distinguish it from standardized assessments. First, rather than performing a test during a short time period, students would work on a single, complex problem over the course of several days. To the extent possible, the task selected would be highly integrated with the curriculum and with teachers' instruction. Students would work on the task during class time and as part of homework. The task would require students to apply a wide variety of cognitive skills each of which would be assessed (to the extent possible). The tasks would be developed such that they require students to reveal their thinking and the rationale for the procedures they employ. In some cases, the task would allow students substantial control over the nature of the topic of exploration and the nature of their final products. In other cases, the topic and nature of the final product would be specified.

Second, as students work on the problem, they would have control over the tools they use throughout the project, including sources they use to collect information, tools they use to organize and analyze information, and the tools they use to produce final products. As part of the assessment process, information would be collected about the tools used during each phase of the project. This information would be used to examine the role technology plays in student work and the relationships between its use and student performance.

Third, the final product is assessed on a variety of dimensions using criteria that are established before the assessment is administered. The criteria would not be specific to the use of technology, but instead would focus on the cognitive skills that students are expected to apply when working on the project. To the extent possible, the dimensions would be construct-based rather than task-based. Thus, the assessment would not focus solely on the quality of the final product, but would provide information about the skills required to produce the final product. Depending on the task, these skills might include the ability to form a hypothesis, the ability to develop a research plan, the ability to perform research, the ability to analyze information, the ability to assimilate information, and the ability to communicate information.

In essence, the PBA model would attempt to hold constant all elements of the assessment process *except* student access to and use of tools and resources. As Becker and Lovitts (2000) state, "It is this 'person-plus' environment (Perkins, 1990) which is to be assessed in this research—that is, it is that variation in access to and ability to use technology resources that makes it possible to answer the 'what difference does it make?' question" (p. 26). So as not to bias the answer to this question, the projects students engage in must be carefully selected so that computers may be used, but are not required for successful completion of the project.

The PBA model can be applied to three distinct classes of assessment:

1. Project Studies in which a class or set of classes engaged in a technology-intensive curriculum unit is compared to a class or set of classes that are studying the same content but are not using the specific technology-intensive tools.

2. Teacher Studies, which compare the performance of students whose teachers make use of technology intensively throughout the year with those students whose teachers use technology less frequently or not at all.

3. School- or Department-wide Studies, which compare the performance of students across schools or departments that use technology intensively with schools or departments that use technology infrequently.

It is through the contrast between high and low technology use settings that information about the added benefits of technology can be gleaned, if they exist. As an example of how a study might be designed, Becker and Lovitts (2000) provide an example of a potential Teacher Study:

> A teacher-level study involves multiple replicates of matched sets of four teachers who teach the same subject to students at the same grade level who are (a) of roughly the same tested abilities and previous school achievement; (b) residing in communities of similar socio-economic status, and; (c) if possible, in the same school district or at least in the same state (for purposes of minimizing differences in curricular objectives between teachers). Within a matched set, each of the four teachers is selected to represent one of four categories of teaching approach: technology-intensive with a student-centered (constructivist) pedagogy; technology-intensive with a content-centered (skills-based and transmission-oriented) pedagogy; "typically limited technology use" combined with a student-centered pedagogy; and "typically limited technology use" combined with a content-centered pedagogy. (p. 28)

Given that word processing and finding information (Becker, 1999) are the two most common uses of computers by students in school and that these activities occur most often in English and Social Studies classes, Becker and Lovitts (2000) suggest that a project undertaken in one of these two subject areas would provide a logical starting place for the use of PBA. Moreover, given the substantial amount of in-class time required for students to work on their project, Becker and Lovitts advocate that the specifications for each PBA be developed with the participating teachers. Although some projects will allow students more flexibility in the topic and format of the project, the process of analyzing is analogous to a science fair competition in which the criteria for assessing the projects is defined and known in advance.

Without question, the PBA model requires a great deal more effort than administering a standardized test. Information must be gathered about instructional practices at the teacher, school, or department level before participating teachers can be selected. Researchers must then work closely with the participating teachers to identify a set of skills that are part of their curriculum and which are worth assessing. Criteria for those skills must then be developed before a project task is defined. A significant amount of class time must be invested for students to work on their projects. Data must be collected about the tools and processes students used while working on their projects. The projects must then be assessed using the pre-specified criteria. And then the data can be analyzed to examine added benefits of technology use.

Although the PBA model has yet to be applied, it holds promise to provide richer and more meaningful information about the impacts of technology on learning as compared to traditional standardized tests. By requiring students to work on an extended project that more closely resembles the work they do with or without technology as part of their regular learning experience and once in the workplace, a PBA is likely to provide a more direct measure of student skills that may be impacted by the use of technology. Moreover, by allowing students the flexibility to use the tools that they use when learning while being assessed, the PBA avoids the modal effects reported by Russell and his colleagues (Russell, 1999; Russell & Haney, 1997a; Russell & Plati, 2001). In addition, by developing complex project tasks, information about multiple constructs can be gleaned and the impact of technology on each of these constructs can be examined. Finally, by purposefully contrasting high-technology-use settings with low-use settings, while holding constant other variables such as prior student achievement, socioeconomic factors, and pedagogical practices, the PBA model allows for direct comparisons of the impact of technology use on student learning rather than less powerful correlations between use and test scores.

Digital Literacy Assessments

In contrast to the Project-based Assessment model which designs tasks for which students are not required to use computers, researchers at the Center for Technology Learning have begun to develop assessments that require computer use. Recognizing that traditional standardized tests are unlikely to capture the types of learning that occur when students engage in inquiry-oriented, technology-based projects, Means et al. (2000) set out to develop prototype assessments designed to capture such learning. As they explain, "We wanted our prototype assessments to capture skills that are not easily assessed with more conventional standardized tests and to demonstrate the capabilities provided by technology for doing more flexible, in-depth assessments" (p. 4). To this end, the research group has developed two types of prototypes. The first requires students to use the World Wide Web to find and assimilate information in order to solve a problem. The second has teachers use a Palm Pilot application to record information about student collaboration as students work in small groups to solve a problem. While both approaches to assessment are novel uses of technology, I focus on the first since it assesses student skills directly through the use of technology.

Given that most standard-setting bodies emphasize the importance of problem-solving and communication skills, the web-based assessment prototype attempts to measure a student's ability to solve a complex problem and then communicate his or her findings to an audience. As Means et al.

(2000) describe, "The assessment prototype presents an engaging, problem-based learning task that integrate technology use with investigations of an authentic problem" (2000, p. 5). Through a student's work on a given problem, three domains are assessed: (a) ability to use appropriate technology like the Internet and productivity tools, (b) reasoning with information, and (c) communication.

The most recent version of the prototype assessment task begins by presenting students with a problem: A group of foreign exchange students wants to come to the United States for the summer and needs to choose one of two cities. The task asks students to research information about the cities and then write a letter to the exchange students recommending a city. To help inform their recommendation, students in middle school are told that the exchange students are concerned about public transportation and recreational opportunities. Students in high school are told that the exchange students are also concerned about the health of the city's economy.

Once presented with the problem, students are provided with URLs of websites for two cities, Knoxville, Tennessee and Fort Collins, Colorado. As students review various web sites, they are asked to evaluate "the credibility of information on particular web pages and to formulate a search query for finding additional, relevant information" (Means et al., 2000, p. 5). When writing their letter to the exchange students, the students are asked to justify their recommendation.

As is the case in Project-Based Assessments, the web-based assessment prototype uses pre-specified analytic scoring rubrics to assess student work. These analytic rubrics focus on several dimensions of student skills and knowledge including their use of technology, ability to evaluate information, reasoning with information, and communication skills. As an example, the pilot rubric for Evaluating Questionable Information rated students' discussion of the questionable information as follows:

1. States that she or he cannot find questionable text, or the text she or he finds appears to be factual and she or he has not explained what she or he finds questionable about it.

2. The student has found questionable text but has not tried to explain why.

3. The student has found questionable text and has tried to explain why, but the explanation has some shortcomings.

4. The student has found questionable text and has adequately explained why. (Means et al., 2000, p. 6)

For a specific task, these general criteria are used to create specific scoring guides that include examples of each score level.

Since developing this first prototype task, Means and her colleagues have used the template to create tasks for other subject areas. As an example, when evaluating the effects of the GLOBE environmental science education program, several web-based assessment tasks were developed. For one of these tasks, students were provided with criteria for selecting the site for the next Winter Olympics. Students were provided with information on several different potential sites and worked in a web-based environment to analyze this information and to create a persuasive presentation complete with graphs of relevant information (Means & Haertel, 2002).

Researchers at the Center for Research on Evaluation, Standards, and Student Testing (CRESST) have also begun developing assessments to assess web-fluency. From CRESST's perspective, web-fluency encompasses the navigational styles, cognitive characteristics, and search behaviors of students when they search for information on the Web. To assess students' web-fluency, Klein, Yarnall, and Glaubke (2001) developed the Web Expertise Assessment (WEA). The WEA is a simulated web environment that includes an online search engine, web-based information window, navigation tools, and an automatic logging capability. To the user, the WEA appears the same as an actual web environment, but the system limits students to approximately 500 pages of information. Thus, the system is a closed information environment.

As students use the WEA to find information to answer a given question, the system records all of the actions students perform to search for and access information. As students find relevant information, they are asked to bookmark pages. Using the record of keystrokes and mouse clicks and the set of bookmarked pages, the system tallies several quantitative measures like the number of searches performed, the number of times each navigational tool was used, the number of steps taken to complete a search, and the number of bookmarks created. Other measures are coded by human judges who examine the search terms students use, the extent to which they redirect or refine searches, the relevance of the bookmarked pages, and the quality of information on the bookmarked pages given the task. In total, 17 separate measures related to web-fluency are recorded for each student. In addition, students complete a questionnaire that asks students about their beliefs regarding information on the World Wide Web. Both sets of measures are combined to form scales that represent different skill sets related to web-fluency. Although the researchers have not yet developed formal names for the skill sets, Table 11.1 displays the measures that form each skill set.

Although both the internet prototype assessments and the WEA are still in the developmental stage, they serve as good working examples of authentic approaches to assessing the skills students are developing through their use of computer-based tools like the World Wide Web. In the

Table 11.1. Web Expertise Assessment Measures

Measure	Description
Number of Steps	The number of steps or mouse clicks made by the student as s/he completed the task.
Number of good searches	Searches were classified as a good search when it was on topic and included keywords, Boolean operators, and/or synonyms.
Number of redirected searches	Searches were classified as redirected when a student attempted a new search before visiting any of the pages included in the initial search's results.
Quality of search	0 indicated no keyword searches or off-topic searches
	1 indicated at least one on-topic search
	2 indicated more than half of the searches were on-topic and included keywords
	3 indicated at least one Boolean keyword search
Bookmark score	0 indicated an off-topic bookmark
	1 indicated a bookmark on topic but not relevant to the task
	2 indicated a bookmark peripherally relevant to the task
	3 indicated an on-topic and directly relevant bookmark
	Note that each bookmark was rated separately
Average bookmark score	The mean bookmark score
Quality of bookmarks	0 irrelevant response set
	1 fair response set
	2 good response set
	3 excellent response set
Search efficiency	Ratio of the number of good bookmarks to the total number of pages visited

case of the WEA, the skills assessed are specific to how well students are able to find information on the Web and, to a lesser extent, assess the appropriateness of that information given a specific question. While the internet prototype aims to assess students search skills, it measures two additional domains—ability to use information to make decisions and communication skills. While more work needs to be done to establish the validity of these two approaches to assessment, they hold promise to add to the variety of measures researchers can use to examine the impact technology use may be having on student learning.

Multi-Level Analysis of Technology Use, Support, and Impact

To date, Becker and his colleagues have performed the most extensive and systematic research on the factors that influence teacher use of technology (Becker, 1999; Ravitz et al., 1999; Ravitz & Wong, 2000). Through analysis of survey responses provided by a nationally representative sample of 3,500 teachers, Becker and his colleagues report that pedagogy, subject area, and grade level are all factors that explain teacher use of technology. Specifically, elementary school-level teachers, teachers of English and Social Studies, and teachers who have more student-centered instructional beliefs generally report higher levels of technology use (Becker, 1999; Ravitz et al., 1999; Ravitz & Wong, 2000).

The use of technology by teachers and students, however, are influenced by factors beyond those that are specific to each individual. As Culp et al. (2000) acknowledge:

> ...the impact of technology in schools is mediated and largely determined by local educational leadership and vision, funding structures, school board politics, and material realities for geography and physical plant....We have learned through our work with a variety of schools that numerous factors influence a school's ability to use technology effectively for student learning. These factors include: Leadership and vision at multiple levels of the system; school- and district-wide goals and expectations for the use of technology in the classroom context; school culture and climate; teachers' beliefs about students and their potential for learning; ongoing professional development for teachers; teachers' prior experience with technology; and availability of technology resources (both infrastructure and human) in the school. (p. 12)

Given the interrelationships among factors that reside at different levels of a school system, student, teacher and school use of technology can be conceptualized in terms of a multi-level and hierarchical framework. Individual students use technology within the context of a classroom; teachers operate within a school and are influenced by its technology policies; and schools, in turn are affected by district level decisions regarding the allocation and use of technology. This natural hierarchy lends itself well to the application of multilevel modeling techniques (Rumberger, 2000).

The simplest multilevel model that can be specified is a two-level model. Individuals within groups are modeled at the first level, and their group membership is modeled at the second level. In the three-level model, the individual is modeled at level one, and their membership in two groups is modeled at levels two and three. For example, students are nested within classrooms and classrooms are nested within schools. Alternatively, teachers are nested within schools, and schools within districts. The sample design employed by any research study dictates the complexity of the multilevel model that can be employed; more complex sample designs allow more levels to be modeled, thus yielding more useful and accurate information about the contexts that affect the outcomes of interest.

Building on the work of Becker and his colleagues, the Technology and Assessment Study Collaborative has collected data from 140 district leaders, 120 principals, 4,400 teachers, and 13,500 students and used this data to build hierarchical models that identify factors that influence teacher and student uses of technology (Russell, Bebell, & O'Dwyer, 2003). To the best of my knowledge, the Use, Support, and Effect of Instructional Technology (USEIT) study is the first large-scale effort to examine technology use from a hierarchical perspective. In addition, the USEIT study has developed several scales that reflect different uses of technology by teachers and students. For teachers, these uses include communication via email, use of technology to prepare for instruction, use of technology to find information outside of class, use of technology to deliver instruction, and assigned use of technology by students during instruction. For students, these uses include use of technology, in and out of school, for school-related activities and for recreation. For each use of technology, the USEIT study is using hierarchical data analysis methods to explain each type of use. Ultimately, the purpose of multilevel regression modeling is to examine the factors that affect the use of technology. Among the factors the USEIT study is examining are:

- District Vision for technology
- School and District Culture
- Leadership
- Technology Resources
- Technology Support
- Professional Development
- Technology Policies and Standards
- Teaching Philosophy/Instructional Model
- Technology Beliefs
- Equity
- Community
- Demographics and Preparedness
- Instructional Uses of Technology
- Technology Use outside of Classrooms
- Barriers to Use

Scales for different types of technology use have been created at the individual student level and at the classroom or teacher level. The schematic in Figure 11.1 shows how student use of technology may be modeled using individual student-level predictors, classroom/teacher-level predic-

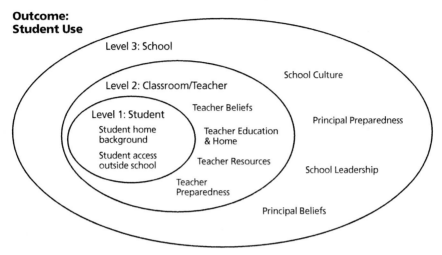

Outcome: Student Use

Figure 11.1.   Three-level model with student use as outcome.

tors, and school-level predictors. This model examines the relationship among student use of technology and student, teacher and school characteristics. The relationship between the predictors and the outcome may vary among classrooms/teachers, schools, or both, as it is expected that schools will differ in terms of the extent to which technology is used. Differences may also occur within groups (within classrooms/teachers or within schools) with regard to the strength of the relationship between the predictors and the outcome. The regression coefficients are examined at each of the three levels to assess these differences.

Figure 11.2 presents an alternative analysis. In this model, the levels are shifted upwards to include the district at the third level. In this model, the relationship among teacher use of technology and teacher, school and district characteristics is examined. Again, there will be differences among teachers in terms of their use of technology and there will be differences within groups in terms of the strength of the relationship between the outcome and the level specific predictors. In addition to the predictors included in the Figures 11.1 and 11.2, barriers to the use of technology are included in each model (although not depicted).

The USEIT study builds on prior research by identifying the factors and interactions between factors that reside at different levels of the school system which influence teacher and student uses of technology. While several organizations, such as the Milken-Exchange on Educational Technology (Lemke & Coughlin, 1998) and the CEO Forum on Education and Technology (2001b) have argued that a small number of dimensions must be in place in order to support effective uses of technology, the USEIT study pro-

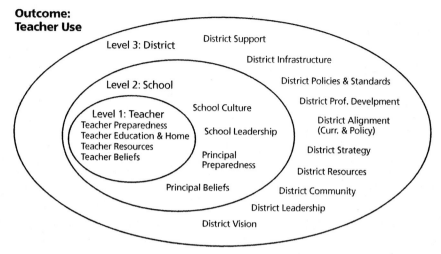

Figure 11.2.   Three-level model with teacher use as outcome.

vides empirical evidence as to which factors are important for specific uses of technology. In addition, the USEIT study extends Becker's work by providing schools and districts with an understanding of the factors under their direct control that influence teacher and student uses of technology (Bebell et al., 2004; O'Dwyer, Russell, & Bebell, 2004; Russell et al., 2003).

Meta-Analysis

Although meta-analysis is not a new methodology and has already been applied to technology research, its full value has yet to be tapped. Meta-analytic procedures refer to a set of statistical techniques used to systematically review and synthesize independent studies within a specific area of research. Gene Glass first proposed such methods and coined the term "meta-analysis" in 1976.

> Meta-analysis refers to the analysis of analyses... to the statistical analysis of a large collection of results from individual studies for the purpose of integrating the findings. It connotes a rigorous alternative to the casual, narrative discussions of research studies which typify our attempts to make sense of the rapidly expanding research literature. (p. 3)

Meta-analysis is particularly useful when a substantial body of research has been conducted on a specific subject area and the findings are inconsistent across studies.

At its core, meta-analysis combines findings from multiple studies to estimate a grand or meta-effect. In any meta-analysis, the first step is to locate all studies performed that are relevant to the topic of interest. As an example, Goldberg, Russell, and Cook (2003) recently conducted a meta-analysis of the effects of computer use on student writing. As a first step, the researchers performed a search of several databases including ERIC, Educational Abstracts, PsychLit, and Dissertation Abstracts, performed a web search using search engines (e.g., Google), searched electronic journals that may not yet be indexed, tracked references cited in related research, and consulted with researchers who have performed research on this topic in the past. In total, their search identified 103 studies related to computers and writing.

The second step in a meta-analysis is to develop criteria for inclusion, review all studies, and then make a decision as to whether the study meets the criteria for inclusion. Among the criteria used by Goldberg and her colleagues were that the study must (a) have been conducted between 1992 and 2002, (b) have reported results in a manner that allows for calculation of effect sizes, (c) include quantitative measures of either quality of writing or quantity of writing, and (d) focus on K–12 students. Two readers reviewed each study and made an independent decision regarding inclusion. Discrepancies were discussed and consensus was reached regarding inclusion. Of the 103 studies initially identified for possible inclusion, 38 were excluded because their focus was off target, 17 were excluded because they did not present original research, 5 were excluded because they were qualitative, and 13 were excluded because they did not report enough information to compute an effect size. Thus, of the 65 studies that were on target, only 43 presented original quantitative research, but only 30 reported sufficient information to allow effect sizes to be calculated.

The third step in a meta analysis is to code various features of the study that may moderate the effect of interest. Often these features include age of the participants, whether or not the study was published in a peer-review journal, sample size, research design, and so forth. These coded features are used during subsequent analysis to examine the extent to which the general findings differ across features.

Fourth, an effect size is calculated for each study. Although there are many different ways to calculate an effect size, Glass' delta is frequently employed. The delta effect size is simply the difference between the experimental group and the control group divided by the standard deviation, of either the control group or the pooled standard deviation (Glass & Hopkins, 1984). Thus, to calculate an effect size, four pieces of information must be provided in the study, including (a) the mean of the control group, (b) the mean of the experimental group, (c) the standard deviation of the control group, and (d) the standard deviation of the experimental group. In the event that a single group is measured at two different points in time, then the mean and standard deviations for the pre- and posttests must be reported. In essence, an effect size represents the difference between group means in standard deviation units.

Once effect sizes have been calculated, the average effect size across all studies is calculated. As Lipsey and Wilson (2001) and Hedges and Olkin (1985) describe in greater detail, there are a number of ways to weight or adjust effect sizes to take into account such factors as differences in sample size or differences in the quality of the study. But irrespective of the method used to calculate the meta-effect, one advantage of meta-analysis is the ability to combine findings from all qualifying studies to produce a single estimate of the effect. For the study conducted by Goldberg, Russell, and Cook (2003), the meta-effect of computer use on writing quality was equivalent to .41 standard deviations. In other words, students who developed writing skills while using computers over an extended period of time produced writing that was .41 standard deviations better than that of students who developed writing skills without using computers.

Despite the utility of combining findings from multiple studies into a single estimate of the effect, some researchers suggest that this single estimate is of limited value. As an example, Becker and Lovitts (2000) write that...

> ...any defensible evaluation of the cost-effectiveness of investments in educational technology cannot rely solely on providing data on mean effect sizes, but must assess the contribution of a wide variety of factors in systematically defining the condition under which consequences of different magnitude arise with reasonable regularity. (p. 4)

Similarly, Culp, Honey and Spielvogel (2000) argue:

> Much of the early research attempting to answer the question, 'Does technology improve student learning?' eliminated from the consideration everything other than the computer itself and evidence of student learning... Teacher practices, student experiences, pedagogical contexts, and even what was actually being done with the computers—all these factors were bracketed out in one way or another. This was done so that the research could make powerful, definitive statements about effects—statements unqualified by the complicated details of actual schooling (p. 4, see also Kulik & Kulik, 1991, who performed a meta-analysis of the effectiveness of computer-based instruction.)

However, despite the sentiment among some researchers that meta-analytic techniques ignore the factors that moderate the mean effect, meta-analysis is well suited for developing such an understanding by examining the extent to which potentially moderating factors have similar effects across studies. In fact, Glass (1976) argues that the most useful aspect of meta-analysis is . . .

> . . . not little single-number summaries such as 'This is what psychotherapy's effect is' but a whole array of study results that show how relationships between treatment and outcome change as a function of all sorts of other conditions—the age of the people in treatment, what kinds of problems they had, the training of the therapist, how long after therapy you're measuring change, and so on. That's what we really want to get—a total portrait of all those changes and shifts, a complicated landscape rather than a single central point. That would be the best contribution we could make. (p. 163)

As an example, the meta-analysis conducted by Goldberg and her colleagues examined the extent to which several variables moderated the effect of computer use on the quantity and quality of student writing. Among the moderating factors the researchers examined included the age of students, peer-editing, teacher feedback, and keyboard skills. Unfortunately, several studies did not report sufficient information about these factors, and when they did, the factor did not vary across studies. Nonetheless, the study did find that grade level was a significant moderating factor, with larger effects occurring in middle and high schools as compared to elementary schools.

As seen in the meta-analysis conducted by Goldberg and her colleagues, the major factor that limits the utility of meta-analysis to provide useful information about intervening factors or conditions does not reside in the methodology itself, but in the studies it is used to assimilate. As Baker and Herman (2000) argue:

> Although individual studies vary in terms of their rigor, size of differences, designs, quality of measures, etc., meta-analyses of technology nonetheless have had some impact on the overall debate (Fletcher, 1990; Kulik, 1994). Even though meta-analysis provides a handy tool, its availability does not supplant the requirements for careful design of evaluations directed to the impact of specific technological interventions. In fact, meta-analyses will be strengthened by careful attention to such studies. (p. 5)

Given the challenges of conducting large-scale, high-quality studies, particularly when randomization is employed, meta-analysis provides a useful and potentially powerful method for assimilating the findings from several smaller-scale, high-quality studies. The value of meta-analysis could be further increased if sets of small studies are thoughtfully developed such that factors believed to moderate the given effect are varied across studies. Finally, if sets of studies are designed simultaneously or in close proximity to one another, the same instruments could be used, thus facilitating the combining of findings across studies.

System of Implementation and Impact Studies

The USEIT study provides a good example of a relatively large-scale research effort designed to explore the multiple factors that operate at different levels of a school system and which may impact various uses of technology by teachers and students. Similarly, meta-analysis techniques provide a useful method for assimilating findings from several studies to both estimate general effects and identify factors that moderate the effects. While large-scale, multi-level studies provide opportunities to learn about the extent to which technology is being used in different ways and the factors that influence these uses, they are not well suited for developing an understanding of how technology may be used in new ways. And while meta-analysis is useful when a body of studies that focus on the impact of technology already exists, the method is of little value during the early stages of developing or implementing a new application of technology in schools.

As discussed earlier, technology research falls into at least four broad categories. First, a new application of technology to teaching and learning is developed. Second, the application is tested in small settings to both improve its use and to begin to develop an understanding of implementation issues. Third, the use of the technology is dispersed to multiple settings and, once in use, the impact of the technology on teaching and learning is examined. (Most often this third stage employs small studies, often in locations where the use has been fully and efficiently adopted.) Fourth, if successful in small settings, larger scale studies are conducted across multiple sites—to date, this step has occurred infrequently, at best. For each category of research, different methods are appropriate. During the early stages, design research, design experiments, case studies, and other qualitative methods are best suited for understanding needs and implementation issues. During the third stage, mixed methods are useful for examining effects on teaching and learning and factors that moderate these effects. During the fourth stage, randomized experimental designs, in some cases combined with survey methods and qualitative methods, are most useful.

Recognizing the different categories of research and the different methods used for each line of inquiry, Hedges, Konstantopoulos, and Thoreson (2000) recommend that technology research be approached as a system of coordinated studies rather than a collection of eclectic individual studies. As they argue, "A comprehensive program of assessment of technology must include a program of interrelated studies. The individual component studies would focus on different aspects of technology, use different methods, and have different purposes and time horizons" (p. 4).

This system's approach to technology research would include four types of studies. At the highest level, large-scale surveys intended to document the availability and use of different types of technology across a nationally representative sample of schools would be conducted. The intent of these large-scale surveys would be threefold. First, they would help document trends over time. Second, they would allow initial inquiries into factors that affect access and use of different types of technology. Third, they would help identify pockets of high and low use.

The second type of research involves intensive research in a sub-sample of schools. This research would be coordinated with the larger scale efforts and would aim to provide more detailed information about how the technology is being used, for what purposes, how the use fits into the curriculum, and what conditions inhibit or facilitate use in different settings. As Becker and Lovitts (2000) have also proposed, the pockets of high and low use identified during larger-scale survey work could provide areas into which more focused inquiry is conducted to understand why this use or non-use has occurred and what effects the use is having on student learning.

The third set of studies would focus on assessing cause and effect of technology use on student achievement, attitudes and behaviors. As Hedges and his colleagues argue (2000), "cross sectional surveys alone simply cannot be used [to] make persuasive causal arguments in this area" (p. 6). To examine cause and effect, a combination of smaller longitudinal and experimental design studies would be conducted. Despite the limited use of randomized experiments discussed above, "Randomized experiments are both desirable and feasible in education and they should be seriously considered as part of a system of work to understand the effects of technology in American education" (p. 6). Given the complexity of conducting randomized experiments and longitudinal studies on a large scale, Hedges recommends several smaller studies.

The final set of studies would focus on developing new methods of assessment and new research designs to provide information on a more timely basis regarding the trends and impact of emerging technologies and uses of technology. These studies would likely require a network of teacher-researchers who work closely to explore new approaches to assessment and technology use. These studies would serve to make others aware of unanticipated trends or uses of technology, identify new data needs, and to provide formative information regarding the use of technology, assessment methods, and the design of future research.

Thus, the aim of this system of studies is to capitalize on the benefits of multiple research methods to provide information about multiple but closely related aspects of technology. Although this system approach to technology assessment has not yet been applied, it serves as a useful model that may help to decrease the fragmented, uncoordinated, and often difficult to interpret findings of past efforts to assess technology in schools.

LOOKING TO THE FUTURE

As described above, over the past two decades, research on educational technology has matured from largely small scale, localized studies to more rigorous and controlled investigations into the factors that affect technology use and the effects of use on teaching and learning. Despite the current emphasis placed on randomized experiments by organizations such as the Federal Institute of Education Sciences, understanding and advancing educational technology requires multiple lines of research that employ methodologies that are appropriate for the research questions posed by researchers and policymakers. To this end, it is important to recognize that the life cycle of a given educational technology has multiple stages that include defining a problem for which technology may be appropriate, developing and refining that technology through small scale design studies, understanding factors that may moderate the effects of the technology's use, and examining the effects of successful implementation of the technology use across a diverse set of learners. Naturally, the research methods used during each stage of development will vary. While randomized experiments may prove useful during the final stages of research on a given technology, investigations during the earlier stages of development may miss important variables that influence the effects of the technology if too much emphasis is placed on controlling all moderating variables.

Similarly, the current emphasis placed on standardized test scores by federal and state legislation poses serious challenges to researchers who are attempting to understand the effects of technology use on student learning. While it is important to understand how technology use affects student learning, it is equally important to employ measures of learning that are sensitive to the types of learning that occur when students use a given technology. It is also vital that the modes of assessment do not mask learning effects by requiring students to demonstrate their knowledge and skills using tools that are unfamiliar to them. This applies both to students who learn with a given technology and are tested without access to that technology (e.g., word processors) and to students who do not learn with a given technology yet are tested with that technology. When comparing the effects of a given technology on student learning, this modal requirement can present significant challenges. Do we need to use a computer-based test for students who learn algebra using a computer-based tutorial system and a paper-based test for students who learn using a traditional paper-based textbook? Do we require students who are taught within a multimedia rich history curriculum to create computer-based multimedia projects while students who are taught with more traditional curricular materials are required to create more traditional paper-based products? Do we require students who learn to write with a word processor to perform a writing test on a computer while students in the comparison group are required to write on paper? If so, how do we know that scores from these different assessments are comparable? And if not, how do we know that the mode of assessment is not introducing construct irrelevant variance to our outcome measures? As I describe more fully above, project-based assessment and digital literacy assessments are two examples of efforts in progress that are attempting to address these assessment issues.

In recent years, researchers have also begun employing a variety of methodologies to develop a better understanding of the use and effect of educational technology. Recognizing that all research has shortcomings, meta-analytic techniques are increasingly being applied to synthesize findings from multiple studies in order to make more generalizable statements about the effects of technology. Similarly, multi-level designs and analytic techniques are beginning to be used to develop a better understanding of how factors that reside at different levels of the education system influence technology use. These techniques are also being used to adjust our estimates of the effects of technology use on student learning so that they reflect factors within students as well as within the educational setting in which this learning occurs. Perhaps the most promising approach to educational technology research, however, will come when separate but coordinated research studies are conducted in multiple settings, and employ common measures that enable results to be both compared between settings and to synthesize findings across settings. Clearly, the extent to which such studies make use of assessment instruments that are aligned with the learning and tools used for learning will further enhance the utility of this coordinated approach to educational technology research. Whereas critics may have found it easy to dismiss early research on educational technology due to methodological limitations, recent advances in the application of more sophisticated methodologies and attempts to develop better aligned measurement instruments holds promise to deepen our understanding of the factors influencing technology use and the effects of these uses.

CHAPTER 12

BRIDGING THE GAPS

There is little doubt that technology and assessment have become important elements of K–12 education in the United States. By some estimates, schools are spending more than $7 billion a year to acquire, maintain and support computer-based technologies. Student use of computers in school and at home has also increased steadily over the past several years with large percentages of students now reporting that they use computers during the school year to write and find information on the Internet for school related assignments (Becker, 1999). To support student use of computers, some states and individual districts have begun implementing 1:1 laptop programs in which all students and their teachers are provided with a laptop computer.

Student assessment has also become a mainstay in educational reform efforts. The No Child Left Behind Act signed into law in the Spring of 2002 requires all states to assess students in grades three through eight on an annual basis. This requirement is layered on top of the testing programs that already exist in the majority of states. Although it is unclear just how much this federally mandated testing will cost, it will certainly run into the billions of dollars each year.

Despite the substantial investments in technology and assessment, observers have questioned whether the full value of these investments is being realized (Cuban, 2001). Although teacher use of computers has increased over the past decade, the percent of teachers who use computers or have their students use computers regularly during instruction is still

Technology and Assessment: The Tale of Two Interpretations, pages 205–217
Copyright © 2006 by Information Age Publishing

relatively small (Becker, 1999; Russell, Bebell, O'Dwyer, & O'Connor, 2003). Moreover, while there are small pockets of evidence that computers are being used to enhance instruction and are having positive impacts on student learning, this evidence is scattered, uncoordinated, and difficult to assimilate into a coherent assessment of the impact of computers on teaching and learning.

Similarly, today's standardized tests are providing schools and policy-makers with reams of data which is useful for identifying students that may be performing at low levels and schools that serve large numbers of low performing students. But the information provided by these tests is of limited value for actually improving instruction. While today's test scores allow teachers and schools to identify areas of the curriculum in which students are performing poorly, the tests do not provide useful insight into why the students are performing poorly in these areas.

In response to increasing emphasis on student performance on standardized tests, teachers and schools are altering their instructional practices. In some cases, instruction is focusing increasingly on the topics assessed by today's standardized tests (Pedulla et al., 2003). Many teachers, schools, and even states are also investing in computer-based tutorials to help prepare students for standardized tests. In other cases, teachers are altering the tools with which students work and the learning activities in which they engage in order to better align learning experiences with testing experiences (Russell & Abrams, 2004; Pedulla et al., 2002).

Increasingly, testing programs are also expanding their use of computer-based technologies in order to increase the efficiency of the testing process (Bennett, 2002). Through computer-based and web-based testing, the efficiency of delivering, scoring, and reporting test results are all increasing. Beyond eliminating the costs of printing, shipping and scanning paper-based test booklets and answer sheets, computer-adaptive tests also provide more reliable estimates of student ability in about half the amount of time. Similarly, computer scoring of student writing dramatically reduces the cost and time of scoring open-ended and essay responses. Although there are a number of issues related to validity that still must be addressed as more and more tests are converted to a computer-based format, it is inevitable that computers will become the primary platform for most standardized tests (Bennett, 2002).

WIDENING GAPS

Despite the increased use of technology in schools and by testing programs, a number of gaps have formed between how computers are used for instruction and assessment. Although schools are increasingly using computer-based tutorials to prepare students for standardized tests, many teachers use computers to develop skills that are not assessed by current tests. As a few examples, teachers have students use the Internet while developing their research skills (Heineke et al., 1999; Russell, 2001). Some teachers also have students use computers to collect, analyze and interpret data. Computer-based simulations are used to help students develop inquiry skills and to understand complex social, economic, and scientific concepts. For many students, computers are used to develop skills communicating with a variety of media including text, sound, still images, and video. Finally, through the use of technology, students develop technology fluency. Although there are several different definitions of technology fluency, there seems to be nearly universal consent among business leaders that technology-fluency is important for success in the workplace (CEO Forum, 2001a). Most standardized tests, however, do not measure many of the skills that students may be developing through instructional uses of computers. And, when they do, they require students to demonstrate their skill using paper-and-pencil.

Two gaps, then, exist between instructional use of technology and the assessment of student learning. First, many of the skills students develop while learning with computers are not measured by today's standardized tests. Second, some of the skills students do develop while learning with computers are mis-measured by standardized tests because students are not allowed to use computers while being tested. Together, these two gaps present a serious challenge to relying on standardized tests to assess the impact that computer-use in school has on student learning. The first gap results in missing information regarding many types of learning. The second gap produces misinformation regarding other types of learning. This problem has been well documented in the area of writing, but may be occurring in other areas of the curriculum as well (Russell, 1999; Russell & Haney, 1997a; Russell & Plati, 2001).

Two gaps also exists between how testing programs are using technology to improve testing and how technology is used in the classroom. First, as has occurred for several decades now, testing programs are using technology to increase the efficiency of current testing practices. Although several state-sponsored tests do use a mix of multiple-choice, open-ended and essay items, these tests tend to focus on discrete knowledge and skills. While these skills are important, they represent only a portion of the full set of skills and knowledge students are expected to develop in school. Thus, while the use of technology for testing may decrease the costs and time required for testing and may return results to schools more quickly, it does not alter the type or range of information provided to teachers about student learning.

Second, recent research on cognition and learning suggests many ways that technology can be used to create conditions believed to enhance learning. These conditions include real-world contexts for learning, connections to outside experts, visualization and analysis tools, scaffolds for problem solving, and opportunities for feedback, reflection, and revision (Means et al., 2000). These types of learning experiences are believed to be particularly helpful for developing students inquiry skills, conceptual understanding, and communication skills. Besides providing poor measures of these types of learning, today's standardized tests do not build these types of conditions into the testing experience. As several observers have argued, today's standardized tests present items in a decontextualized manner, do not allow students access to tools and additional information that may help them solve a complex problem, do not attempt to scaffold problems, do not require students to reflect on or revise their responses, and generally provide feedback long after the test is completed. Thus, while current tests do lead teachers to alter the content and skills upon which they focus, they do little to provide feedback to teachers and students in a timely manner which can be used to improve students' understanding of a given concept or ability to apply a given skill.

In turn, these four gaps produce two potentially troubling problems. First, test data does not provide any insight into the instructional practices that positively impact student learning, particularly when technology is used as part of the instructional process. As a result, policymakers, researchers, and the general public lack sufficient information to make informed decisions about the impact technology is having on student learning.

Second, teachers are employing potentially questionable practices regarding instructional uses of computers. Despite evidence that use of computers for writing has a positive impact on student writing skills, some teachers are decreasing this use in response to paper-based tests (Russell & Abrams, 2004). In hopes of increasing student performance in the areas assessed by standardized tests, teachers are also increasing their use of computers to help students learn discrete skills and knowledge. While it is important for all students to develop basic skills in mathematics and reading and to perform well on these standardized tests when high-stakes decisions are made based on their test scores, growing use of test preparation tutorials is likely coming at the expense of computer use aimed at enhancing learning, improving technology fluency, and developing higher order research, reasoning, and communication skills.

CHALLENGES TO ASSESSING TECHNOLOGY

In addition to problems caused by the gap between instructional use of technology and assessment, several additional challenges complicate efforts to assess the effects of instructional technology. These additional challenges fall into two categories: Understanding Context and Lack of Coordinated High Quality Research.

Understanding Context

A large body of research developed over the past century demonstrates that simply placing any type of educational technology, whether it is film, radio, television, or computer-based, into an educational setting does not result in use of that technology (Cuban, 1986; Saettler, 1990). Rather, regular and sustained use of educational technology is dependent upon many conditions. Teachers must see how the technology supports the curriculum and must be trained to use the technology, both in a technical manner and in an instructional manner. Teachers must have or must develop positive beliefs about the educational value of the technology. School and curriculum leaders must support and champion the use of the technology. The technology must be easily accessed and reliable. And the positive effects that the use of the technology may bring to students must be valued by the larger community (Lemke & Coughlin, 1998; O'Dwyer et al., 2004). Given the variety of factors that affect the success with which educational technology becomes integrated into the teaching and learning process, it is important that research on the effects of technology is not limited to the outcomes that result from that technology. Instead studies must place those outcomes in the context of the conditions in which the technology was (or was not) used. This requires research to examine both the outcomes and the extent to which the conditions that support the use of that technology exist.

With the current emphasis on randomized experiments, there is a danger that a given technology or technology-based program will be assigned to a set of sites and denied to other sites. Sometime later, outcome measures will be compared and conclusions about the effectiveness of that technology will be drawn. Inevitably, the effectiveness of the technology will vary across participating sites. This variation will likely result from different levels of use of that technology which in turn will be related to the extent to which the factors supporting that use were present in a given site. Unless randomized experiments employ a broad focus that extends beyond simply placing technology in one setting and not in another, and instead includes working with sites to create the conditions that support the use of that technology, it seems likely that the extent to which the technology is used will vary widely across sites placed in the experimental group. Similarly, unless such studies include data that focuses on the extent to which the conditions that support the technology use are present in participating sites and that this data is used during analyses, an incomplete understanding of the effects of the technology under different conditions will result.

Uncoordinated, Variable Quality Research

Over the past two decades, a considerable body of research has examined computer-based educational technologies. As I discussed in greater detail in Chapter 10, the quality and focus of this research vary considerably. As a result, policy makers and educational leaders face a confusing, often contradictory, and incomplete set of findings regarding the value of investing in educational technologies.

The U.S. Department of Education's current focus on scientifically-based evidence holds promise to increase the quality of future research. The current emphasis on student achievement also holds promise to more closely focus educational technology research on measurable impacts of the educational technology use on student learning. Moreover, the Department of Education's efforts to play a more active role in defining research priorities and in monitoring the quality of research studies could promote a more coordinated line of research that focuses on issues the Department believes are of critical importance. Ideally, these issues would include exploring the needs educational technology might meet, examining the effect a specific technology or a technology program has on teaching and learning, and deepening our understanding of the contexts in which these technologies and programs are most successful.

Unfortunately, it appears unlikely that issues such as these will be at the center of large-scale research efforts since the priorities established by the Department of Education and the Institute of Education Sciences often focus more on methodology than defining a research agenda. As an example, a number of grant programs developed over the past few years have awarded priority points based on the use of randomized experimental designs rather than the extent to which the proposal examines the application of educational technology to meet a critical need. Thus, rather than creating an atmosphere in which researchers focus their attention on important issues related to the use and effects of educational technology, the current priority is likely to spur researchers and educational technology programs to modify the focus of their research and programs such that they can more easily be examined via a randomized experiment. Given that many of the factors that affect the extent to which educational technology is used cannot be manipulated, further research on these issues may be curtailed. Similarly, since it is unreasonable to employ a randomized experiment when first developing and piloting a new educational technology, the development of new technologies may also become less supported. Finally, since it is far easier to design a randomized experiment that focuses on a single piece of educational technology, such as a piece of software, research on technology programs, including 1:1 laptop or PalmPilots or on-line learning, may diminish. Thus, while current trends in federal support for research on technology may sharpen the focus on examining the effects of educational technology on student learning and will encourage the use of randomized experimental designs, it is unclear whether this emerging body of research will address the critical issues related to implementing, supporting, and maximizing the potentially positive effects of educational technology.

SLOW PROGRESS DEVELOPING NEW FORMS OF ASSESSMENT

Throughout the 1990s, there was growing interest in advancing the technology of testing through the development of computer-based tests. This potential became an important component of the National Research Council's 2001 report titled *Knowing What Students Know.* Following the release of the NRC report, momentum built to make major investments in exploring a variety of ways in which computer-based technologies could be used to advance the state of the art in student assessment. This potential was evidenced by the National Science Foundation's development of the Science of Learning Centers grant program which, among other areas, included a focus on assessment in its program announcement. Similarly, the US Department of Education's Enhancing State Assessment Program provides opportunities for states to explore ways to improve their testing programs through novel applications of computers to testing. In addition, several states have begun exploring and, in a few cases, employing computer-based tests as part of their accountability systems.

Today, however, momentum to advance the technology of testing has given way to pressures to increase the efficiency with which traditional types of tests are administered, scored, and reported upon. While the Enhancing State Assessment Program did fund a small set of studies aimed at exploring applications of computers to increase accessibility to test items and the resulting validity of score inferences, only a small portion of this program's funds have been used to explore issues related to computer-based testing. Similarly, despite sparking interest in forming centers that focus specifically on applications of technology to student assessment, the NSF Science of Learning program has not resulted in significant funding for this topic. And, while an increasing number of states are transitioning to computer-based tests, these moves entail either transferring paper-based tests to a computer-delivered mode or developing computer-adaptive tests.

To be clear, federal programs have provided funds to several organizations to support the development of new applications of computers to testing. As an example, the Educational Testing Service is using federal funds to develop a flexible delivery system that could enable test takers to access items in a variety of formats such that construct irrelevant variance is reduced. Similarly, the Technology and Assessment Study Collaborative has received funding to develop computer-adaptive tests designed to diagnose misconceptions that interfere with students' understanding of important algebraic concepts. In addition, organizations such as the Center for Research on Evaluation, Standards, and Student Testing, the Center for Technology and Learning, and Carnegie Mellon's Pittsburgh Advanced Cognitive Tutor Center have continued to receive funding to explore applications of computers to the assessment process. While each of these projects, as well as many others, hold promise to enhance current assessment practices, a failure to provide significant funding to explore ways to advance the technology of testing through applications of computers is resulting in a fractured program of research that likely will not carry with it the political clout to impact large-scale testing programs or have widespread penetration into schools. Instead, testing programs appear to be investing considerably more time and effort in increasing the efficiency of practices developed several decades ago.

BELIEFS MATTER

Whether we focus on the role of technology for student assessment or the role of tests in assessing the impacts of technology, fundamental beliefs about testing and technology underlie the policies and practices that drive accountability systems and educational technology programs. As I describe in the first chapter, there are two divergent beliefs driving the use of technology in schools. On one side, some educational leaders believe that educational technology holds promise to drive educational reform. People like Seymour Papert and Angus King (the former Governor of Maine who launched a statewide laptop program) believe that educational technology can create new ways of and opportunities for learning. In contrast, others believe that computer-based technology is best applied to help students develop the basic skills associated with reading and mathematics.

Similar differences exist regarding the role student assessment should play in schools. Some assessment experts, like Grant Wiggins, Walt Haney, and Jim Popham, believe that student assessment's most valuable role is to inform a teacher's instructional practices and provide formative feedback to students. These leaders see student assessment as a process that is closely linked with instruction and occurs on a more frequent and refined manner. Many policy makers, however, believe that tests are best used to hold students, teachers, and schools accountable for teaching and learning a core set of skills and knowledge. They believe that assessing a specific subset of skills and knowledge on an annual basis will spur schools to focus instruction on this subset of skills and knowledge. In turn, this increased focus will improve student learning in these areas.

When beliefs regarding the role of technology and the role of assessment intersect, two principle viewpoints emerge. From one perspective, technology is seen as a tool that can be used to better prepare students for state tests while state tests are seen as a tool that can be used to assess the effectiveness of educational technology. From this viewpoint, the relationship between technology and student assessment is circular with technology being used to prepare students to perform on the outcome measure that is used to evaluate the value of technology.

A different perspective, however, views technology as a tool that opens possibilities, both for learning and for assessment. By providing students access to a wider variety of resources, educational experiences, and interactions, technology enables a wide variety of learning. At the same time, by providing teachers with relevant and timely information about student learning, technology-enabled assessments provide teachers with timely information that they can use to refine their instruction to better meet students' needs. In this way, technology-based assessment and technology-based learning become more closely intertwined.

What distinguishes these two perspectives are the time and place during which student assessment occurs. The first perspective views student assessment as a summative activity, the results of which inform practices that occur in the more distant future. The second perspective views student assessment as a formative activity that is often embedded into the instructional process, the results of which are applied immediately. Operating under the first perspective, decisions about the effectiveness of a given technology hinge on changes in summative test scores. In contrast, under the second perspective, a more holistic approach is taken when examining the effectiveness of a given technology. This holistic approach may include an analysis of summative state test scores, but also includes more refined and aligned measures of learning that is impacted as students engage with a given technology. Recognizing that the ways in which students interact with a given technology will likely vary across contexts, the second perspective is likely to be more open to examining a range of impacts across a variety of contexts.

A STRATEGY TO CLOSE THE GAP

Bridging the gap between the assessment of student achievement and research on educational technology requires collaboration between those who develop assessment tools and those who conduct research on educational technology. Test developers need to develop their understanding of the technological capacity of today's schools and how these capacities are altering the ways in which teaching and learning occur in some settings. Through this awareness, test developers will be better positioned to develop assessment instruments that enable students to employ the computer-based tools they have become accustomed to using during the learning process. Similarly, by becoming more familiar with the skills and knowledge developed through the use of educational technology, test developers will be better positioned to develop instruments that are more closely aligned with the domains technology researchers are interested in measuring.

The burden, however, for developing instruments that are more aligned and, potentially, sensitive to the types of learning that may occur through the use of educational technology does not lie solely on test developers. Educational technology researchers must also take steps to strengthen the psychometric properties of the instruments they developed as part of their research efforts. While the recent focus on scientifically-based research may overemphasize the role of randomized experiments, the push for rigorous, high-quality quantitative data collection creates opportunities for educational technology researchers to begin developing assessment instruments that, if of high quality, may become more attractive to policy makers and educational leaders as valid outcome measures. In many cases, however, the development of instruments that meet the standards of those endorsing scientifically-based research will require that educational technology researchers work more closely with researchers who have greater expertise in instrument develop and psychometrics.

In many ways, the need for educational technology researchers and test developers to work together more closely is consistent with the recommendations for more collaborative assessment development made by the authors of *Knowing What Students Know.* While these authors focused on the development of cognitively-based assessment instruments and recommended closer working relationships between cognitive scientists, test developers, and educators, the same principle holds for educational technology research. By bringing together educators who are at the cutting edge of instructional technology uses with researchers and test developers, greater potential will exist for the development of sound instruments that are aligned with the learning processes and outcomes in these technology-rich settings.

Currently, there are multiple opportunities to support collaboration between educators, educational technology researchers, and measurement experts. As described earlier, the National Science Foundation's Science of Learning Center program could provide substantial funding over an extended period of time to bring experts from these disciplines together to develop assessment instruments that capitalize on educational technology and which provide more valid measures of student learning in technology-enable learning environments. Although on a significantly smaller scale, the IES's Cognition and Student Learning program also holds promise to bring cognitive scientists, measurement experts, and educational technology specialists together to develop instruments that capitalize on educational technology and provide more robust measures of student learning.

To deepen understanding of how and why teaching and learning may change in technology-rich environments, the Science of Learning Center program could also provide funding for a sustained examination of instruction and learning outcomes in such environments. Although not a stated priority, the Institute of Education Sciences' National Research and Development Centers competition also holds potential to provide substantial sustained funding for this line of research.

On a smaller scale, the Department of Education's Enhance State Assessment Grants program provides opportunities for test developers, educational technology experts, and state education leaders to collaborate on state-level assessment development efforts that aim to enhance the validity and utility of state assessment programs. Already, funding from this program has been used to support research on uses of computer-based technology to increase the validity of test scores for students with a variety of test accommodation needs. This program, however, could also provide funding to develop assessment tasks that enable students to employ computer-based technologies during testing and which measure the constructs students may develop while learning with technology.

With increased emphasis placed in several IES grant programs on demonstrating the validity of measurement used for federally funded research, opportunities also exist to build instrument development and validation into research proposals. Funding for instrument development and validation could provide opportunities for educational technology researchers to work closely with measurement experts during this development phase. Given that this language is included in the Reading and Writing Education Research and the Mathematics and Science Education Research programs, funding to support both research on educational technologies applied within each of these content areas and the development of psychometrically sound learning outcome measures exists.

Despite these multiple opportunities to provide funding that brings educational technology researchers and measurement experts together to develop new assessment instruments, little funding is available to conduct large-scale sustained research on comprehensive technology-based programs. Without question, the IES's Reading and Writing and Mathematics and Science programs could provide funding for research on technology-based interventions. However, given both the limited size of these programs and the emphasis placed on randomized experiments, research supported by these programs is limited to interventions that focus on a specific and relatively inexpensive technology-based tool such as an algebra tutor or reading software. While high-quality research on such tools is needed, research on larger and less clearly defined interventions such as a 1:1 laptop program or hand-held computing devices is unlikely to be supported by these funding sources due to the high costs associated with conducting a randomized experiment in which large numbers of classrooms or schools are provided with laptops or handheld devices.

As discussed in Chapter 11, what is needed is a coordinated line of research that is capable of conducting a variety educational technology studies. These studies would range from carefully controlled large-scale studies in which specific components of a technology program are manipulated to smaller studies that investigate uses of technology that emerge at the local level. To facilitate this range of research, I envision a two-tiered research program that would include a single national coordinating center and a set of regional research centers. Based upon recommendations of a national advisory panel, the regional centers would conduct a limited set of large-scale studies. Responsibility for directing these large-scale priority studies would be designated to the national coordinating center while data collection would be conducted by researchers in the regional centers. In addition, the national coordinating center would employ a team of measurement experts that would develop and validate data collection instruments that would be employed by the regional centers. In this way, large-scale research could be conducted in representative samples of schools from across the nation using common measures, each of which have been thoroughly validated for a given study.

To avoid limiting educational technology research to well-established technology interventions, regional centers would also have discretionary funding that could be used to conduct smaller-scale research on issues emerging in the schools within their region. By working with state educational technology leaders and developing working relationships with local school districts that actively explore new ways to employ educational technology, regional centers could solicit requests from local schools and districts for small-scale research studies that focus on emerging uses of technology. Similarly, educational technology developers could submit requests for research on products and interventions that they have developed. To inform decisions regarding which studies to undertake, the regional centers would acquire advice from their advisory board. In addition, to avoid duplicating studies across regions, the national coordinating center would also provide advice on the small-scale studies performed by the regional centers. Finally, to increase the quality of data collection, the regional centers would work with the measurement specialists within the national coordinating center to develop and validate data collection tools. From this coordinated, yet flexible, research effort, it is likely that a body of student assessment tools that are aligned with the learning outcomes that may occur through the use of educational technology will emerge. As the utility of these measurement tools is demonstrated through research studies, they may also become models for the types of student assessment instruments used as part of school accountability programs. Although this two-tiered research structure would be expensive and require careful oversight, I believe it holds potential to begin closing the gap between the role of technology for student assessment and student learning while also providing the quality of evidence required to examine the effectiveness of a wide variety of applications of educational technology to teaching and learning.

REFERENCES

Adams, A.S. (1961). The pace of change. In Educational Testing Service, *Proceedings of the 1960 Invitational Conference on Testing Problems* (pp. 74–84). Princeton, NJ: Educational Testing Service.

Airasian, P. (1997). *Classroom assessment.* New York: McGraw-Hill.

Allington, R.L., & McGill-Franzen, A. (1992). Unintended effects of reform in New York. *Educational Policy, 4,* 397–414.

Alman, J.E. (1954). The university service bureau. In Educational Testing Service, *Proceedings of the 1953 Invitational Conference on Testing Problems* (pp. 147–150). Princeton, NJ: Educational Testing Service.

Almond, R.G., Steinberg, L.S., & Mislevy, R.J. (2002). Enhancing the design and delivery of assessment systems: A four-process architecture. *Journal of Technology, Learning, and Assessment, 1*(5). Available from http://www.jtla.org

Amrein, A.L. & Berliner, D.C. (2002, March 28). High-stakes testing, uncertainty, and student learning. *Educational Policy Analysis Archives, 10*(18). Retrieved May 15, 2002, from http://epaa.asu.edu/epaa/v10n18/

Anderson, J.R., Corbett, A.T., Koedinger, K., & Pelletier, R. (1995). Cognitive tutors: Lessons learned. *Journal of Learning Sciences, 4,* 167–207.

Andrich, D. (in press). Georg Rasch: Mathematician and Statistician. In the *Encyclopedia of social measurement.* San Diego, CA: Academic Press.

Angrist, J., & Lavy, V. (2001). *New evidence on classroom computers and pupil learning.* Bonn: Institute for the Study of Labor.

Azevedo, R., & Bernard, R.M. (1995a). Assessing the effects of feedback in computer-assisted learning. *British Journal of Educational Technology, 26*(1), 57–58.

Azevedo, R., & Bernard, R.M. (1995b). A meta-analysis of the effect of feedback in computer-based instruction. *Journal of Educational Computing Research, 13*(2), 109–125.

Baker, E. (1999). *Technology: How do we know it works?* Paper for the Secretary's Conference on Educational Technology, Washington, DC. Available from http://www.ed.gov/Technology/TechConf/1999/whitepapers/paper5.html

Baker, E., & Herman, J. (2000). *Technology and evaluation.* Paper presented at the SRI Design Meeting on Design Issues in Evaluating Educational Technologies.

Technology and Assessment: The Tale of Two Interpretations, pages 219–235
Copyright © 2006 by Information Age Publishing
All rights of reproduction in any form reserved.

Retrieved December 4, 2002, from http://www.sri.com/policy/designkt/baker1.pdf

Baker, E., Herman, J., & Gearhart, M. (1996). Does technology work in school? Why evaluation cannot tell the full story. In C. Fisher, D. Dwyer, & K. Yocam (Eds.), *Education and technology: Reflections on computing in classrooms* (pp. 185–202). San Francisco: Apple Press.

Bangert-Drowns, R.L. (1993). The word processor as an instructional tool: A meta-analysis of word processing in writing instruction. *Review of Educational Research, 63*(1), 69–93.

Barron, B.J., Schwartz, D.L., Vye, N.J., Moore, A., Petrosino, A., Zech, L., & Bransford, J.D. (1998). Doing with understanding: Lessons from research on problem and project-based learning. *Journal of Learning Sciences, 7*(3), 271–312.

Barry, A. (1994). Advertising and Channel One: Controversial partnership of business and education. In A. DeVaney (Ed.), *Watching Channel One: The convergence of students, technology, and private business* (p. 102–136). Albany: State University of New York Press.

Bebell, D., Russell, M., & O'Dwyer, L. (2004). Measuring teachers' technology uses: Why multiple-measures are more revealing. *Journal of Research on Technology in Education, 37*(1) 45–64.

Becker, H.J. (1999). *Internet use by teachers: Conditions of professional use and teacher-directed student use.* Irvine, CA: Center for Research on Information Technology and Organizations.

Becker, H.J., & Lovitts, B. (2000). *A project-based assessment model for judging the effects of technology use in comparison group studies.* Paper presented at the SRI Design Meeting on Design Issues in Evaluating Educational Technologies. Retrieved December 4, 2002, from http://www.sri.com/policy/designkt/becker2.pdf

Bennett, R.E. & Persky, H. (2002). *NAEP technology-based assessment project.* Princeton, NJ: Educational Testing Service.

Bennett, R.E. (1995). *Computer-based testing for examinees with disabilities: On the road to generalized accommodation* (RM-95-1). Princeton, NJ: Educational Testing Service.

Bennett, R.E. (1998a). *Reinventing assessment: Speculations on the future of large-scale educational testing.* Princeton, NJ: Educational Testing Service, Policy Information Center. Retrieved January 27, 2001, from http://www.ets.org/research/pic/bennett.html

Bennett, R.E. (1998b). *Speculations on the future of large-scale educational testing.* Princeton, NJ: Educational Testing Service.

Bennett, R.E. (1999a). Computer-based testing of examinees with disabilities: On the road to generalized accommodation. In S. Messick (Ed.), *Assessment in higher education: Issues of access, quality, student development, and public policy.* Mahwah, NJ: Lawrence Erlbaum Associates.

Bennett, R.E. (1999b). Using new technology to improve assessment. *Educational Measurement, 18*(3), 5–12.

Bennett, R.E. (2001). How the Internet will help large-scale assessment reinvent itself. *Education Policy Analysis Archives, 9*(5). Retrieved February 15, 2001, from http://epaa.asu.edu/epaa/v9n5.html

Bennett, R.E. (2002). Inexorable and inevitable: The continuing story of technology assessment. *Journal of Technology, Learning, and Assessment, 1*(1). Retrieved August 10, 2003, from http://www.bc.edu/research/intasc/jtla/journal/v1n1.shtml

Bereiter, C., & Scardamalia, M. (1989). Intentional learning as a goal of instruction. In L. Resnick (Ed.), *Knowing, learning, and instruction: Essays in Honor of Robert Glaser* (pp. 361–392). Hillsdale, NJ: Lawrence Erlbaum Associates.

Bodily, S., & Mitchell, K. (1997). *Evaluating challenge grants for technology in education: A sourcebook.* Santa Monica, CA: Rand.

Bradley, P.H. (1954). Speaking for international business machines. In Educational Testing Service, *Proceedings of the 1953 Invitational Conference on Testing Problems* (pp. 169–172). Princeton, NJ: Educational Testing Service.

Brown-Chidsey, R., & Boscardin, M.L. (1999). *Computers as accessibility tools for students with and without learning disabilities.* Amherst: University of Massachusetts.

Bruer, J. (1998). Let's put brain science on the back burner. *NASSP Bulletin, 82*, 9–19.

Bunderson, C., Inouye, D., & Olsen, J. (1989). The four generations of computerized educational measurement. In Linn, R. L. (Ed.), *Educational measurement* (3rd ed., pp. 367–408). Washington, DC: American Council on Education.

Burstein, J. (2001). *Automated Essay Scoring @ ETS.* Available from http://www.ets.org/research/erater/sld001.htm

Callahan, R. (1956). *An introduction to education in American society.* New York: Alfred A. Knopf.

Carnegie Learning. (2002). *Frequently asked questions about Cognitive Tutor® Curricula and Carnegie Learning's place in the classroom.* Retrieved July 29, 2002, from http://www.carnegielearning.com/faq/

Center for Universal Design. (1997). *What is universal design?* Retrieved August 1, 2002, from http://www.design.ncsu.edu/cud/univ_design/ud.htm

CEO Forum on Education and Technology. (2001a). *Key building blocks for student achievement in the 21st century: Assessment, alignment, accountability, access, analysis* (Year 4 Report). Washington, DC: Author. Available from http://www.ceoforum.org/reports.html

CEO Forum on Educational Technology. (2001b). *STaR Chart: A tool for school technology and readiness.* Retrieved December 29, 2002, from http://www.iste.org/starchart/index.cfm

Christensen, C.M. (1997). *The innovator's dilemma: When new technologies cause great firms to fail.* Boston: Harvard University Press.

Clarke, M., Madaus, G., Horn, C., & Ramos, M. (2001). The marketplace for educational testing. *National Board on Educational Testing and Public Policy Statements, 2*(3).

Coalition of Essential Schools. (2002). *CES national affiliate schools.* Retrieved June 6, 2002, from http://www.essentialschools.org/cs/schools/query/q/562?x-r=runnew

Cochran-Smith, M, Paris, C., & Kahn, J. (1991). *Learning to write differently: Beginning writers and word processing.* Norwood, NJ: Ablex.

Cohen, D.K., & Hill, H.C. (2001). *Learning policy: When state education reform works.* New Haven, CT: Yale University Press.

Connell, D., Turner, R., & Mason, E. (1985). Summary of findings of the school health education evaluation: Health promotion effectiveness, implementation and costs. *Journal of School Health, 55*, 316–321.

Cook, T. (2000). *Reappraising the arguments against randomized experiments in education: An analysis of the culture of evaluation in American schools of education.* Paper presented at the SRI Design Meeting on Design Issues in Evaluating Educational Technologies. Retrieved on December 4, 2002, from http://www.sri.com/policy/designkt/cokfinal.pdf

Cook, T., Anson, A., & Walchli, S. (1993). From causal description to causal explanation: Improving three already good evaluations of adolescent health programs. In S.G. Millstein, A.C. Petersen, & E.O. Nightengale (Eds.), *Promoting the health of adolescents: New directions for the twenty-first century.* New York: Oxford University Press.

Cook, T., Habib, F., Phillips, J., Settersten, R., Shagle, S., & Degirmencioglu, S. (1999). Comer's school development program in Prince George's County, Maryland: A theory-based evaluation. *American Educational Research Journal, 36*(3), 543–597.

Cook, T., Hunt, H., & Murphy, R. (1999). *Comer's school development program in Chicago: A theory based evaluation.* Working paper, Institute for Policy Research, Northwestern University, Chicago, IL.

Corbet, A. (2002). Cognitive Tutor Algebra I: Adaptive student modeling in widespread classroom use. In the National Research Council's *Technology and assessment: Thinking ahead—proceedings from a workshop* (pp. 50–62). Washington, DC: National Academies Press.

Cronbach, L.J. (1982). *Designing evaluations of educational and social programs.* San Francisco: Jossey-Bass.

Cronbach, L.J., & Snow, R.E. (1977). *Aptitudes and instructional methods: A handbook for research on interactions.* New York: Irvington.

Cronbach, L.J., Ambron, S.R., Dornbusch, S.M., Hess, R.D., Hornik, R.C., Phillips, D.C., et al. (1980). *Toward reform of program evaluation.* San Francisco: Jossey-Bass.

Cuban, L. (1986). *Teachers and machines: The classroom use of technology since 1920.* New York: Teachers College Press.

Cuban, L. (2001). *Oversold & underused: Computers in the classroom.* Cambridge, MA: Harvard University Press.

Culp, K., Honey, M., & Spielvogel, R. (2000). *Local relevance and generalizability: Linking evaluation to school improvement.* Paper presented at the SRI Design Meeting on Design Issues in Evaluating Educational Technologies. Retrieved December 4, 2002, from http://www.sri.com/policy/designkt/chs.pdf

Daiute, C. (1986). Physical and cognitive factors in revising: Insights from studies with computers. *Research in the Teaching of English, 20*, 141–159.

Daniel, J. (2000). *The Internet and higher education: Preparing for change.* Presentation at the Internet Revolution Conference, London. Retrieved August 4, 2002, from http://www.open.ac.uk/vcs-speeches/IntEdRev.html

Danitz, T. (2001). *Special Report: States pay $400 million for tests in 2001.* Retrieved June 20, 2002, from Stateline.org Web site: http://www.stateline.org/stateline/?pa=story&sa=showStoryInfo&id=116627

Danitz, T. (2002). *States challenged by education bill.* Retrieved June 20, 2002, from Stateline.org Web site: http://www.stateline.org/stateline/?pa=story&sa=show-StoryInfo&id=215350

Darling-Hammond, L., Ancess, J., & Falk, B. (1995). *Authentic assessment in action: Studies of schools and students at work.* New York: Teachers College Press.

de la Mare, P. (1997). *An industry born.* Retrieved October 29, 2003, from http://www.dotprint.com/fgen/history1.htm

Debra P. v. Turlington, 474 F. Supp. 244 (M.D. FL 1979).

deGraaf, C., Ridout, S., & Riehl, J. (1993). Technology in education: Creatively using computers in the language arts. In N. Estes & M. Thomas (Eds.), *Rethinking the roles of technology in education* (Vol. 2). Cambridge, MA: Massachusetts Institute of Technology.

Downey, M.T. (1965). *Ben Wood: Educational reformer.* Princeton, NJ: Educational Testing Service.

Drasgow, F., & Olson-Buchanan, J.B. (1999). *Innovations in computerized assessment.* Mahwah, NJ: Lawrence Erlbaum Associates.

Dunham, P.H., & Dick, T.P. (1994). Research on graphing calculators. *The Mathematics Teacher, 87,* 440–445.

Durlak, J., & Wells, A. (1997). Primary prevention mental health programs: The future is exciting. *American Journal of Community Psychology, 25,* 233–241.

Dwyer, D. (1996). Learning in the age of technology. In C. Fisher, D. Dwyer, & K. Yocam (Eds.), *Education and technology: Reflections on computing in classrooms* (pp. 15–34). San Francisco: Apple Press.

Educational Testing Service. (1954). *Proceedings of the 1953 Invitational Conference on Testing Problems.* Princeton, NJ: Author.

Etchinson, C. (1989). Word processing: A helpful tool for basic writers. *Computers and Composition, 6*(2), 33–43.

Finn, J., & Achilles, C. (1990). Answers and questions about class size: A statewide experiment. *American Educational Research Journal, 27*(3), 557–577.

Fisher, C., Dwyer, D., & Yocam, K. (1996). *Education and technology: Reflections on computing in classrooms.* San Francisco: Apple Press.

Fletcher, J.D. (1990). *Effectiveness and cost of interactive videodisc instruction in defense training and education* (IDA Paper P-2372). Alexandria, VA: Institute for Defense Analyses.

Foltz, W., Gilliam, S., & Kendall, S. (2000). Supporting content-based feedback in on-line writing evaluation with LSA. *Interactive Learning Environments, 8,* 111–128.

Franke, W. (1960). *The reform and abolition of the traditional Chinese examination system.* Cambridge, MA: Harvard University Press.

Frederiksen, N., Mislevy, R., & Bejar, I. (1993). *Test theory for a new generation of tests.* Hillsdale, NJ: Lawrence Erlbaum Associates.

Futrell, M., & Rotberg, I. (2002, October 2). Predictable casualties. *Education Week on the Web.* Retrieved November 11, 2002, from http://www.edweek.org/ew/ewstory.cfm?slug=05futrell.h22&keywords=diploma

Glass, G.V. (1976). Primary, secondary, and meta-analysis of research. *Educational Researcher, 5,* 3–8.

Glass, G., & Hopkins, K. (1984). *Statistical methods in education and psychology.* Boston: Allyn and Bacon.

Glennan, T.K., & Melmed, A. (1996). *Fostering the use of educational technology: Elements of a national strategy.* Santa Monica, CA: Rand.

Goldberg, A., O'Connor, K., & Russell, M. (2002). *Teachers' perceived use, access, support, and obstacles in using instructional technology.* Chestnut Hill, MA: Technology and Assessment Study Collaborative. Available from http://www.bc.edu/research/intasc/studies/USEIT/description.shtml

Goldberg, A., Russell, M., & Cook, A. (2002). *Meta-analysis: Writing with computers 1992–2002.* Chestnut Hill, MA: Boston College, Technology and Assessment Study Collaborative. Retrieved January 21, 2003, from http://www.bc.edu/research/intasc/PDF/Meta_WritingComputers.pdf

Goldberg, A., Russell, M., & Cook, A. (2003). The effect of computers on student writing: A meta-analysis of studies from 1992 to 2002. *Journal of Technology, Learning, and Assessment, 2*(1). Available from http://www.jtla.org

Goldman-Segall, R. (1998). *Points of viewing children's thinking: A digital ethnographer's journey.* Mahwah, NJ: Lawrence Erlbaum Associates.

Good, H., & Teller, J. (1973). *A history of American education.* New York: Macmillan.

Goodnough, A. (2002, September 25). If test scores in New York swell, so may superintendents' wallets. *New York Times,* pp. A1, A22.

Gould, S.J. (1996). *The mismeasure of man.* New York: W.W. Norton & Company.

Greenfield, P.M., & Cocking, R.R. (Eds). (1996). *Interacting with video.* Greenwich, CT: Ablex.

Guba, E.G., & Lincoln, Y. (1982). *Effective evaluation.* San Francisco: Jossey-Bass.

Gutek, G. (1986). *Education in the United States: An historical perspective.* Englewood Cliffs, NJ: Prentice Hall.

Haas, C., & Hayes, J.R. (1986). What did I just say? Reading problems in writing with the machine. *Research in the Teaching of English, 20*(1), 22–35.

Hambelton, R., Swaminathan, H., & Rogers, H. (1991). *Fundamentals of item response theory.* Newbury Park, CA: Sage.

Haney, W. (2000). The myth of the Texas miracle in education. *Educational Policy Analysis Archives, 8*(41). Retrieved October 20, 2002, from http://epaa.asu.edu/epaa/v8n41/

Haney, W.M., Madaus, G.F., & Lyons, R. (1993). *The fractured marketplace for standardized testing.* Boston: Kluwer Academic.

Haney, W., & Raczek, A. (1994). *Surmounting outcomes accountability in education.* Paper prepared for the U.S. Congress, Office of Technology Assessment, Washington, DC.

Hankes, E.J. (1954). New developments in test scoring machines. In Educational Testing Service, *Proceedings of the 1953 Invitational Conference on Testing Problems* (pp. 157–159). Princeton, NJ: Educational Testing Service.

Hannafin, M., & Dalton, D. (1987). The effects of word processing on written composition. *The Journal of Educational Research, 80,* 338–342.

Hanson, M.A., Borman, W.C., Mogilka, H.J., Manning, C., & Hedge, J.W. (1999). In F. Drasgow & J. B. Olson-Buchanan (Eds.), *Innovations in computerized assessment* (pp. 151–176). Mahwah, NJ: Lawrence Erlbaum Associates.

Harman, H.H., & Harper, B.P. (1954). AGO machines for test analysis. In Educational Testing Service, *Proceedings of the 1953 Invitational Conference on Testing Problems* (pp. 154–156). Princeton, NJ: Educational Testing Service.

Healy, J. (1999). *Failure to connect.* New York: Simon & Schuster.

Hedges, L., & Olkin, I. (1985). *Statistical methods for meta-analysis.* Orlando, FL: Academic Press.

Hedges, L., Konstantopoulos, S., & Thoreson, A. (2000). *Designing studies to measure the implementation and impact of technology in American schools.* Paper presented at the SRI Design Meeting on Design Issues in Evaluating Educational Technologies. Retrieved December 4, 2002, from http://www.sri.com/policy/designkt/hedges2.pdf

Heinecke, W., Blasi, L., Milman, N., & Washington, L. (1999). *New directions in the evaluation of the effectiveness of educational technology.* Paper presented at the Secretary's Conference on Educational Technology, Washington, DC.

Herman, J.L. (1994). Evaluating the effects of technology in school reform. In B. Means (Ed.), *Technology and education reform: The reality behind the promise.* San Francisco: Jossey-Bass. Available from http://www.ed.gov/Technology/TechConf/1999/whitepapers/paper8.html

Hickey, D.T., Kindfield, A.C.H., & Horwitz, P. (1999, August). *Large-scale implementation and assessment of the GenScope learning environment: Issue, solutions, and results.* Paper presented at the meeting of the European Association for Research on Learning and Instruction, Goteborg, Sweden.

Hieronymus, A.N. (1972). Today's testing: What do we know how to do? In Educational Testing Service, *Educational Change: Implications for Measurement, Proceedings of the 1971 Invitational Conference on Testing Problems* (pp. 57–68). Princeton, NJ: Educational Testing Service.

Hoban, C.F., & Van Ormer, E.B. (1950). *Instructional film research, 1918–1950* (Tech. Rep. No. SDC 269-7-19). Port Washington, NY: U.S. Naval Special Devices Center. (ERIC Document Reproduction Service No. ED 647255)

Hollenbeck, K., Tindal, G., Harniss, M., & Almond, P. (1999). Reliability and decision consistency: An analysis of writing mode at two times on a statewide test. *Educational Assessment, 6*(1), 23–40.

Hunter, B. (1998). *Vanguard for learning: Linking across boundaries.* Amissville, VA: Piedmont Research Institute. Retrieved November 2, 2002, from http://www.piedmontresearch.org/bib/linking.html

Hunter, C. (1998). *Technology in the classroom: Haven't we heard this before?* Retrieved August 3, 2002, from http://www.asc.upenn.edu/usr/chunter/edtech.html

International Society for Technology Education Association. (2000). *National Educational Technology Standards for Students—Connecting curriculum and technology.* Washington, DC: Author. Available from http://iste.org/bookstore/detail.cfm?sku=netsb2

Irvine, S.H., & Kyllonen, P.C. (2002). *Item generation for test development.* Mahwah, NJ: Lawrence Erlbaum Associates.

Johnson, D.W., & Johnson, R. (1975). *Learning together and alone: Cooperation, competition, and individualization.* Englewood Cliffs, NJ: Prentice-Hall.

Katz, I.R., Martinez, M.E., Sheehan, K.M., & Tatsuoka, K.K. (1998). Extending the rule space model to a semantically-rich domain: Diagnostic assessment in architecture. *Journal of Educational and Behavioral Statistics, 23*, 254–278.

Kay, H., Dodd, B., & Sime, M. (1968). *Teaching machines and programmed instruction.* Middlesex, England: Penguin Books.

Kenelly, J. (1990). Implementing the standards: Using calculators in the standardized testing of mathematics. *Mathematics Teacher, 83*(9), 716–720.

Kerchner, L., & Kistinger, B. (1984). Language processing/word processing: Written expression, computers, and learning disabled students. *Learning Disability Quarterly, 7*(4), 329–335.

Klahr, D., & Carver, S.M. (1988). Cognitive objectives in a LOGO debugging curriculum: Instruction, learning, and transfer. *Cognitive Psychology, 20*(3), 362–404.

Klein, D., Yarnall, L., & Glaubke, C. (2001). *Using technology to assess students' web expertise* (Technical Report 544). Retrieved December 4, 2002, from http://www.cse.ucla.edu/CRESST/Reports/TECH544.pdf

Knott, T. (1993). The role of evaluation in the educational reformation. In N. Estes & M. Thomas (Eds.), *Rethinking the roles of technology in education.* Cambridge, MA: Massachusetts Institute of Technology.

Koedinger, K., Anderson, J., Hadley, W., & Mark, M. (1997). Intelligent Tutoring goes to school in the Big City. *International Journal of Artificial Intelligence in Education, 8*, 30–43.

Kulik, C.C., & Kulik, J. (1991). Effectiveness of computer-based instruction: An updated analysis. *Computers in Human Behavior, 7*(12), 75–94.

Kulik, J.A. (1994). Meta-analytic studies of findings on computer-based instruction. In E.L. Baker & H.F. O'Neil, Jr. (Eds.), *Technology assessment in education and training* (pp. 9–33). Hillsdale, NJ: Lawrence Erlbaum Associates.

Kurtz, M., & Vaishnav, A. (2002, December 5). Student's MCAS answer means 449 others pass. *The Boston Globe*, p. A1.

Landau, S., Russell, M., Gourgey, K., Erin, J., & Cowan, J. (2003). Use of the talking tactile tablet in mathematics testing. *Journal of Visual Impairment and Blindness, 97*(2), 85–96.

Lemke, C. (2002). *21st century skills: The EnGauge framework.* Naperville, IL: North Central Regional Educational Laboratory. Available from North Central Region Education Laboratory Web site, http://www.ncrel.org/engauge/skills/skills.htm

Lemke, C., & Coughlin, E. (1998). *Technology in American schools: Seven dimensions for gauging progress.* Santa Monica, CA: Milken Family Foundation, Milken Exchange on Educational Technology. Retrieved December 4, 2002, from http://www.mff.org/pubs/ME158.pdf

Levin, D., & Arafeh, S. (2002). *The digital disconnect: The widening gap between Internet-savvy students and their schools.* Washington, DC: Pew Internet and American Life Project. Retrieved October 29, 2003, from http://www.pewInternet.org/reports/toc.asp?Report=67

Lindquist, E.F. (1954). The Iowa electronic test processing equipment. In Educational Testing Service, *Proceedings of the 1953 Invitational Conference on Testing Problems* (pp. 160–168). Princeton, NJ: Educational Testing Service.

Lipsey, M., & Wilson, D. (2001). *Practical meta-analysis* (Vol. 49). Thousand Oaks, CA: Sage.

Madaus, G.F. (1993). A national testing system: Manna from above? An historical/technological perspective. *Educational Assessment, 1*(1), 9–26.

Madaus, G.F. (2001). Educational testing as a technology. *National Board on Educational Testing and Public Policy Statements, 2*(1).

Madaus, G.F., & O'Dwyer, L.M. (1999). A short history of performance assessment: Lessons learned. *Phi Delta Kappan, 80*(9), 688–695.

Madaus, G.F., Raczek, A.E., & Clarke, M.M. (1997). The historical and policy foundations of the assessment movement. In A.L. Goodwin (Ed.), *Assessment for equity and inclusion: Embracing all our children* (pp. 1–33). New York: Routledge.

Maduas, G.F., Stufflebeam, D.L., & Scriven, M.S. (1993). Program evaluation: A historical overview. In G.F. Madaus, M.S. Scriven, & D.L. Stufflebeam (Eds.), *Evaluation models: Viewpoints on educational and human services evaluation* (pp. 3–22). Boston: Kluwer-Nijhoff.

Maine Learning Technology Initiative. (2002). Retrieved November 19, 2002, from http://www.state.me.us/mlte/

Mann, D., Shakeshaft, C., Becker, J., & Kottkamp, R. (1999). *West Virginia story: Achievement gains from a statewide comprehensive instructional technology program.* Santa Monica, CA: A Milken Family Foundation Monograph. (ED429575) http://www.mff.org/publications/publications.taf?page=155

Market Data Retrieval. (1999). *Technology in education 1999.* Shelton, CT: Author.

Market Data Retrieval. (2001). *Technology in education 2001.* Shelton, CT: Author.

Martinez, M. (2002). *Lee Cronbach's and Richard Snow's important lessons from the past: Historical perspective.* Retrieved November 7, 2002, from http://www.training-place.com/source/research/cronbach.htm

Massachusetts Department of Education. (2002). *Online MCAS tutorials for the Class of 2003 and 2004.* Retrieved September 10, 2002, from http://www.doe.mass.edu/mcas/tutors/tutorial_memo.html

Massachusetts Department of Education. (2003). *Requirements for the participation of students with disabilities in MCAS.* Malden, MA: Authors. Retrieved December 10, 2003, from http://www.doe.mass.edu/mcas/alt/spedreq.pdf

McDonnell, L.M., McLaughlin, M.W., & Morison, P. (Eds.). (1997). *Educating one and all: Students with disabilities and standards-based reform.* Washington, DC: National Academies Press.

McFarlane, A.E., Friedler, Y., Warwick, P., & Chaplain, R. (1995). Developing an understanding of the meaning of line graphs in primary science investigations, using portable computers and data logging software. *Journal of Computers in Mathematics and Science Teaching, 14*(4), 461–480.

McGrew, K.S., Thurlow, M.L., Shriner, J.G., & Spiegel, A.N. (1992). *Students with disabilities in national and state data collection programs.* Minneapolis: University of Minnesota, National Center on Educational Outcomes.

McNabb, M., Hawkes, M., & Rouk, U. (1999). *Critical issues in evaluating the effectiveness of technology* [Report on the Secretary's Conference on Educational Technology 1999]. Washington, DC: U.S. Department of Education. Available from U.S. Department of Education Web site, http://www.ed.gov/rschstat/eval/tech/techconf99/confsum.html

Mead, A., & Drasgow, F. (1993). Equivalence of computerized and paper-and-pencil cognitive ability tests: A meta-analysis. *Psychological Bulletin, 114*(3), 449–58.

Means, B. (1994). *Technology and education reform: The reality behind the promise.* San Francisco: Jossey-Bass.

Means, B., & Haertel, G. (2002). Technology supports for assessing science inquiry. In the National Research Council's *Technology and assessment: Thinking ahead—Proceedings from a workshop* (pp. 12–25). Washington, DC: National Academies Press.

Means, B., Penuel, B., & Quellmalz, E. (2000). *Developing assessments for tomorrow's classrooms.* Paper presented at the Secretary's Conference on Educational Technology 2000, Washington, DC. Retrieved December 4, 2002, from http://www.ed.gov/Technology/techconf/2000/means_paper.html

Means, B., Penuel, B., & Quellmalz, E. (2001). Developing assessments for tomorrow's classrooms. In W.F. Heinecke & L. Blasi (Eds.), *Methods of evaluating educational technology* (pp. 149–160). Greenwich, CT: Information Age Publishing.

Meskill, J. (1963). *The Chinese Civil Service: Career open to talent.* Boston: Heath.

Meyer, L., Orlofsky, G., Skinner, R., & Spicer, S. (2002). Quality counts 2002: The state of the states. *Education Week, 21*, 68–70.

Microsoft. (2002, March 4). *Microsoft technology hits the road in BMW 7 Series.* Retrieved May 16, 2002, from http://www.microsoft.com/presspass/press/2002/Mar02/03-04BMWpr.asp

Mills, C.N., Potenza, M.T., Fremer, J.J., & Ward, W.C. (2002). *Computer-based testing: Building the foundation for future assessments.* Mahwah, NJ: Lawrence Erlbaum Associates.

Minstrell, J., Stimpson, V., & Hunt, E. (1992, April). *Instructional design and tools to assist teachers in addressing students' understanding and reasoning.* Paper presented at the meeting of the American Educational Research Association, San Francisco.

Mislevy, R.J. (1993). Foundations of a new test theory. In N. Frederiksen, R.J. Mislevy, & I.I. Bejar (Eds.). *Test theory for a new generation of tests* (pp. 19–40). Hillsdale, NJ: Lawrence Erlbaum Associates.

Mosteller, F., Light, R., & Sachs, J. (1996). Sustained inquiry in education: Lessons from skill grouping and class size. *Harvard Educational Review, 66*, 797–842.

Mouran, R.R., Lakshmanan, R., & Chantadisai, R. (1981). Visual fatigue and Cathode Ray Tube display terminals. *Human Factors, 23*(5), 529–540.

National Center for Education Statistics. (2002). *Internet access in U.S. public schools and classrooms: 1994–2001.* Washington, DC: Author.

National Center for Education Statistics. (2003). *Technology-Based Assessment Project.* Retrieved March 22, 2003, from http://nces.ed.gov/nationsreportcard/studies/tbaproject.asp

National Commission on Excellence in Education. (1983). *A nation at risk: The imperative for education reform.* Washington, DC: U.S. Government Printing Press. Retrieved November 11, 2002, from http://www.ed.gov/pubs/NatAtRisk/risk.html

National Governors Association. (2002). *Using electronic assessment to measure student performance.* Washington, DC: NGA Center for Best Practices, Education Policy

Studies Division. Retrieved September 4, 2002, from http://www.nga.org/cda/files/ELECTRONICASSESSMENT.pdf

National Research Council. (2000). *How people learn: Brain, mind, experience, and school.* Washington, DC: National Academy Press.

National Research Council. (2001). *Knowing what students know: The science and design of educational assessment.* Washington, DC: National Academy Press.

Nave, B., Miech, E. I. J., & Mosteller, F. (1999). *A rare design: The role of field trials in evaluating school practices.* Paper presented at the American Academy of Arts and Sciences at Harvard University.

Newburger, E. (2001). *Home computers and Internet use in the United States: August 2000. Special studies current population reports.* Washington, DC: U.S. Department of Commerce Economics and Statistics Administration, U.S. Census Bureau. Retrieved November 19, 2002, from http://www.census.gov/prod/2001pubs/p23-207.pdf

Nichols, P.D., & Brennan, R.L. (1995). Preface. In P. D. Nichols, S. F. Chipman, & R. L. Brennan (Eds.), *Cognitively diagnostic assessment.* Hillsdale, NJ: Lawrence Erlbaum Associates.

Nichols, P.D., Chipman, S.F., & Brennan, R.L. (Eds.). (1995). *Cognitively diagnostic assessment.* Hillsdale, NJ: Lawrence Erlbaum Associates.

North Carolina Department of Public Instruction. (2000). Calculator requirements for the North Carolina Testing Program. *Assessment Brief, 7*(1). Retrieved October 20, 2002, from http://www.ncpublicschools.org/accountability/testing/briefs/CalculatorRe quirements/

O'Dwyer, L., Russell, M. & Bebell, D. (2004). Identifying teacher, school and district characteristics associated with teachers' use of technology: A multilevel perspective. *Educational Policy Analysis Archives, 12*(48). Available: http://epaa.asu.edu/epaa/v12n48/v12n48.pdf

Oppenheimer, T. (20003). *The flickering mind: The false promise of technology in the classroom and how learning can be saved.* New York: Random House.

Orlofsky, G.F., & Olson, L. (2001). The state of the states. *Education Week, 20*(17), 86–88.

Page, E. (1966). The imminence of grading essays by computer. *Phi Delta Kappan, 47,* 238–243.

Page, E. (1968). The use of computers in analyzing student essays. *International Review of Education, 14*(2), 210–221.

Page, E. (1995, August). *Computer grading of essays: A different kind of testing?* Paper presented at the meeting of the American Psychological Association, New York.

Papert, S. (1993). *The children's machine: Rethinking school in the age of the computer.* New York: Basic Books.

Pedulla, J., Abrams, L., Madaus, G., Russell, M., Ramos, M., & Miao, J. (2003). *Perceived effects of state-mandated testing programs on teaching and learning: Findings from a national survey of teachers.* Chestnut Hill, MA: Boston College, National Board on Educational Testing and Public Policy. Retrieved April 29, 2003, from http://www.bc.edu/research/nbetpp/statements/nbr2.pdf

Pellegrino. J., Chudowsky, N., & Glaser, R. (2001). *Knowing what students know: The science and design of educational assessments.* Washington, DC: National Academy Press.

Perkins, D.N. (1990). *Person plus: A distributed view of thinking and learning.* Paper presented at the meeting of the American Educational Research Association, Boston.

Peters, R., & McMahon, R. (Eds.). (1996). *Preventing childhood disorders, substance abuse, and delinquency.* Thousand Oaks, CA: Sage.

Peterson, P., Greene, J., Howell, W., & McCready, W. (1998). *Initial findings from an evaluation of school choice programs in Washington, D.C.* Cambridge, MA: Harvard University, Program on Education Policy and Governance.

Popham, W. (1988). *Educational evaluation.* Englewood Cliffs, NJ: Prentice-Hall.

Powers, D., Fowles, M, Farnum, M, & Ramsey, P. (1994). Will they think less of my handwritten essay if others word process theirs? Effects on essay scores of intermingling handwritten and word-processed essays. *Journal of Educational Measurement, 31*(3), 220–233.

Ramirez, M., & Althouse, P. (1995). Fresh thinking: GIS in environmental education. *THE Journal, 23*(2), 87–90.

Rasch G. (1980). *Probabilistic model for some intelligence and attainment tests.* Chicago: University of Chicago Press. (Original work published 1960)

Ravitch, D. (1995). *National standards in American schools.* Washington, DC: Brookings Institute.

Ravitz, J L., Mergendoller, J., & Rush, W. (2002). *What's school got to do with it? Cautionary tales about correlations between student computer use and academic achievement.* Paper presented at the meeting of the American Educational Research Association, New Orleans, LA.

Ravitz, J., & Wong, Y. (2000). How teaching philosophies relevant to computer use originate: Effects of educational background, teaching responsibilities, and computer experience. In H. Becker (Chair), *When does computer use contribute to pedagogical reform?* Paper presented at the meeting of the American Educational Research Association, New Orleans, LA.

Ravitz, J., Wong, Y., & Becker, H. (1998). *Teaching, learning, and computing: A national survey of schools and teachers describing their best practices, teaching philosophies, and uses of technology.* Irvine, CA: Center for Research on Information Technology and Organizations.

Ravitz, J., Wong, Y., & Becker, H. (1999). *Teacher and teacher directed student use of computers and software.* Irvine, CA: Center for Research on Information Technology and Organizations.

Rockman, S. (2000). *A lesson from Richard Nixon: Observations about technology policy and practice in education.* Paper presented at the Secretary's Conference on Educational Technology 2000, Washington, DC. Available from U.S. Department of Education Web site, http://www.ed.gov/rschstat/eval/tech/techconf00/rockman_paper.html

Rubinstein, J. (1999). Printing: History and development. *Jones telecommunications & multimedia encyclopedia.* Retrieved August 3, 2003, from http://www.digital-century.com/encyclo/update/print.html

Rudner, L. (2001). *Computer grading using Bayesian Networks—Overview.* Retrieved March 2, 2004, from http://edres.org/betsy/bayesian_ov.htm

Rudner, L.M., & Liang, T. (2002). Automated essay scoring using Bayes' theorem. *Journal of Technology, Learning, and Assessment, 1*(2). Retrieved December 29, 2002, from http://www.jtla.org

Rudner, L., & Liang, T. (2002, April). *Automated essay scoring using Bayes' theorem.* Paper presented at the meeting of the National Council on Measurement in Education, New Orleans, LA.

Rumberger, R. (2000). *A multi-level, longitudinal approach to evaluating the effectiveness of educational technology.* Paper presented at the SRI Design Meeting on Design Issues in Evaluating Educational Technologies. Retrieved December 4, 2002, from http://www.sri.com/policy/designkt/rumberg5.pdf

Russell, M. (1999). Testing writing on computers: A follow-up study comparing performance on computer and on paper. *Education Policy Analysis Archives, 7*(20). Retrieved December 15, 2001, from http://epaa.asu.edu/epaa/v7n20/

Russell, M. (2000). *Wellesley Public Schools curriculum technology program evaluation report.* Wellesley, MA: Wellesley Public Schools.

Russell, M. (2001). Framing technology program evaluations. In W. Heinecke & J. Willis, *Methods of Evaluating Educational Technology* (pp.149–162). Greenwich, CT: Information Age.

Russell, M. (2002). It's time to upgrade: Tests and administration procedures for the new millenium. *Essays in Education, 1.* Retrieved March 2, 2004, from http://www.usca.edu/essays/vol12002/time_to_upgrade_revised.pdf

Russell, M., & Abrams, L. (2004). Instructional uses of computers for writing: How some teachers alter instructional practices in response to state testing. *Teachers College Record, 106*(6) 1332–1357.

Russell, M., Bebell, D., Cowan, J., & Corbelli, M. (2003). An AlphaSmart for each student: Does teaching and learning change with full access to word processors? *Computers and Composition, 20,* 51–76.

Russell, M., Bebell, D., & O'Dwyer, L. (2003) *Use, support, and effect of intructional technology study: An overview of the USEIT study and the participating districts.* Chestnut Hill, MA: Boston College, Technology and Assessment Study Collaborative. Retrieved July 10, 2003, from http://www.bc.edu/research/intasc/studies/USEIT/pdf/USEIT_r1.pdf

Russell, M., Bebell, D., O'Dwyer, L., & O'Connor, K. (2003). Examining teacher technology use: Implications for pre-service and in-service teacher preparation. *Journal of Teacher Education, 54*(4) 297–310.

Russell, M., Goldberg, A., & O'Connor, K. (2003). Computer-based testing and validity: A look back and into the future. *Assessment in Education, 10*(3), 279–293.

Russell, M., & Haney, W. (1997a). Testing writing on computers: An experiment comparing student performance on tests conducted via computer and via paper-and-pencil. *Education Policy Analysis Archives, 5*(3). Retrieved December 4, 2002, from http://epaa.asu.edu/epaa/v5n3.html

Russell, M., & Haney, W. (1997b, March). *Promoting school level reflection: The Co-NECT School Accountability Model.* Paper presented at the meeting of the American Education Research Association, Chicago, IL.

Russell, M., & Haney, W. (2000). Bridging the gap between testing and technology in schools. *Education Policy Analysis Archives, 8*(19). Retrieved March 20, 2002, from http://epaa.asu.edu/epaa/v8n19.html

Russell, M., & Plati, T. (2000). *Mode of administration effects on MCAS composition performance for grades four, eight and ten.* Report prepared for the Massachusetts Department of Education. Retrieved December 15, 2001, from http://www.bc.edu/research/nbetpp/statements/ws052200.pdf

Russell, M., & Plati, T. (2001). Effects of computer versus paper administration of a state-mandated writing assessment. *Teachers College Record.* Retrieved December 26, 2001, from http://www.tcrecord.org/Content.asp?ContentID=10709

Russell, M., & Tao. W. (2004a). Effects of handwriting and computer-print on composition scores: A follow-up to Powers et al. *Practical Assessment, Research, and Evaluation, 9*(1).

Russell, M., & Tao. W. (2004b). The influence of computer-print on rater scores. *Practical Assessment, Research, and Evaluation, 9*(3).

Saettler, P. (1990). *The evolution of American educational technology.* Englewood, CO: Libraries Unlimited.

Salomon, G., Perkins, D.N., & Globerson, T. (1991). Partners in cognition: Extending human intelligence with intelligent technologies. *Educational Researcher, 20,* 2–9.

Satava, R. (2001, July). *Metrics for objective assessment of surgical skills workshop: Developing quantitative measurements through surgical simulation.* Draft report for meeting in Scottsdale, AZ.

Schiff, T.W., & Lewis, C.S. (1999). *California Digital High School process evaluation: Year one report.* Santa Monica, CA: Milken Family Foundation, Educational Technology Project. Available from the Milken Family Foundation Web site, http://www.mff.org/publications/publications.taf?page=258

Schofield, J. (1995). *Computers and classroom culture.* New York: Cambridge University Press.

Schwartz, D.L., Lin X., Brophy, S., & Bransford, J.D. (1999). Toward the development of flexibly adaptive instructional designs. In C.M. Reigelut (Ed.), *Instructional design theories and models: Volume II* (pp. 183–213). Hillsdale, NJ: Lawrence Erlbaum Associates.

Scriven, M. (1972). Pros and cons about goal-free evaluation. *Evaluation Comments, 3*(4).

Secretary's Commission on Achieving Necessary Skills. (1991) *What work requires of schools: A SCANS report for America 2000.* Washington, DC: U.S. Department of Labor. Retrieved November 15, 2002, from http://wdr.doleta.gov/SCANS/whatwork/whatwork.html

Seels, B., Berry. L., Fullerton, K., & Horn, L.C. (1996). Research on learning from television. In D. Jonassen (Ed.), *Handbook for research on educational communications and technology* (pp. 299–377). New York: Macmillan.

Semple, B. M. (1992, July). *Performance assessment: An international experiment* (International Assessment of Educational Achievement Report No. 22-CAEP-06). Princeton, NJ: Educational Testing Service.

Shade, D. (2001). Introduction. *Information Technology in Childhood Education Annual 2001, 1,* 1–3.

Shepard, L. (1990). Inflated test score gains: Is the problem old norms or teaching the test? *Educational Measurement: Issues and Practice, 9*(3), 15–22.

Shriner, J.G., & Thurlow, M.L. (1992). *State special education outcomes 1991.* Minneapolis: University of Minnesota, National Center on Educational Outcomes.

Sivin-Kachala, J., & Bialo, E. (1994). *Report on the effectiveness of technology in schools, 1990–1994.* Washington, DC: Software Publishers Association.

Slavin, R. (1987a). Grouping for instruction in the elementary school: Equity and effectiveness. *Equity and Excellence, 23,* 31–36.

Slavin, R. E. (1987b). Mastery Learning reconsidered. *Review of Educational Research, 57,* 175–213.

Spalding, E. (2000). Performance assessment and the New Standards Project: A story of serendipitous success. *Phi Delta Kappan, 81,* 758–764.

Spencer, K. (1999). Educational technology—an unstoppable force: A selective review of research into the effectiveness of educational media. *Educational Technology & Society, 2,* 23–34.

St. Pierre, R., Cook, T., & Straw, R. (1981). An evaluation of the nutrition education and training program: Findings from Nebraska. *Evaluation and Program Planning, 4,* 335–344.

Stake, R. (1967). The countenance of educational evaluation. *Teachers College Record, 68,* 523–540.

Standage, T. (2002). *The Turk: The life and times of the famous eighteenth-century chess-playing machine.* New York: Walker & Company.

Steamship. (2001). In *Columbia Encyclopedia* (6th ed.). New York: Columbia University Press. Retrieved November 12, 2002, from http://www.bartleby.com/65/st/steamshi.html

Stigler, S.M. (1986). *The history of statistics.* Cambridge, MA: Harvard University Press.

Stoll, C. (1999). *High-tech heretic.* New York: Random House.

Tatsuoka, K.K. (1983). Rule space: An approach for dealing with misconceptions based on item response theory. *Journal of Educational Measurement, 20,* 345–354.

Tatsuoka, K.K. (1991). *Boolean algebra to determination of the universal set of knowledge states* (ETS Technical Report ONR-91-1). Princeton, NJ: Educational Testing Service.

Thomas, D. (2002). *Report on scientifically-based research supported by U.S. Department of Education* [Press release]. Retrieved November 19, 2002, from http://www.ed.gov/news/pressreleases/2002/11/11182002b.html

Thompson, S. J., Thurlow, M. L., Quenemoen, R. F., & Lehr, C. A. (2002). *Access to computer-based testing for students with disabilities* (Synthesis Report 45). University of Minnesota, National Center on Educational Outcomes. Retrieved July 10, 2002, from http://education.umn.edu/nceo/OnlinePubs/Synthesis45.html

Thurlow, M.L., Scott, D.L., & Ysseldyke, J.E. (1995a). *A compilation of state's guidelines for accommodations in assessments for students with disabilities* (Synthesis Report 18). Minneapolis: University of Minnesota, National Center on Educational Outcomes. Retrieved February 29, 2004, from http://education.umn.edu/nceo/OnlinePubs/SynthRep18.pdf

Thurlow, M.L., Scott, D.L., & Ysseldyke, J.E. (1995b). *A compilation of states' guidelines for including students with disabilities in assessments* (Synthesis Report 17). Minneapolis: University of Minnesota, National Center on Educational Outcomes.

Tierney, R. (1996). Redefining computer appropriation: A five-year study of ACOT students. In C. Fisher, D. Dwyer, & K. Yocam (Eds.), *Education and technology: Reflections on computing in classrooms* (pp. 169–184). San Francisco: Apple Press.

Tindal, G., & Fuchs, L. (1999). *A summary of research on test changes: An empirical basis for defining accommodations.* Lexington, KY: Mid-South Regional Resource Center.

Traxler, A.E. (1954). The IBM Test Scoring Machine: An evaluation. In Educational Testing Service, *Proceedings of the 1953 Invitational Conference on Testing Problems* (pp. 139-146). Princeton, NJ: Educational Testing Service.

Trotter, A. (2003). A question of direction: 'Adaptive' testing puts federal officials and experts at odds. *Education Week, 22*(35), 17–21.

Tyler, R. (1949). *Basic principles of curriculum and instruction.* Chicago: University of Chicago Press.

U.S. Congress, Office of Technology Assessment. (1992). *Testing in American schools: Asking the right questions* (Publication No. OTA-SET-519). Washington, DC: U.S. Government Printing Office. (NTIS No. PB92-170091)

U.S. Department of Commerce. (2002). *A nation online: How Americans are expanding their use of the Internet.* Washington, DC: Author. Retrieved April 19, 2002, from http://www.ntia.doc.gov/ntiahome/dn/nationonline_020502.htm

U.S. Department of Education. (2002). *Grant opportunities and history: 2002 PT3 funding.* Retrieved November 11, 2002, from http://mirror.eschina.bnu.edu.cn/Mirror/ed.gov/www.ed.gov/offices/OPE/PPI/teachtech/pt32002.html

Vacc, N. (1987). Word processor versus handwriting: A comparative study of writing samples produced by mildly mentally handicapped students. *Exceptional Children, 54*(2), 156–165.

Varandi, F., & Tatsuoka, K.K. (1989). *BUGLIB* [Computer software]. Princeton, NJ: Educational Testing Service.

Vendlinski, T., & Stevens, R. (2000). The use of artificial neural nets (ANN) to help evaluate student problem solving strategies. In B. Fishman & S. O'Connor-Divelbiss (Eds.), *Proceedings of the fourth international conference of the learning sciences* (pp. 108–114). Mahwah, NJ: Lawrence Erlbaum Associates.

Vendlinski, T., & Stevens, R. (2002). Assessing student problem-solving skills with complex computer-based tasks. *Journal of Technology, Learning, and Assessment.* Retrieved July 10, 2002, from http://www.bc.edu/research/intasc/jtla/journal/v1n3.shtml

Wenglinsky, H. (1998). *Does it compute?: The relationship between educational technology and student achievement in mathematics.* Princeton, NJ: Educational Testing Service. Retrieved January 9, 2002, from ftp://ftp.ets.org/pub/res/technolog.pdf

White House, The. (2001). *President honors nation's leading math and science teachers.* Retrieved December 2, 2003, from http://www.ed.gov/news/pressreleases/2001/03/wh-0305.html

White House, The. (2002). *Fact sheet: No Child Left Behind Act.* Retrieved February 29, 2004, from http://www.whitehouse.gov/news/releases/2002/01/20020108.html

Wiggins, G. (1993). Assessment: Authenticity, context, and validity. *Phi Delta Kappan, 75*, 210–214.

Williamson, M.L., & Pence, P. (1989). Word processing and student writers. In B.K. Britton & S.M. Glynn (Eds.), *Computer writing environments: Theory, research, and design* (pp. 96–127). Hillsdale, NJ: Lawrence Erlbaum Associates.

Wilson, M., & Sloane, K. (2000). From principles to practice: An embedded assessment system. *Applied Measurement in Education, 13*(2), 181–208.

Witte, J. (1998). The Milwaukee voucher experiment. *Educational Evaluation and Policy Analysis, 20,* 229–251.

Woelfel, N., & Tyler, I. (1945). *Radio and the school.* Hudson, NY: World Book.

Wood, B., & Freeman, F. (1929). *Motion pictures in the classroom: An experiment to measure the value of motion pictures as supplementary aids in regular classroom instruction.* Boston: Houghton Mifflin.

Wood, B., & Freeman, F. (1932). *An experimental study of the educational influences of the typewriter in the elementary school classroom.* New York: Macmillan.

Wright, B.D., & Stone, M.H. (1979). *Best test design: Rasch measurement.* Chicago: Mesa Press.

Ysseldyke, J., Thurlow, M., McGrew, K., & Shriner, J. (1994). *Recommendations for making decisions about the participation of students with disabilities in statewide assessment programs* (Synthesis Report 15). Minneapolis, MN: University of Minnesota, National Center on Educational Outcomes.

Zandvliet, D., & Farragher, P. (1997). A comparison of computer-administered and written tests. *Journal of Research on Computing in Education, 29*(4), 423–438.

Zlatos, B. (1994). Don't test, don't tell: Is "academic red-shirting" skewing the way we rank our schools? *American School Board Journal, 181*(11), 24–28.

INDEX

A

A Nation at Risk, 12
  influence of, 13
  long-term response to, 18
Accountability systems
  and focus on content/curriculum
    framework, 3
  impact on computer skills develop-
    ment, 70–72
  prior to NCLB, 12
  See also Education Week's annual qual-
    ity rating by state; *No Child
    Left Behind (NCLB)*
Adams, Arthur, concerns over machine
  testing, 45
Algebra Cognitive Tutor, 149
Alman, John, 39
AlpahSmarts, 165
American Association for the Advance-
  ment of Sciences (AAAS),
  "national" standards/bench-
  marks (development of), 13
Apple Classrooms of Tomorrow
  (ACOT) project, 132
Architecture Exam (ETS), 105–107
Assessment applications, 101–102
  Architecture Exam (ETS), 105–107
  development challenge, 211–212
  diagnostically adaptive assessments,
    119–120

Interactive Multi-Media Exercises
  (IMMEX), 107–109
K–12 learning environments,
  113–119
  BioLogica, 115–119, 116f, 117f
National Assessment of Education
  Progress (NAEP) study for
  ETS, 104–105
surgical simulation, 109–113, 110f,
  111f, 112f
Assessment of student learning, 206
  challenges to, 120
    political, 122–123
    practical, 123–124
    technical, 120–121
  and current political context, 8
  evolution of as educational reform
    strategy, 11
  factors limiting change (state level),
    17–18
  as justification of high computer
    costs in schools, 6
  machine scoring (reservations
    about), 44–47
  publications exploring new direc-
    tions, 101
  shortcomings in current technology
    of testing, 102–104
  See also Assessment applications;
    Computer-based technolo-
    gies/testing; Diagnostic

Technology and Assessment: The Tale of Two Interpretations, pages 237–243
Copyright © 2006 by Information Age Publishing

DH

371.
260
285
RUS

Printed in the United States
44986LVS00002B/39-92

9 781593 110383